Rel 1022

Jesus the Teacher

Jesus the Teacher

A SOCIO-RHETORICAL INTERPRETATION OF MARK

VERNON K. ROBBINS

FORTRESS PRESS   PHILADELPHIA

COPYRIGHT © 1984 BY FORTRESS PRESS

Library of Congress Cataloging in Publication Data

Robbins, Vernon K. (Vernon Kay), 1939–
  Jesus the teacher.

  Bibliography: p.
  Includes indexes.
  1. Bible. N.T. Mark—Criticism, interpretation, etc.
I. Title.
BS2585.2.R58 1984   226'.306   83–16504
ISBN 0–8006–0719–8

K479G83 Printed in the United States of America 1–719

IN MEMORIAM
Norman Perrin
My Doctoral Father

ET IN HONOREM
Earl W. Robbins
and
Mildred I. Hanson Robbins
My Parental Father and Mother
During their Fiftieth Year of Marriage

Contents

Abbreviations

JAC	*Jahrbuch für Antike und Christentum*
JAF	*Journal of American Folklore*
JBL	*Journal of Biblical Literature*
JJS	*Journal of Jewish Studies*
JR	*Journal of Religion*
JRH	*Journal of Religious History*
JSNTSup	Journal for the Study of the New Testament—Supplement Series
JSOTSup	Journal for the Study of the Old Testament—Supplement Series
KBANT	Kommentar und Beiträge zum Alten und Neuen Testament
KNT	Kommentar zum Neuen Testament
LCL	Loeb Classical Library
LingBib	*Linguistica Biblica*
LXX	Septuagint
MBT	Münsterische Beiträge zur Theologie
MT	Masoretic Text
NICNT	New International Commentary on the New Testament
NovT	*Novum Testamentum*
NovTSup	NovT—Supplements
NT	New Testament
NTAbh	Neutestamentliche Abhandlungen
NTL	New Testament Library
NTS	*New Testament Studies*
OCD	*Oxford Classical Dictionary*
OT	Old Testament
PRS	*Perspectives in Religious Studies*
PRS—SSS	PRS—Special Studies Series
RevB	*Revista Biblica*
RP	Religious Perspectives
RSR	*Religious Studies Review*
RTR	*Reformed Theological Review*
SANT	Studien zum Alten und Neuen Testament
SBL	Society of Biblical Literature
SBLSBS	SBL Sources for Biblical Study
SBLDS	SBL Dissertation Series
SBLMS	SBL Monograph Series
SBM	Stuttgarter biblische Monographien
SCHNT	Studia ad corpus hellenisticum novi testamenti
SHR—Numen Supp.	Studies in the History of Religions—Numen Supplements

SJLA	Studies of Judaism in Late Antiquity
SPB	Studia Post-Biblica
SRSup	Studies in Religion/Sciences religieuses—Supplement
SS	Semeia Studies
SUNT	Studien zur Umwelt des Neuen Testaments
TAPA	*Transactions of the American Philological Association*
TBAW	Tübinger Beiträge zur Altertumswissenschaft
TDNT	G. Kittel and G. Friedrich (eds.), *Theological Dictionary of the New Testament*
TH	Théologie Historique
TU	Texte und Untersuchungen
TUMSR	Trinity University Monograph Series in Religion
VT	*Vetus Testamentum*
WMANT	Wissenschaftliche Monographien zum Alten und Neuen Testament
ZAW	*Zeitschrift für die alttestamentliche Wissenschaft*
ZDA	*Zeitschrift für deutsches Altertum und deutsche Literatur*
ZNW	*Zeitschrift für die neutestamentliche Wissenschaft*
ZTK	*Zeitschrift für Theologie und Kirche*

Preface

Approximately seventeen years ago I became interested in the problems of research surrounding the Gospel of Mark. To a great extent, this book represents my methodological journey since the time when, after being trained in the Jewish background of the New Testament, I was appointed to teach New Testament language and literature in a state university with a joint appointment in a program in religious studies and a department of the classics.

My research, then, has been influenced by the setting of a state university where a school of humanities and a classics department have been major points of reference. In this setting, interpretations considered virtually sacrosanct within biblical scholarship have left me without answers to basic questions that have arisen from students and colleagues. As I found myself grappling for answers to "more general" questions, I tried to find a mode of interpretation that was neither sectarian nor anti-theological, and one that offered insights into the interrelation of religious life and culture not only during the first century but also during the twentieth century.

It is my impression that we need a paradigm for research that keeps us in touch with Greek and Greco-Roman literature, as well as biblical and Jewish literature, as we interpret Mark. In order to do this, it is necessary to have a concept of "form" different from the one in the disciplines of form and redaction criticism. After developing an alternative concept of "form" inductively as I have read and reread biblical, Jewish, Hellenic, and Greco-Roman literature interchangeably for about a decade, I discovered that a portion of Kenneth Burke's work provided a framework for integrating the phenomena I had found. My own inductive approach to the texts, along with insights gained from ancient and modern treatises on rhetoric, has determined the particular kind of socio-rhetorical analysis in which I engage, and may suggest an arena in which the approach can be improved.

The publication of this manuscript gives me an opportunity to acknowledge my indebtedness to a number of people and institutions. To the late Merl W. Harner, and to Irvin W. Batdorf, Harold H. Platz, Wayne E. Barr, and George W. Frey I owe my beginnings in biblical languages and interpretation at United Theological Seminary. Then to the late Norman

Perrin I owe a great debt for creating a stimulating and supportive environment at the University of Chicago Divinity School. Finally, to William R. Schoedel, Gary G. Porton, and David L. Petersen, colleagues in religious studies dedicated to intellectual interchange and growth, and to my colleagues in the Classics Department at the University of Illinois, I express my gratitude for their engagement in intellectual pursuits that have informed my efforts.

In addition, I wish to mention individuals and groups who have welcomed, supported, and challenged my thoughts in untold ways: Richard and Carol Saller, Irene Vassos Davis, Dennis Davis, Sarah Glenn De-Maris, Richard E. DeMaris, Dennis Duling, James A. Wilde, and David Rhoads. Charles H. Talbert and David E. Aune graciously critiqued portions of the manuscript during its earlier stages. More recently, conversations with Burton L. Mack have been informative and directive. I am also grateful to the people who invited me to present portions of this material in the Gussie Smock Maher Bible Lectures at the Monticello United Methodist Church; the Adult Seminars at the First United Presbyterian Church in Urbana; the Dropsie University Lecture Series; the Biblical Seminar in Buffalo, New York, supported by Canisius College and Daemen College; the Religious Studies Lectures at the University of Rochester; and the New Testament Seminar at the Claremont Graduate College. The Institute for Ecumenical and Cultural Research, Collegeville, Minnesota, with its dedicated staff, provided a most pleasant spring in 1975 for me and my family, during which I first discerned patterns in Xenophon's *Memorabilia* that I considered important for analysis of Mark. The Max Richter Conversations in Judaism at Brown University, under the informed leadership of Jacob Neusner, provided me with an opportunity to clarify similarities and differences between religious, social, and cultural traditions in antiquity. The Research Board of the University of Illinois at Urbana-Champaign, and my colleague Thomas M. Conley, provided me with the opportunity to study rhetorical literature and theory under a grant for Study in a Second Discipline during the fall of 1981. The Institute for Antiquity and Christianity at Claremont, under the joint funding of the Society of Biblical Literature–Claremont Fellowship, provided the academic setting during the spring of 1982 that stimulated final revisions of the manuscript. To the people in these settings—many must go unnamed—who were responsible for making these opportunities available to me, I express my gratitude for supporting the fragile life of scholarship in an often bewildering world.

Then, too, to Elizabeth Woolverton and Mary Crawford, who diligently typed final copy, and to Martha Buck DeLaTorre, who accepted the role of critic and editor when my own energies had reached an end, I shall always be grateful. After the manuscript was completed, John A. Hollar, Therese D. Boyd, and their staff provided important copyediting and final production. At the very last stage—when I was located in Trondheim, Norway, under the joint sponsorship of the US Educational Foundation in Norway (Fulbright Commission) and the Religionsvitenskapelig Institutt at Universitetet i Trondheim—Barbara Penney graciously accepted the challenge of the index of passages and Peder Borgen and Dagfinn Rian helped to obtain access and funding which allowed me to use a Nord 100 computer to print the index.

Finally, I express my gratitude to Rick and Chimene, our children, and to Deanna, my wife, for their kindness, patience, and respect through this endeavor. And I dedicate this book to my parents, who have encouraged and loved the one to whom they gave birth, and to Norman Perrin, who gave birth to my academic career.

Vernon K. Robbins
University of Illinois at Urbana-Champaign

1
Comparative Analysis
of the
Gospel of Mark

Comparison, the existence of similarity, is the inescapable presupposition of
historical research.[1]

The era of source, form, and redaction criticism of the gospels has
revealed myriads of developments within Jewish tradition prior to and
during the time in which Christianity came into being. These efforts have
corrected many erroneous claims about earliest Christianity and have
shown that Christianity began as one more group—a sect, voluntary
association, or renewal movement[2]—within Palestinian Judaism.

These very methods, however, became so self-conscious about explicit
historical developments within Christian circles that they failed to keep in
touch with basic social and cultural phenomena in the Mediterranean
world that created the environment in which Christianity lived and moved
and had its being. Few NT documents have suffered more in this regard
than the Gospel of Mark. The standard commentaries show little attempt
to glean information from Greco-Roman literature as well as biblical and
Jewish literature in order to explicate its contents.

Within recent years, interpreters have plumbed Greco-Roman literature as well as biblical and Jewish literature in order to establish a
comparative base for explicating NT documents other than the Gospel of
Mark. Certainly the Pauline letters have attracted this kind of investigation. Analysis of Greco-Roman letters has revealed various aspects of
Paul's letters that reflect contemporary literary conventions.[3] Also, analysis of social data in the letters has opened new discussions concerning the
engagement of Paul and Pauline Christianity with Greco-Roman society.[4]
Next in line has been Luke-Acts. Investigations by Henry J. Cadbury have
attracted renewed interest,[5] and new approaches have uncovered phenomena previously untapped for understanding this two-volume work.[6] In
addition, various studies unrelated to the Pauline letters or Luke-Acts
have analyzed Greco-Roman spheres of understanding and action for the
purpose of broadening NT investigation.[7] Some studies of portions of

Mark have attempted to open a new era in the study of Mark,[8] but there has been little movement toward a systematic use of data from Greco-Roman, biblical, and Jewish literature in commentaries on its form and content.

A major challenge for an interpreter of a NT document is to discern the particular manner in which patterns of thought and action characteristic both of Jewish and of Greco-Roman social, religious, or literary traditions and conventions are exhibited in the document. In other words, an interpreter of a NT document must not only compare the text he or she is interpreting with biblical and Jewish data but also with Greek and Greco-Roman data. Biblical traditions and conventions had a major influence on earliest Christianity. Also, however, the social and cultural milieu of the first century C.E. had been influenced by traditions and conventions that had emerged from Hellenic society. Hellenistic culture had a widespread influence after the exploits of Alexander the Great (331–323 B.C.E.), and even in Judea the anti-Hellenistic reaction under the Maccabean priest-kings could not reverse the inertia of the progressive, universalistic cultural movement that was pervading the Mediterranean world.[9] Within this setting, two movements within Judaism survived the Jewish-Roman wars of 66–70 and 132–135 C.E.—Pharisaism and Christianity. While Pharisaism was a successful renewal movement within ethnic Jewish culture, Christianity adapted Jewish monotheism with its beliefs, values, ethics, traditions, and rituals to Greco-Roman culture.[10] Accordingly, the authors of the NT gospels wrote documents that exhibit a fascinating intermingling of Jewish and Greco-Roman patterns of thought and action.

Despite the variations within Mediterranean culture, certain common patterns of interaction and communication existed throughout the cultural milieu in which Christianity was born. Rhetorical forms and the figure and concept of the sage intersected with established traditions to provide a common cultural base for Greek, Roman, Jewish, and Christian communities. Within this setting, small forms like the proverb, the apophthegma, and the chreia provided a bridge between oral and written culture. A great variety of larger literary forms—oration, diatribe, essay, symposium, epistle, and biography—represented the meeting ground for rhetorical forms and patterns of influence from the wise personages in the culture.[11]

From a cultural standpoint, it is no accident that the type of Christianity that lived on in the Greco-Roman world selected a NT comprised of five biographical documents (the gospels and Acts) and twenty-one epistles (or essays in the form of epistles). Even the one document that is neither a biography nor an epistle, the Apocalypse (Revelation), contains seven epistles in the first three chapters. Biography and epistle constitute two of the most common literary forms in the culture and were ready-made for gathering smaller literary forms into a broader literary framework. The smaller oral and literary units were gathered together into larger generic structures that were heavily influenced by oratorical and biographical patterns of interaction and understanding.[12] The NT documents contain patterns, forms, and structures that exhibit the emergence of the Christian movement in the cultural sphere of late Mediterranean antiquity.

Yet the interest in the broader cultural environment faces a persistent deterrent in NT studies. Interpreters study the OT and expand the analysis to intertestamental and rabbinic Jewish literature without consulting Greco-Roman literature. Since no Greco-Roman literature is contained in the Bible, the literature does not have the religious sanctions that Jewish literature shares with Christian literature. To accept Greco-Roman data in the analysis requires a broader orientation toward the cultural involvement of earliest Christianity than many NT interpreters have been willing to entertain.

INTERPRETATION OF THE GOSPEL OF MARK

Only with the rise of modern scholarship has there been an attempt to discover the social and cultural environment of the Gospel of Mark. The earliest traditions suggested that this gospel was written by a close associate of Peter. This associate, John Mark, simply translated and wrote down, as accurately as he could, the things that Peter preached about Jesus.[13] Such an interest in reliable transmission of tradition ignores dimensions of cultural influence in the document. For many interpreters, a fundamental shift in interpretation began in 1901 with William Wrede's analysis of the statement of secrecy in Mark.[14] His analysis proposed that the secrecy motif had been placed within the narrative by its author to explain why people did not know, during Jesus' ministry, that he was the Messiah. Such an interpretation broke the focus of attention on Mark as reliable history. Since Wrede's work, interpreters have faced the challenge of explicating this gospel in the religiohistorical environment in which the document was written, namely, earliest Christianity.

In the ensuing years, investigations of Mark have focused on Jewish dimensions within early Christian traditions about Jesus so intently that too little attention has been given to Mediterranean culture of late antiquity, which represents the overall context in which this gospel emerged. Recently, analysis of techniques of composition and of plot development in Mark has suggested that the author wrote a document that represents a creative literary achievement.[15] Still, this insight has not allowed most interpreters to understand Mark within the cultural setting of late Mediterranean antiquity. Either the relation of Mark to Jewish traditions or the internal literary characteristics of Mark dominates analysis so completely that perceptions about broader cultural influences are virtually absent from commentary on Mark.

When interpreters have analyzed Mark in relation to Jewish literature, they have been struck by the absence of such a literary form in the antecedent tradition. For this reason, a description internal to Christian traditions themselves has attracted the greatest approval. Rudolf Bultmann's proposal that Mark presents the end product of the proclamation of the kerygma[16] still reigns supreme, with modifications, among interpreters. In fact, however, Mark's gospel does not look especially strange among all the different kinds of biographical compositions during the Hellenistic era. A few interpreters have been aware all along that the gospels contain significant parallels to contemporary Greco-Roman biographies,[17] but their insights have gone unheeded.

During the era of form and redaction criticism, most interpreters were—and many still are—impressed with the uniqueness of the Gospel of Mark rather than the similarities it shares with biographical literature within Jewish and Greco-Roman circles during the first and second centuries C.E.[18] Observations of uniqueness, however, should not turn an interpreter away from analysis of similarities that a document shares with other literature in its cultural setting. Any document containing significant literary dimensions is unique to itself. This uniqueness reflects the creativity of a writer who formulates a literary account somehow different from the literature available to him.

The claims about uniqueness in Mark are linked with two strongholds of opinion: (1) that Mark is the first gospel written within earliest Christianity, and (2) that the gospels are unparalleled in Jewish literature. Whether written first, second, or third, a document that was composed in the *lingua franca* of the culture and that functioned as a mediary between ethnic Jewish traditions and general Greco-Roman traditions should be expected to contain influences from general streams of tradition. The lack of an exact parallel in Jewish or Greco-Roman literature is a pertinent item for the investigation of Mark, but this lack should encourage analysis of broader cultural influences rather than exaggerated claims about uniqueness. On the one hand, much of Greco-Roman literature was "unique" in the sense that many different constituent forms and styles were united into "new" wholes. On the other hand, the uniqueness of any document is an achievement within a sociocultural environment that furnishes patterns of understanding and action through which the document communicates.[19] For this reason, items that appear to be unique often reflect, on closer analysis, manifold dimensions in common with cultural phenomena contemporary with it.

The thesis of this investigation is that the fusion of religious traditions, folklore, and ethical pronouncements in the Gospel of Mark contains parallels both in Jewish and in Greco-Roman circles during the first century. Examination of Greco-Roman literature featuring religio-ethical teachers suggests that fundamental sociocultural influences in Mediterranean culture intermingled with Jewish influences to provide the overall integration of Jesus traditions in Mark. The analysis presupposes the distinctiveness of Mark in the setting of Jewish and Greco-Roman literature. Distinctiveness, however, in contrast to uniqueness, does not presuppose isolation from popular sociocultural influences. Undoubtedly the study requires modification of statements about the uniqueness of Mark, but the major goal is to explore the literary and social environment in which this gospel was written.

TOOLS FOR ANALYSIS

While various studies have given us a beginning point for a new era of investigation of the gospels,[20] the type of research that will reveal the intersection, fusion, and transmutation of cultural streams of tradition within the early Christian movement only recently has gained momentum. The "quests" and new "methods" that liberated the text of the Gospel of Mark during a previous era of scholarship need to be revised and adapted to allow a new reading that positions the text amidst sociocultural patterns of understanding and action as they were perpetuated by biblical, Jewish, Greek, and Greco-Roman traditions and are available to us in extant literature.

My approach is supported most explicitly by the method of interpretation of literature and culture formulated by Kenneth Burke and Clifford Geertz.[21] The concept of culture espoused by the approach is semiotic. In other words, the stories, sayings, and editorial comment that we read are the signifiers—signs, symbols, or expressions (i.e., *semeia*)—of cultural understanding. Underlying the semiotic approach is a belief that "man is an animal suspended in webs of significance he himself has spun."[22] Culture is constituted by "those webs, and the analysis of it [is] . . . an interpretive one in search of meaning."[23] Our analysis presupposes, therefore, that our data consists of "our own constructions of other people's constructions of what they and their compatriots are up to."[24] The data with which we are primarily concerned are in the Gospel of Mark. The text of Mark presents a construction by another person, that is, the author of the text and the concerns of the author. This "other person's construction" recites a "flow of behavior" which is symbolic action, that is, the recital of action is social discourse that exhibits cultural forms of understanding. The recital of the flow of behavior in Mark exhibits webs of significance that accompanied some early Christians as they engaged in the thinking and doing that perpetuated the patterns of belief and action that came to be called Christianity.

The time is ripe, therefore, to construct a reading of the Gospel of Mark in a setting of significant engagement with a range of data from ancient Mediterranean culture. A sense of the distinctiveness of Mark must not turn one away from analysis of social and cultural influences in the document. The interpreter needs to use disciplines that reach beyond the confines of the traditional forms of NT criticism to explicate the intermingling of social, religious, and literary traditions and conventions in the Gospel of Mark. This study goes beyond previous analysis by employing a socio-rhetorical method of interpretation. Rhetoric refers to the art of persuasion.[25] Rhetorical interpretation, therefore, is concerned with strategies that change attitudes and induce action. While much rhetorical analysis concentrates on overt techniques of persuasion, socio-rhetorical analysis emphasizes the wide range of strategies, both overt and covert, that constitute persuasive communication.

It is natural for rhetorical strategies to occur in settings characterized by "strife, enmity and faction,"[26] and the Gospel of Mark is filled with such combativeness. But sole concentration on overt rhetorical strategies may fail to reveal that "opponents can join battle only through a mediatory ground that makes their communication possible."[27] The mediatory ground is constituted by "a general body of identifications that owe their convincingness much more to trivial repetition and dull daily reënforcement than to exceptional skill."[28] In other words, changing attitudes and inducing actions are matters of identifying oneself with particular images, people, actions, or perceptions. Following the lead of Kenneth Burke, our rhetorical approach emphasizes that an author persuades his readers not only by the use of overt techniques of ordering and emphasizing but also "by the use of stylistic identifications; his act of persuasion may be for the purpose of causing the audience to identify itself with the speaker's interests; and the speaker draws on identification of interests to establish rapport between himself and his audience."[29] A socio-rhetorical approach, therefore, analyzes the text as a strategic statement in a situation characterized by "webs of significance" containing an intermingling of social, cultural, religious, and literary traditions and conventions in the Mediterranean world.

SOCIO-RHETORICAL FORMS
IN MARK

Within the setting of socio-rhetorical analysis, four kinds of form play a role: (a) progressive form; (b) repetitive form; (c) conventional form; and (d) minor form. The term "form" in our usage shares some common ground with the meaning of the term in form criticism. Yet most form criticism became interested in specific categories of form, that is, *Gattungen,* rather than with the rhetorical dimensions of form that change attitudes and induce actions.[30] In my analysis I concur with Burke: "A work has form in so far as one part of it leads a reader to anticipate another part, to be gratified by the sequence."[31] Thus rhetorical criticism concerns the arousal and fulfillment of expectations and desires within the reader. Form is present where there is a strategy of communication that causes the reader to become an active participant in the process, anticipating sequences, gaining familiarity through repetition, and identifying with certain people and causes.

From the perspective of socio-rhetorical analysis, most NT criticism during the past century has concerned itself with minor forms in the Gospel of Mark. Certainly the practitioners of form criticism knew that most pericopes in Mark "manifest sufficient evidences of episodic distinctness to bear consideration apart from their context."[32] In other words, forms like controversy stories, miracles, and parables arouse one or more expectations that are satisfactorily fulfilled within the span of the pericope itself, and many forms like this are present in Mark. Also, a series or a chiasmus is a minor form. During the era of form criticism, extended series of controversy stories (Mark 2:1—3:6; 11—12), parables (4:1–34), miracle stories (4:35—5:43), sayings (9:42–50; 13:1–37), and passion events (14—15) attracted attention, and they have received renewed attention with the rise of redaction and composition criticism.[33] Also, recent interest in literary criticism has attracted greater attention to minor forms like metaphor, antithesis, and parallelism.[34]

From the perspective of socio-rhetorical interpretation, the minor forms in the Gospel of Mark represent folklore from sectors of early Christianity that participated in the Jesus movement, as described so well by Gerd Theissen.[35] As the reader now encounters the folklore in this gospel, overarching rhetorical forms produced by the composition of the document have a powerful rhetorical hold on the minor forms contained within it. Nevertheless, the minor forms continue to function both within the document and outside it as "formal events"[36] that perpetuate the identity of the movement through the transmission of sayings and stories attributed to Jesus of Nazareth.

The folklore present in Mark's gospel created a social cohesion within sectors of early Christianity by articulating the antagonisms felt by the movement. The recitation of stories and sayings that perpetuated the antagonisms created a social drama, and at the core of social drama is agonistic interaction.[37] Within any social drama, certain people are identified as adversaries. These stories celebrate fleeting moments of victory and grieve over moments of defeat. While some of the adversaries may be relatively powerless, the majority are established members of society who perpetuate values and norms that are perceived to victimize the ones who transmit the folklore. The minor forms in this gospel express the egotism and hostility of the movement through stories in which Jesus responds with witty, proverbial speech in settings where scribes, Pharisees, Sadducees, chief priests, elders, and Herodians are present.[38]

Through the recitation of the social drama in the folklore, a group like the Jesus movement ensures conformity to its own accepted norms. The folklore establishes continuity from generation to generation through its role in education.[39] Folklore, therefore, is recited:

> to inculcate the customs and ethical standards in the young, and as an adult to reward him with praise when he conforms, to punish him with ridicule or criticism when he deviates, to provide him with rationalizations when the institutions and conventions are challenged or questioned, to suggest that he be content with things as they are, and to provide him with a compensatory escape from the "hardships, the injustices" of everyday life.[40]

Many of the minor forms in Mark, therefore, are items of folklore that perpetuated the identity of a socioreligious group over against established leaders within Jewish society. The proverbial sayings, parables, and aphoristic stories "work by providing a charter for action, by legislating, by justifying, by educating, by applying social pressure, by providing socially approved outlets for anti-social motives."[41] The folklore within Mark declares its vision to be new and rebellious. Within early Christianity itself, however, it served a traditional, conservative function. The sayings and stories perpetuated the established norms of a recently founded group within eastern Mediterranean society during the first century of the Common Era, simultaneously providing the means for the group to break away from Jewish society and to establish its own identity in the sphere of Mediterranean society.

While practitioners of form criticism were interested in the minor forms outside their setting in the gospels, practitioners of redaction criticism considered the minor forms to be tradition incidental to the redaction that revealed the theology of evangelists. The present investigation is concerned with the role of the minor forms in the setting of three primary rhetorical forms in the overall document: (a) progressive form; (b) repetitive form; and (c) conventional form.

In recent interpretation of the Gospel of Mark, interpreters have shown an interest in progressive form in the narrative. Progressive form, according to Burke, can be of two kinds: (1) logical progression, which has "the form of a perfectly conducted argument, advancing step by step";[42] or (2) qualitative progression, in which "the presence of one quality prepares us for the introduction of another."[43] On the one hand, Norman Petersen's presentation of temporal plotting is a beginning point for seeing the existence of "logical progression" in Mark.[44] As the narrative proceeds, assertions are made that create specific expectations within the reader. Once the reader sees that many of these assertions are fulfilled within a short span of the text, he or she expects a logical progression within the text that reliably fulfills all the assertions. My analysis suggests that the logic of assertion and fulfillment in Mark has its ultimate source in the logic of promise and fulfillment in biblical literature. In the Gospel of Mark, however, the logic of promise and fulfillment is generalized by allowing assertions both of the narrator and of Jesus to function as powerfully as statements of God or one of his prophets. Thus, when Jesus says that "the bridegroom will be taken away" (2:20) and when the narrator says that the Pharisees and Herodians held counsel to destroy Jesus (3:6), the reader expects as specific a fulfillment of these assertions as he or she does of God's statement through Isaiah that he sends a messenger to prepare the way for the Messiah (1:2). Assertions by God, by the narrator, and by Jesus create logical progressions in the narrative as specific expectations are created and fulfilled in the narrative sequence.

In contrast to logical progressions stand qualitative progressions. Robert Tannehill has identified qualitative progressions where he has observed what he calls "unexpected developments" or "reversal of expectations" in Mark.[45] Qualitative progressions occur when an attribute of speech or action, which the reader had no reason to expect on the basis of a previous assertion, emerges in relation to one or more characters in the narrative. When new attributes and new titles emerge in the portrayal of Jesus, the narrative acquires qualitative progressive form. Likewise, when the disciples react differently from what the reader expects, a qualitative rhetorical progression is occurring in the narrative. Theodore J. Weeden analyzed qualitative progressive form in the portrayal of the disciples when he observed the development from unperceptiveness to misconception and finally to fear and flight.[46] A qualitative progression has occurred when the reader accepts the misconception and flight as an appropriate sequence, and the reader will accept the sequence only if the previous narrative has created the proper state of mind for it. In contrast to a logical

progression, then, the reader recognizes the appropriateness of the progression only after the events have occurred.

While Petersen and Tannehill have given us a start with logical and
qualitative progressive form in Mark, much less has been done in recent
scholarship with repetitive form in this gospel. Repetitive form is "the
consistent maintaining of a principle in new guises, . . . [a] restatement of
the same thing in different ways."[47] When current interpreters investigate
repetitive form, they may be inclined to engage in a structural rather than
a rhetorical analysis of Mark. Yet virtually every commentary on Mark
mentions the threefold repetition of the prediction of the passion and
resurrection in Mark 8:31; 9:31; and 10:32–34. Also, the repetition of
certain words and phrases reveals significant aspects of Markan theology.
Usually, however, only minor repetitive forms are analyzed whereas my
investigation concerns repetitive form that extends throughout. Therefore, I begin with analysis of a repetitive pattern that spans the document
and provides a formal structure for the Gospel of Mark.

In addition to progressive forms and repetitive forms, conventional
forms have an important place in socio-rhetorical analysis. In contrast to
progressive and repetitive forms, which arouse expectations during the
process of reading, conventional forms may exist as a "categorical expectancy . . . anterior to the reading."[48] Great attention has, of course, been
given to conventional forms within the minor forms in the gospels. "Any
form can become conventional,"[49] and forms like the parable, the eschatological saying, and the miracle story became conventional forms within
early Christianity. My investigation, however, concerns the overall document as a rhetorical form and probes the relation of overarching forms in
Mark to conventional forms within Mediterranean circles.

I begin with the observation that the Gospel of Mark partakes of the
form of a biography that depicts a disciple-gathering teacher—from the
high point of his career to his death.[50] This form, it is discovered, existed
as a conventional form in circles that perpetuated their patterns of belief
through biographical accounts of people who taught and enacted a particular system of thought and action. Within Greco-Roman circles, the
literature about Socrates, written during the fourth century B.C.E. and
undergoing a revival during the first centuries B.C.E. and C.E., especially
provides important comparative data for analysis of conventional forms in
Mark. In Jewish circles, the literature about Elijah and Elisha provides
especially important comparative data for analysis of conventional forms in
Mark.

INTERRELATION AND CONFLICT OF FORMS

With the presence of progressive, repetitive, conventional, and minor
forms in a piece of literature, both interrelation and conflict arise between

rhetorical forms in the document.[51] In other words, expectations raised by one form may either interrelate with or conflict with expectations raised by another form. To a great extent, the success of the Gospel of Mark is attributable to its complex interrelation of rhetorical forms. This investigation is designed to clarify some of the interrelations. For example, Mark's portrayal of Jesus interrelates logical progression—from conflict to crucifixion—with qualitative progression—from a wonder-working prophet-teacher to a messiah-king who rises after he is killed. Logical progression is manifest in the dramatic plot that portrays the crucifixion as an expected outcome of the conflict that attends Jesus' teaching and action from the beginning. Qualitative progression is present in the systematic unfolding of Jesus' identity through both speech and action that prepares the reader for the next stage of events. The sequences in the qualitative progressions are not perceived by the reader to be necessary results of previous events, but they are perceived as appropriate when they occur. In the setting of logical and qualitative progression, repetitive form features Jesus issuing commands that imply that the appropriate response to the imminence of the kingdom of God is to follow the system of thought and action attributed to Jesus. A great achievement of the author is the successful interrelation of these progressive and repetitive forms in the narrative.

Perhaps the greatest challenge for socio-rhetorical analysis is to sort out the interrelation, and possible conflict, among conventional forms, progressive forms, and repetitive forms in Mark. Analysis of the conventional forms is complicated by the intermingling of ethnic Jewish forms with more general social and cultural forms. Yet this kind of analysis could prove to be the most rewarding of all. My analysis suggests that the portrayal of a cycle of relationships between teacher and disciple from the moment of the call to discipleship until the time of the death of the teacher is a conventional form in Mediterranean literature. This conventional form appears to be well established in Greco-Roman society vis-à-vis the religiophilosophical schools and their traditions. Taking the Elijah-Elisha narrative as a clue on the side of Jewish traditions, it appears obvious that the relation of Elijah to Elisha opened the way for a natural merger of Jewish prophetic narrative with this conventional Greco-Roman cycle. No conflict among conventional, progressive, and repetitive forms therefore appears in the portrayal of Jesus. The presence of the Elijah-Elisha cycle introduces miracle working as a natural part of the activity of the prophet-teacher. Similarly, the presence of the Greco-Roman cycle concerning teachers and disciple-companions introduces repeated scenes of interaction between Jesus and his disciples.

The Gospel of Mark, therefore, is characterized by a major story line that skillfully interrelates progressive, repetitive, and conventional forms.

A subsidiary story line about the disciples, however, portrays a qualitative progression that conflicts with a conventional form in Mediterranean culture. The qualitative progression that prepares the reader for the shift from eager following to flight and denial conflicts with a conventional form. In this conventional form, there is an expectation that faithful disciples will gain a reasonably clear understanding of their teacher's system of thought and action by the end of their time together, even though they resist their teacher's acceptance of death through an unjust verdict. The interrelation of the well-integrated major story line with the unexpected and undesired features of the subsidiary story line creates the particular rhetorical effect of the gospel.

After the analysis of repetitive, progressive, and conventional forms, I will explore the socio-rhetorical implications of the interrelation and conflict of forms in Mark (chapter seven). My thesis concerning messiahship will be compared with the thesis concerning discipleship to see if the same kind of assertion is made about both. From these observations, conclusions will be drawn about the socio-rhetorical nature of Mark's gospel in the milieu of late Mediterranean antiquity.

GOALS

In summary, the ultimate goal of this investigation is to read the Gospel of Mark in the context of a wider range of literature from the Mediterranean world than is usual in Markan scholarship. Rather than reading Mark simply in the context of biblical and Jewish literature, I intend to read this gospel in the context of literature that lies both within and outside Jewish and Christian circles of influence. Documents like Josephus's *Antiquities* and Philo's *Life of Moses* are taken into account, as well as Xenophon's *Memorabilia*, Plato's dialogues, and Philostratus's *Life of Apollonius of Tyana*. This range of literature provides the setting for discovering features that are in common and features that separate the documents from one another.

In order to understand the Gospel of Mark within this broader sphere, it is necessary to use a comparative method of analysis[52] rather than the traditional methods of source, form, and redaction criticism. The method is called socio-rhetorical criticism. From the perspective of socio-rhetorical analysis, the entire literary product is the result of the compositional activity of an author. The question for the analysis is not so much What changes did Mark effect within traditions about Jesus? as How is the Gospel of Mark similar to and different from other literature about people who are considered by certain sectors within the culture to be important leaders or heroes? Whether the author of Mark has collected, copied, or freely composed the material which he has written down, he himself has performed an act of selection, arrangement, revision, and composition that has created a literary document—somehow like and somehow unlike other literary documents in the sphere of Mediterranean culture.

The socio-rhetorical analysis used here is perceived to be a bridge between traditional exegetical interpretation and more recent literary and structuralist approaches. The approach provides a means for biblical scholarship to move beyond the limitations in its present methods without breaking radically with previous achievements. One of the results of the shift in method is to consider the distinction between narration and discourse more important than the distinction between tradition and redaction. This approach allows the interpreter to utilize widespread rhetorical procedures of analysis which are more amenable to social and anthropological investigations than source, form, and redaction criticism.

This project is envisioned as a contribution to the social, cultural, literary, and religious history of early Christianity. The approach begins by exhibiting the formal structure, or outline, of Mark that arises through repetitive forms in the document. Chapter two, therefore, explores well-known repetitive forms in Mark to show the means by which the narrative contains an introduction followed by six sections of material and a conclusion. The next step is to analyze the relation of repetitive forms in Mark to conventional repetitive forms in the portrayal of prophets and teachers in the literature of Mediterranean antiquity. Chapter three, therefore, contains an analysis of repetitive forms in prophetic literature, Xenophon's *Memorabilia*, and the Gospel of Mark. After the analysis of repetitive forms in Mark, progressive forms are analyzed in relation to conventional forms in biblical, Jewish, and Greek literature. This leads to the observation that logical and qualitative progressions disclose the role of Jesus and the role of the disciples through the sequence of a teacher/disciple cycle that begins with summons and response, continues with teaching and learning, and ends with farewell and death. Chapters four through six probe the intermingling of biblical and Jewish patterns of understanding with Greek and Hellenistic patterns of understanding in order to discover the sociocultural perceptions that provided an environment of plausibility for the portrayal of Jesus and his disciples within first-century Mediterranean culture and society.

Chapter seven summarizes the rhetorical argument of Mark's gospel about Jesus and about the disciples, and it attempts to answer why the Gospel of Mark was preserved when 99 percent of it is duplicated in Matthew and Luke. The thesis is launched that the Gospel of Mark played a significant role within early Christianity by successfully meeting Jewish messianic expectations with role enactment that was widely known and esteemed in popular Greco-Roman culture. Instead of prophetic expectation and historical fulfillment, Mark's gospel is dominated by messianic expectation and cultural fulfillment. The fluid concept of the Jewish Messiah during the first century was filled with activity by a religious teacher who was killed as a result of his teaching and action.[53] Since a majority of the people in the Mediterranean world valued the role of the religio-ethical teacher and understood that he might have to accept an unjust death in order to maintain congruence between his words and his actions, they could accept Jesus' activity as a significant fulfillment of their own expectations.

NOTES

1. J. Z. Smith, *Map Is Not Territory*, 242.
2. For discussion of the social nature of early Christianity, see W. A. Meeks, "The Man from Heaven in Johannine Sectarianism"; R. Scroggs, "The Earliest Christian Communities as Sectarian Movement"; A. Malherbe, *Social Aspects of Early Christianity*; W. A. Meeks and R. L. Wilken, *Jews and Christians in Antioch in the First Four Centuries of the Common Era*; G. Theissen, *Sociology of Early Palestinian Christianity*; L. E. Keck, "On the Ethos of Early Christians"; idem, *The New Testament Experience of Faith*; J. Gager, *Kingdom and Community: The Social World of Early Christianity*; J. A. Wilde, "The Social World of Mark's Gospel."
3. E.g., C.-H. Kim, *Form and Structure of the Familiar Greek Letter of Recommendation*; J. L. White, *The Form and Function of the Body of the Greek Letter*; idem, *The Form and Structure of the Official Petition*; J. L. White and K. A. Kensinger, "Categories of Greek Papyrus Letters"; H. D. Betz, *Der Apostel Paulus und die Sokratische Tradition*; idem, "The Literary Composition and Function of Paul's Letter to the Galatians"; idem, "In Defense of the Spirit"; F. F. Church, "Rhetorical Structure and Design in Paul's Letter to Philemon"; W. H. Wuellner, "Paul's Rhetoric of Argumentation in Romans."
4. G. Theissen, *The Social Setting of Pauline Christianity*; E. A. Judge, *The Social Pattern of the Christian Groups in the First Century*; idem, "The Early Christians as a Scholastic Community"; idem, "Contemporary Political Models for the Inter-relations of the New Testament Churches"; idem, "Paul's Boasting in Relation to Contemporary Professional Practice"; idem, "St. Paul and Classical Society"; idem, "St. Paul and Socrates"; idem, "St. Paul as a Radical Critic of Society"; R. F. Hock, *The Social Context of Paul's Ministry*; idem, "Paul's Tent-making and the Problem of His Social Class"; idem, "Simon the Shoemaker as an Ideal Cynic."
5. H. J. Cadbury, *The Style and Literary Method of Luke*; idem, *The Making of Luke-Acts*; idem, *The Book of Acts in History*.
6. E. Plümacher, *Lukas als hellenistischer Schriftsteller*; C. H. Talbert, *Literary Patterns, Theological Themes and the Genre of Luke-Acts*; idem, *What Is a Gospel?* F. W. Danker, *Luke*; F. Veltman, "The Defense Speeches of Paul in Acts";

V. K. Robbins, "By Land and By Sea: The We-Passages and Ancient Sea Voyages"; idem, "Prefaces in Greco-Roman Biography and Luke-Acts"; idem, "Laudation Stories in the Gospel of Luke and Plutarch's *Alexander*"; M. Hengel, *Acts and the History of Earliest Christianity;* W. S. Kurz, "Hellenistic Rhetoric in the Christological Proof of Luke-Acts"; D. Ladoucleer, "Hellenistic Preconceptions of Shipwreck and Pollution as a Context for Acts 27—28"; G. B. Miles and G. B. Trompf, "Luke and Antiphon."

7. E.g., D. L. Tiede, *The Charismatic Figure as Miracle Worker;* H. D. Betz, ed., *Plutarch's Theological Writings and Early Christian Literature;* idem, *Plutarch's Ethical Writings and Early Christian Literature;* J. H. Elliott, *A Home for the Homeless;* W. H. Wuellner, "Der Jakobusbrief im Licht der Rhetorik und Textpragmatik."

8. S. Schulz, "Die Bedeutung des Markus für die Theologiegeschichte des Urchristentums"; L. E. Keck, "Mark 3:7–12 and Mark's Christology"; H. D. Betz, "Jesus as Divine Man"; P. J. Achtemeier, "Toward the Isolation of Pre-Markan Miracle Catenae"; idem, "Gospel Miracle Tradition and the Divine Man"; idem, "The Origin and Function of the Pre-Marcan Miracle Catenae"; M. Smith, "Prolegomena to a Discussion of Aretalogies, Divine Men, the Gospels and Jesus"; and H. C. Kee, "Aretalogy and Gospel."

9. S. Lieberman, *Greek in Jewish Palestine;* idem, *Hellenism in Jewish Palestine;* M. Hadas, *Hellenistic Culture;* M. Hengel, *Judaism and Hellenism;* idem, *Jews, Greeks and Barbarians.*

10. For a selection of works on Pharisaic participation in Greco-Roman culture, see L. Baeck, *The Pharisees and Other Essays;* D. Daube, "Rabbinic Methods of Interpretation and Hellenistic Rhetoric"; idem, "Alexandrian Methods of Interpretation and the Rabbis"; S. Stein, "The Influence of Symposia Literature and the Literary Form of the Pesach Haggadah"; E. J. Bickerman, "The Maxim of Antigonus of Socho"; idem, "The Civil Prayer for Jerusalem"; M. Smith, "Palestinian Judaism in the First Century"; idem, "The Image of God"; H. A. Fischel, "Story and History"; idem, "Studies in Cynicism and the Ancient Near East"; idem, *Rabbinic Literature and Greco-Roman Philosophy;* idem, *Essays in Greco-Roman and Related Talmudic-Midrashic Literature.*

11. Fischel, "Story and History," 61–63.

12. Ibid., 60–61.

13. For discussions of this early tradition, see B. W. Bacon, *The Gospel of Mark,* 22–49; W. R. Schoedel, *Polycarp, Martyrdom of Polycarp, Fragments of Papias,* 105–9.

14. W. Wrede, *The Messianic Secret.*

15. The first clear signs of this point of view emerged in N. Perrin's *What is Redaction Criticism?* and T. J. Weeden's *Mark—Traditions in Conflict.* Now a more specifically literary analysis of Mark is available in N. R. Petersen's *Literary Criticism for New Testament Critics* and in D. Rhoads and D. Michie's *Mark as Story.*

16. R. Bultmann, *History of the Synoptic Tradition,* 347.

17. The most comprehensive statement of the parallels was made by C. W.

Votaw, *The Gospels and Contemporary Biographies in the Greco-Roman World*. Cf. D. Georgi, "The Records of Jesus in Light of Ancient Accounts of Revered Men," 541–42.

18. The stage was set for emphasis on the uniqueness of Mark by K. L. Schmidt, "Die Stellung der Evangelien in der allgemeinen Literaturgeschichte." Bultmann shared this point of view, *Synoptic Tradition*. 371–74. For recent work, see N. Perrin, "The Literary *Gattung* 'Gospel' "; H. Koester, "One Jesus and Four Primitive Gospels," 161–62. For a survey of assertions that Mark is unique, see V. K. Robbins, "Mark as Genre."

19. See Talbert, *What Is a Gospel?* 11; A. Fowler, "The Life and Death of Literary Forms," 77.

20. See R. C. Tannehill, *The Sword of His Mouth;* idem, "The Disciples in Mark"; idem, "The Gospel of Mark as Narrative Christology"; C. H. Talbert, *What Is a Gospel?* idem, "Biographies of Philosophers and Rulers as Instruments of Religious Propaganda in Mediterranean Antiquity"; idem, "Prophecies of Future Greatness"; H. D. Betz, "The Sermon on the Mount."

21. Works by K. Burke especially pertinent for analysis in this book include *Counter-Statement, A Rhetoric of Motives*, and *Language as Symbolic Action*. See the major work of C. Geertz in *The Interpretation of Cultures*. For the relation of Geertz's work to literary analysis, see G. Gunn, "The Semiotics of Culture and the Interpretation of Literature."

22. Geertz, *Interpretation of Cultures*, 5.

23. Ibid.

24. Ibid., 9.

25. Burke, *Rhetoric of Motives*, 49–55.

26. Ibid., 20.

27. Ibid., 25.

28. Ibid., 26.

29. Ibid., 46.

30. M. Dibelius, *From Tradition to Gospel*, 7; Bultmann, *Synoptic Tradition*, 2–7. Cf. J. A. Wilcoxen, "Narrative."

31. Burke, *Counter-Statement*, 124.

32. Ibid., 127.

33. See M. Albertz, *Die synoptischen Streitgespräche;* Achtemeier, "Isolation of Pre-Markan Miracle Catenae"; idem, "Origin and Function of Pre-Marcan Miracle Catenae"; H.-W. Kuhn, *Ältere Sammlungen in Markusevangelium;* R. Pesch, *Naherwartungen;* W. H. Kelber, ed., *The Passion in Mark*.

34. Tannehill, *The Sword of His Mouth*.

35. Theissen, "Itinerant Radicalism"; idem, *Sociology of Early Palestinian Christianity*.

36. Burke, *Counter-Statement*, 127.

37. R. D. Abrahams, "Introductory Remarks to a Rhetorical Theory of Folklore," 147.

38. In the Gospel of Mark, scribes, Pharisees, Sadducees, chief priests, elders, and Herodians stand in the place of policemen, mayors, sheriffs, and ethnic minorities in American folklore.

39. W. Bascom, "Four Functions of Folklore," 349.

40. Ibid.

41. Abrahams, *Rhetorical Theory of Folklore*, 147.

42. Burke, *Counter-Statement*, 124.

43. Ibid., 125.

44. Petersen, *Literary Criticism*, 49–80; idem, "The Composition of Mark 4:1—8:26." Apart from Petersen's analysis, logical progression has usually been investigated from the perspective of tragic plot in Mark. See G. G. Bilezikian, *The Liberated Gospel*; H. B. Carre, "The Literary Structure of the Gospel of Mark"; E. W. Burch, "Tragic Action in the Second Gospel"; D. W. Riddle, *The Gospels*, 141–45; C. Beach, *The Gospel of Mark*; F. G. Lang, "Kompositionsanalyse des Markusevangeliums," 21–22.

45. Tannehill, "The Disciples in Mark"; idem, "The Gospel of Mark."

46. Weeden, *Mark—Traditions in Conflict*, 26–51.

47. Burke, *Counter-Statement*, 125.

48. Ibid., 127.

49. Ibid., 126.

50. The recent discussion of "aretalogy" has sparked interest in overarching conventional form in Mark. See M. Hadas and M. Smith, *Heroes and Gods*. Recently, C. H. Talbert has shifted the discussion of conventional form to biography. See *What Is a Gospel?* idem, "Biographies of Philosophers and Rulers."

51. Burke, *Counter-Statement*, 128–30.

52. D. L. Barr uses the term "comparative analysis" to describe his generic comparison of Plato's *Crito, Phaedo,* and *Apology* with the synoptic gospels in "Toward a Definition of the Gospel Genre." He compares both bodies of literature with "a known genre that has been adequately described, tragedy as defined by Aristotle in his *Poetics*" (p. iii). By contrast, I attempt to encourage "comparative socio-rhetorical analysis" whereby specific passages in the gospels are analyzed in the setting of specific passages in both the biblical-Jewish and Greco-Roman literature. Such a form of exegesis moves beyond analysis of specific literary and cognitive influences (historical perpetuation of tradition) into analysis of sociocultural patterns and conventions known to us from extant literature. For other examples of comparative socio-rhetorical analysis, see V. K. Robbins, "Mark I.14–20"; idem, "Laudation Stories."

53. For an excellent discussion of the fluidity of the concept of Messiah during the first century, see M. de Jonge, "The Use of the Word 'Anointed' in the Time of Jesus."

2

The Formal Structure of Mark

In making a poem a poet is forced to follow a more or less tight formal plan; and he is forced to follow it more or less consciously.[1]

My analysis begins with the observation that repetitive forms in Mark lead to the formal structure, or outline, of Mark. Virtually every literary document has a formal structure that is a planned framework, and the framework is likely to provide a clue to the interrelation of forms in the document.[2] In modern times such a framework is usually displayed in an outline that reveals the author's division of the document into chapters and subunits. This outline helps the reader to comprehend the scope and progression of the document and allows him or her to read portions of the document according to thought units. The reader may either stop at the end of a chapter, if the book should be read from beginning to end, or select a portion that interests him or her, if the book is something like a manual or encyclopedia.

If the author of the Gospel of Mark divided the text into units, that activity has been lost to us. After the fourth century the text was transmitted with divisions and titles imposed by individual scribes.[3] Not until Stephanus's fourth edition (1551) was the text divided into verses, and the story is perpetrated that some of the arbitrariness of the divisions arose from the jogging of Stephanus's horse as he marked the verses on horseback.[4] The main purpose of the markings through the centuries has been to aid a person in finding a particular passage or statement with ease.

During the past century, interpreters have outlined the gospels for the purpose of organizing commentaries on the text. Increasing attention to the details of each gospel characterizes the investigations.[5] During the last twenty-five years, interpreters have attempted to produce a highly refined outline of Mark. While arguments over details have been abundant, something of a basic consensus has emerged that the narrative divides into sections somewhere between the beginning and middle of chapters 1, 3, 6, and 8, and around the beginning of chapters 11 and 14.[6] This consensus is responsive to the narrative movement in the gospel. Interpreters have located the basic areas where the narrative takes a new direction, but they disagree over the exact dividing points in the narrative.

My outline of the Gospel of Mark suggests that repetitive forms are the vehicle for the portrayal of a qualitative progression in the identity of Jesus. A qualitative progression, the reader will recall, does not advance step by step like a perfectly conducted argument, but presents one quality as preparation for the introduction of another.[7] In Mark, repetitive forms containing three units are the means for unfolding the attributes of Jesus and the implications of those attributes for discipleship. This feature of Mark is discovered by merging composition criticism with rhetorical criticism. Repetitive style in Mark reveals the presence of repetitive rhetorical forms. First, simple series of three and scenes composed of three units of action reveal repetition that often ends with an emphatic statement in the third unit. Second, three-step progressions that provide the framework for the three passion predictions (8:31; 9:31; and 10:32–34) reveal a special kind of sequence in settings where Jesus summons people to follow him. Third, analysis of three-step progressions with a framework analogous to the framework for the three passion predictions reveals the formal structure, or outline, of the narrative. Explication of the formal structure occupies the remainder of the chapter.

REPETITIVE FORM IN SERIES AND SCENES

The primary clues for establishing the formal structure of Mark emerge from stylistic traits within the Markan narrative. Frans Neirynck's analysis of repetitive phrases in Mark allows the interpreter to see the importance of repetitive form in the narrative. Most important for this study is the analysis of "series of three."[8] At the most primary level of composition, a repetitive form occurs when three people, things, or phrases occur in a series where the second and third items are connected to the first by means of the simple conjunction *kai* (and).[9] There are sixteen examples of this phenomenon:

1. 3:32:   your mother and your brothers (and your sisters);[10]
2. 3:35:   my brother and sister and mother;
3. 4:8:   thirtyfold and sixtyfold and hundredfold;
4. 4:20:   thirtyfold and sixtyfold and hundredfold;
5. 5:37:   Peter and James and John;
6. 9:2:   Peter and James and John;
7. 14:33:   Peter and James and John;
8. 6:4:   in his own country and among his own kin and in his own house;
9. 6:21:   his courtiers and the officers and the leading men of Galilee;

10. 8:31:   by the elders and the chief priests and the scribes;
11. 9:5:   three booths, one for you and one for Moses and one for Elijah;
12. 11:27:   the chief priests and the scribes and the elders;
13. 14:43:   from the chief priests and the scribes and the elders;
14. 14:53:   all the chief priests and the elders and the scribes;
15. 15:1:   the chief priests with the elders and the scribes and the whole Sanhedrin;
16. 16:1   Mary Magdalene and Mary the mother of James and Salome.[11]

Example fifteen (15:1) shows how the series may be arranged to make the final member in the series emphatic. In contrast to the constructions in 8:31; 11:27; 14:43; and 14:53, the construction in 15:1 joins the chief priests with the elders so the series can end with "the whole Sanhedrin."

At a second level, the series of three provides the framework for entire scenes. A well-known example is the denial of Peter in 14:66–72:

1. *One of the maids* of the high priest came; and *seeing Peter* . . . she looked at him, and *said,* "You also were with the Nazarene, Jesus." *But he denied it,* saying, "I neither know nor understand what you mean" (14:66–68);
2. And *the maid saw him,* and *began again to say* to the bystanders, "This man is one of them." *But again he denied it* (14:69–70a);
3. And after a little while *again the bystanders said to Peter,* "Certainly you are one of them; for you are a Galilean." *But he began to invoke a curse on himself and to swear,* "I do not know this man of whom you speak" (14:69b–71).

In this scene, repetitive form appears in three units of action. In the first unit, one of the maids sees Peter and speaks to him. When the maid identifies Peter as an associate of Jesus, he denies her identification. The narration in the second unit repeats the sequence with a variation whereby the maid speaks to the bystanders instead of Peter. Even with the variation, Peter hears the maid and again denies the identification. The narration in the third unit introduces a second variation whereby the bystanders, rather than the maid, make the statement that associates Peter with Jesus. The third time Peter replies with an emphatic denial by invoking a curse on himself and swearing that he has no knowledge whatsoever of Jesus. This last response dramatically closes the series.

Thus, three units of action present a repetitive series that ends with a vehement and vigorous denial by Peter. [12]

A similar repetitive form occurs in the scene in Gethsemane (14:32–42), and the third unit of action again is emphatic:

1. And *going a little farther,* he fell on the ground *and prayed* that, if it were possible, the hour might pass from him. *And he said,* "Abba, Father, all things are possible to thee; remove this cup from me; yet not what I will, but what thou wilt." And *he came and found them sleeping, and he said* to Peter, "Simon, *are you asleep?* Could you not watch one hour? Watch and pray that you may not enter into temptation; the spirit indeed is willing, but the flesh is weak" (14:35–38);

2. And *again he went away and prayed, saying the same words. And again he came and found them sleeping,* for their eyes were very heavy; and *they did not know what to answer him* (14:39–40);

3. And *he came the third time,* and *said to them,* "Are you still sleeping and taking your rest? It is enough; the hour has come; the Son of man is betrayed into the hands of sinners. Rise, let us be going; see, my betrayer is at hand" (14:41–42).

The scene contains three repetitive units of action. The first unit introduces the basic sequence: Jesus goes a distance away from the disciples, prays, comes back, finds the disciples sleeping, and speaks to the disciples. The second unit condenses the action into straightforward, simple narration without any direct or indirect speech. The lack of speech exhibits the stark, repetitive nature of the unit: Jesus goes away, prays saying the same words, comes back, finds the disciples sleeping, and speaks to them. The third unit abbreviates the narration so that the reader has to supply Jesus' going away and praying before coming back "the third time." Also, the reader has to infer from Jesus' speech that the disciples again were asleep when Jesus returned. The third unit is dominated by the direct speech of Jesus. In his speech he emphatically ends the scene with a reprimand of the disciples for sleeping, an announcement that the hour has come, an interpretation of the hour as the moment of the arrest of the Son of man, and a command to arise and depart. The scene has repetitive form as variations occur in the midst of three units containing the same sequence of actions. [13]

PASSION PREDICTIONS AND THREE-STEP PROGRESSIONS

Repetitive forms containing three units are present not only in series and scenes but also in extended portions of the text. The most well known example, surely, is the triple repetition of the passion predictions in Mark 8:31; 9:31; and 10:32–34. [14] The first two passion predictions contain

twenty-five and seventeen Greek words respectively as they rehearse the
basic events of the passion:

1. *The Son of man* must suffer many things, and be rejected by the elders
   and the chief priests and the scribes, *and be killed, and after three days
   rise again* (8:31);
2. *"The Son of man* will be delivered into the hands of men, *and they will kill
   him; and,* when he is killed, *after three days he will rise"* (9:31).

The units repeat three basic actions: the Son of man will be publicly
mistreated; he will be killed; and after three days he will rise. Variation in
wording and in reference to the ones who mistreat Jesus occurs within a
framework that repeats the same basic actions.

The third unit contains forty Greek words as it brings Jesus' description
of the passion events to its most emphatic and full expression:

3. "Behold we are going up to Jerusalem, and *the Son of man* will be
   delivered to the chief priests and the scribes, and they will condemn him
   to death, and deliver him to the Gentiles; and they will mock him, and
   spit upon him, and scourge him, *and kill him; and after three days he will
   rise"* (10:33–34).

Again the three basic actions of public mistreatment, killing, and rising
occur. Before a recital of these actions, however, Jesus tells the disciples,
"Behold we are going up to Jerusalem." The announcement of the travel
direction and of the mutual participation in the entry into the city of
Jewish authority and power emphasizes the end result of their activity
together and the mutual involvement in the outcome. Then a detailed list
of the activities in Jerusalem emphasizes the ignominious nature of the
events that are to follow. In this final unit of the sequence, the rehearsal of
arrest, trial, and conviction by the Temple hierarchy—followed by mocking, spitting, and whipping by Gentiles—emphasizes the horrible nature
of the events prior to the death and resurrection of Jesus.

While many have noticed that the three passion predictions are repetitive forms, fewer have observed that each passion prediction resides in
a framework that contains a three-step progression.[15] A three-step progression is a sequence of three units of action that build upon one another
like building blocks. Each unit of action adds information that contributes
to the meaning and significance of the final unit in the progression. Each
of the passion predictions resides in a sequence that contains three units
of action, and each final unit of action portrays Jesus summoning (*proskaleisthai*) or calling (*phōnein*) his disciples. The first unit (8:27—9:1)
reveals the three-step progression in this manner:

1. And *Jesus went on with his disciples* . . . and . . . he asked his disciples . . . and he asked them . . . and he charged them . . . (8:27–30);
2. *And he began to teach them* . . . and he said this plainly . . . But turning and seeing his disciples, he rebuked Peter, and said . . . (8:31–33);
3. *And he called to him* [*proskalesamenos*] the multitude with his disciples, and said to them . . . (8:34—9:1).

The first unit of the sequence begins with a statement that Jesus was going from one place to another, and it explicitly mentions the presence of the disciples with Jesus. The second unit introduces more intensive interaction between Jesus and his disciples. The third unit brings the sequence to a dramatic closure as Jesus summons (*proskaleisthai*) the multitude with his disciples and teaches the implications of discipleship through a series of sayings, which are some of the most memorable and most often quoted sayings from the Gospel of Mark.

The second passion prediction also occurs in a sequence containing three units of action, and the sequence again presents a three-step progression which leads to a final unit that contains teaching about discipleship:

1. *They went on from there* and passed through Galilee. And he would not have anyone know it; for he was teaching *his disciples*, saying to them . . . (9:30–32);
2. And they came to Capernaum; and *when he was in the house he asked them* . . . But they were silent; for on the way they had discussed with one another who was the greatest (9:33–34);
3. And *he sat down and called* [*ephōnēsen*] the twelve; and he said to them . . . and . . . he said to them . . . But Jesus said . . . (9:35–50).

Again the first unit portrays Jesus traveling from one place to another, and it is explicitly mentioned that the disciples are present with Jesus. The second unit features interaction between Jesus and the disciples that sets the stage for the third unit. The third and final unit features Jesus calling (*phōnein*) the Twelve and urging them to understand the responsibilities of discipleship. As the third unit of action in 8:27—9:1 features a series of sayings in which Jesus teaches about discipleship, so the third unit in 9:30–50 features Jesus teaching the disciples the intricacies of discipleship through a series of sayings supported by demonstrative action.

Mark 10:32–45, the three-step progression in which the final passion prediction occurs, brings the section to a dramatic conclusion. The structure of the unit is analogous to the form in 8:27—9:1 and 9:30–50.

1. And *they were on the road, going up to Jerusalem,* and Jesus was walking ahead of them; . . . and *those who followed* were afraid. And taking the twelve again, he began to tell them . . . (10:32–34);

2. And *James and John . . . came forward to him, and said to him . . .* and he said to them . . . But Jesus said to them . . . And Jesus said to them . . . (10:35–40);

3. And when the ten heard it, they began to be indignant . . . And *Jesus called them to him* [*proskalesamenos*] and said to them . . . (10:41–45).

Again in this sequence the first unit indicates the movement of Jesus, and the presence of the Twelve with Jesus is explicitly mentioned by the narrator. The second unit creates interaction between Jesus and his disciples that sets the stage for the concluding unit. The third and final unit features Jesus summoning (*proskaleisthai*) his disciples to him and stating to them a sequence of sayings (again some of the most memorable ones in Mark) that summarizes the entire section from 8:27 to 10:45.

The three-step progressions that provide the framework for the repetition of the passion predictions have repetitive form at a different level of narration than the simple series and the scenes. On the one hand, the simple series of three arouses and fulfills an expectation within such a short span of text that the movement and rhythm of the sequence achieve their purpose apart from the reader's mental reflection or suspense. Repetitive form in scenes that contain three units of action, on the other hand, relies on a principle of elongation. By lengthening the scene to three repetitive units, the narrator introduces a moment of suspense that sets the stage for an emphatic conclusion. At still another level of the text, three-step progressions use three units of action to portray Jesus going to new places with his disciples, engaging in particular kinds of interaction, and summoning his disciples for special purposes.

THREE-STEP PROGRESSIONS AND THE FORMAL STRUCTURE OF MARK

The kind of three-step progression that provides the framework for each passion prediction leads to the formal structure, or outline, of Mark.[16] This formal structure appears to be a planned framework that systematically unfolds "the gospel of Jesus Christ, the Son of God." The initial three-step progression occurs in 1:14–20, and subsequent three-step progressions occur in 3:7–19; 6:1–13; 8:27—9:1; 10:46—11:11; and 13:1–37.[17] These three-step progressions move Jesus through a similar sequence of actions at points where major shifts occur in the narrative. The pattern is as follows: (1) Jesus goes to a new place with his disciples; (2) he engages in a special situation of interaction; and (3) as a result of this interaction he summons his disciples anew. These three-step progressions show Jesus "repeating his identity . . . under changing situations."[18] In other words, Jesus repeatedly engages in the same pattern of behavior when the story moves to a time and place where a new phase of activity begins. In Mark, therefore, three-step progressions are repetitive forms that employ a familiar behavior pattern in order to allow new attributes of Jesus' action and speech to emerge in the narrative sequence.

Since three-step progressions provide a framework for new attributes of Jesus to emerge in new settings, they function as major vehicles for the qualitative progressions that occur in the narrative. Attributes of both Jesus and the disciples unfold in the setting of the three-step progressions as Jesus transfers the attributes of his own activity to his disciple-companions. The qualitative progressions in the portrayal of Jesus set the stage for the qualitative progressions in the portrayal of the disciples. Therefore, the qualitative progressions in the portrayal of Jesus are primary in the narrative, and the qualitative progressions in the portrayal of the disciples are coordinate to the portrayal of Jesus.

The three-step progressions that provide the formal structure of the narrative introduce basic attributes of Jesus to the reader and set the stage for subsequent three-step progressions. In each three-step progression, themes from preceding material are restated in a new situation and themes appear that will be developed in succeeding material. The three-step progressions are, therefore, transitional in character. The intermingling of new themes with preceding material allows the progressions to function for the reader as units that introduce new sections of material. Qualitative progression in the identity of Jesus occurs as new attributes and titles portraying qualities of Jesus' character emerge in situations that are somehow reminiscent of previous situations in the narrative. The three-step progressions unfold the attributes of Jesus in the following manner. Jesus is:

1. a prophet-teacher who follows one who was arrested (and will be killed), who authoritatively preaches the gospel of God, and who calls people to be his disciple-companions (1:14–20);
2. a miracle worker appropriately called Son of God who authoritatively names twelve disciples to be with him, to be sent out to preach, and to have authority to cast out demons (3:7–19);
3. a rejected prophet who sends disciples out with preparation for settings in which they will be rejected (6:1–13);
4. a Messiah/Son of man who—after submitting to arrest, public humiliation, servanthood, and death—will arise and come again (8:27—9:1);
5. an authoritative Son of David who enters the Jerusalem Temple and remolds expectations concerning its religious role (10:46—11:11);
6. a messianic prophet-teacher who transmits his system of thought

and action to his followers and will come again as the heavenly Son of man to verify his statements (13:1–37).

This sequence of three-step progressions introduces a qualitative progression in the portrayal of Jesus. The pattern of behavior that Jesus repeats again and again reveals his social role as an itinerant teacher who transmits his system of thought and action to a group of disciple-companions. In the setting of this repetition, special attributes and titles of honor emerge to exhibit the distinctive character of his thought and action. The three-step progressions, therefore, gradually unfold a complete picture of Jesus as new dimensions of his thought and activity emerge. Using the three-step progressions as a clue to the formal structure of Mark, we arrive at the following outline:

The Gospel of Jesus Christ, the Son of God

Introduction: Jesus and the Baptist (Mark 1:1–13)
1. Jesus and the Gospel of God (Mark 1:14—3:6);
2. The Healing Son of God (Mark 3:7—5:43);
3. The Rejected Prophet (Mark 6:1—8:26);
4. The Suffering, Dying, Rising Son of Man (Mark 8:27—10:45);
5. The Authoritative Son of David (Mark 10:46—12:44);
6. The Future Son of Man and the Dying Messiah-King (Mark 13:1—15:47);
Conclusion (Mark 16:1–8).

Each section of the narrative begins with a three-step progression that represents another stage in the author's elaboration of "the Gospel of Jesus Christ, the Son of God." These sections show Jesus challenging a general populace to accept new responsibilities and directing a group of disciple-companions toward specific duties. Let us now analyze these three-step progressions to see how the author builds upon themes from the preceding narrative in a three-step framework that unfolds new attributes of Jesus and coordinates these attributes with the responsibilities of discipleship.

Jesus and the Gospel of God:
Mark 1:14–15, 16–18, 19–20

The first three-step progression in the narrative provides a transition from Jesus' temptation in the wilderness (1:12–13) to the opening of his ministry in a synagogue in Capernaum (1:21–28). The three units in the progression emerge as follows:

1. Now . . . *Jesus came* into Galilee, *preaching . . . and saying* . . . (1:14–15);
2. *And passing along* by the Sea of Galilee, *he saw* . . . *And Jesus said* to them . . . And immediately they left . . . and followed him (1:16–18);
3. *And going on a little farther, he saw* . . . *And immediately he called them;* and they left . . . and followed him (1:19–20).

The first unit in the progression features Jesus coming into Galilee, announcing the kingdom of God, and issuing an exhortation to repent and believe (1:14–15). This unit of action introduces the basic ethos of Jesus as one who announces a prophetic message and challenges people to adopt a particular system of thought and action in response to the message. The second unit of action portrays Jesus going to the Sea of Galilee and commanding Simon and Andrew, two fishermen, to follow him (1:16–18). This unit adapts the general thought and action in the first unit to a setting of direct encounter with people. With the encounter, imperative speech is repeated, and the repetitive form of speech provides the medium for the shift from "repent and believe" to "follow me." The third unit repeats the sequence of action in the second unit with a variation in vocabulary that describes Jesus' activity in terms of "calling" (*kalein*) people. [19]

With this three-step progression the author introduces a rhetorical pattern that is a repetitive form throughout the narrative. The form exhibits Jesus' movement as an itinerant prophet-teacher and Jesus' transference of thought and behavior from himself to his disciple-companions. All three units of action in 1:14–20 begin with a statement indicating Jesus' movement as an itinerant prophet-teacher:

1. Jesus came into Galilee (1:14);
2. And passing along by the Sea of Galilee (1:16);
3. And going on a little farther (1:18).

All three units also exhibit a mode of imperative speech:

1. "Repent, and believe in the gospel" (1:15);
2. "Come after me" (1:17);
3. And immediately he called them (1:20).

The variations within the progression unfold a dimension of Jesus' thought and activity that is central to the portrayal of Jesus throughout the narrative. While Jesus may issue general commands as he does in the first unit of action, his real *modus vivendi* is specific encounter. The second and third units introduce the basic vocabulary upon which the narrator builds as he moves Jesus, the disciple-gathering prophet-teacher, through the action and speech that unfolds his identity. On the one hand, the response of people to Jesus' encounter is described as "leaving" (*aphienai*) their present circumstances, "following" (*akolouthein*), or "going away after him" (*aperchesthai opisō autou*). On the other hand, Jesus' encounter is described in the third unit as "calling" (*kalein*), and this vocabulary sets the stage for Jesus' repetitive "calling to" or "summoning" (*proskaleisthai*) of his disciples and the crowds in the remaining narrative.

The language and subject matter of the three units of action show that this three-step progression is a compositional means by which the author begins to elaborate the topic that is announced in the first verse of the narrative: "the gospel of Jesus Christ, the Son of God."[20] Evidence from the rhetorical treatises and the *Progymnasmata* suggests that the author of the Gospel of Mark learned this procedure in the setting where he learned to compose in Greek.[21] As early as the beginning of the first century B.C.E., students were trained to elaborate a thesis by means of a procedure called the *exergasia* (Latin: *expolitio*).[22] The elaboration procedure (*exergasia*) "consists in dwelling on the same topic and yet seeming to say something ever new. . . . We shall not repeat the same thing precisely—for that, to be sure, would weary the hearer and not elaborate the idea—but with changes" (*Ad Herennium* 4.42.54). In a narrative setting, an author elaborates the topic by presenting a sequence of units that systematically unfold the system of thought and action presupposed in the topic.

Mark 1:14–20 is the first three-step progression in which the author formally elaborates the topic introduced in Mark 1:1: "the gospel of Jesus Christ, the Son of God." The initial unit of action uses three of the five major terms in Mark 1:1 for the elaboration. Therefore, three terms stand in common between 1:1 and 1:14–15:

1. Jesus (1:1, 14);
2. the gospel (1:1, 14, 15);
3. God (1:1, 15).

Six other words and phrases in the unit occur in the verses that come between 1:1 and 1:14–15:

1. John (1:4, 6, 9);
2. Jesus came (1:9);
3. Galilee (1:9);
4. preaching (1:4, 7);
5. saying (1:7);
6. repentance (1:4).

The author gathers these words and phrases together in a scene that restates Mark 1:1 in a new setting.[23] The unit elaborates the earlier

statement through the addition of four items that are entirely new in the
narrative:

1. the arrest (*paradidonai*) of John (1:14);
2. the fulfillment of time (1:15);
3. the kingdom of God (1:15);
4. a command to "believe" (1:15).

As the statement in Mark 1:1 is reformulated, the ethos of Jesus is
manifest in speech and action specifically characteristic of him. The
particular nature of his speech and action is clarified through comparison
with the speech and action of John the Baptist. Both Jesus and John
preach and both issue a call to repentance (1:4, 15). Since, however, Jesus
preaches a subject matter called "the gospel of God" (1:14) rather than "a
baptism of repentance for the forgiveness of sins" (1:4), a distinctive
picture of Jesus' speech and action begins to emerge. Also, John the
Baptist points to Jesus in his speech, while Jesus points to the fulfillment
of time, the kingdom of God, and belief in the gospel (1:15).

Mark 1:14–15 is simply the first step in the elaboration of Mark 1:1.
Through the three-step procedure characteristic of the narrative, the
import of 1:14–15 is adapted to the specific setting of discipleship. Mark
1:16–18 portrays the form and effect of Jesus' speech and action when it
occurs in a setting where potential disciple-companions are present.
When Jesus encounters two fishermen who are casting their nets in the
sea, the imperative form of his speech carries over from Mark 1:15, but
the content is adapted to the new situation. The general command to
"repent and believe" changes to "come after me." The rationale for the
command is presented in the form of a promise that he will make them
into something they now are not, namely, "fishers of men." The result of
Jesus' encounter is successful. The narration tells the reader that the two
fishermen immediately left their nets and followed him (1:18).

After the second unit places the action and speech of Jesus in a situation
of specific encounter, the third unit repeats the movement, encounter,
and response present in the second unit. Jesus goes along a little farther,
sees two more fishermen, and confronts them. The two leave everything
and go away after Jesus. In the setting of repetition, the narrator describes
Jesus' action as "calling" (*kalein*: 1:20). Immediately when called, the two
men leave their father, their associates, and their vocation to follow Jesus.

The sequence transfers the teaching and action of Jesus to the setting of
discipleship prior to the narrative program that displays Jesus' ability to
attain an obedient response both from people and from unclean spirits.[24]
In this progression the Markan narrative introduces Jesus of Nazareth in
the well-known cultural role of an itinerant prophet-teacher who gathers

disciple-companions as he travels. The progression emphasizes the initial moment in the relation between a prophet-teacher and a disciple-companion.

The Healing Son of God:
Mark 3:7–8, 9–12, 13–19

Mark 3:7–19 constitutes the second three-step progression that establishes the formal structure of the narrative.[25] The framework of the progression is as follows:

1. *Jesus withdrew* with his *disciples* . . . and a great multitude . . . *followed* . . . and . . . a great multitude . . . *came to him* (3:7–8);
2. And *he told his disciples* . . . for he had healed many . . . [and] the unclean spirits . . . fell down before him and cried out . . . and he strictly ordered them . . . (3:9–12);
3. And *he went up* . . . and *called to him those whom he desired;* and they came . . . And he appointed twelve, to be with him, and to be sent out to preach and have authority to cast out demons (3:13–19).

The first unit of the progression is a restatement of Mark 1:14–20 in a manner similar to the restatement of Mark 1:1 at 1:14–15. The unit elaborates Mark 1:14–20 through a restatement of five themes present in the earlier progression:

1. Jesus (1:14, 17);
2. his disciples (1:17–20);
3. the sea (1:16);
4. Galilee (1:14, 16);
5. followed (1:18, 20).

Jesus' name is not repeated in the opening verse of a scene from 1:14 until 3:7, even though it occurs seven times in the narrative between the two progressions (1:24, 25; 2:5, 8, 15, 17, 19). Mark 3:7–8, however, contains a specific reference not only to Jesus but also to his disciples (at least the four he called in 1:16–20 and Levi whom he called in 2:15). Then, just as Jesus comes from Galilee in 1:9 and goes back into Galilee in 1:14, so Jesus gathers his disciples along the sea in 1:16–20 and goes with them back to the sea in 3:7. Moreover, while in 1:14–20 Simon, Andrew, James, and John begin to follow Jesus, in 3:7–8 a large multitude from Galilee, Judea, Jerusalem, Idumea, beyond the Jordan, and beyond Tyre and Sidon come to him (or follow him).[26] The enumeration is noticeable. Much as 1:16–20 had described the four fishermen—Simon, Andrew the brother of Simon, James the son of Zebedee, and John his brother (1:16, 19)—so 3:7–8 gives an itemized account of the groups following Jesus.

The only verse between 1:21 and 3:6 that contains similar enumeration is 1:29 where the names of Simon, Andrew, James, and John are reiterated. Enumeration is a prominent technique in the three-step progressions. With the enumeration in this unit the author restates and amplifies the theme of following. Mark 3:7–8 elaborates 1:14–20 by means of the response of the crowds to whom Jesus has preached since the initial three-step progression.

The second unit of the progression, Mark 3:9–12, introduces a new dimension by gathering features from 1:21—3:6 together and introducing a specific title for Jesus in relation to this activity. The unit begins with a command by Jesus to the disciples to prepare a boat on account of the crowd, lest they crush him. Then, much as 1:16 presents a rationale for Simon and Andrew's casting of nets into the sea ("for they were fishermen"), 3:10 provides a rationale for Jesus' command to the disciples ("for he had healed many, so that all who had diseases pressed upon him to touch him"). In the second progression, however, the rationale is a restatement of the activity of Jesus in 1:21—3:6 with the addition of new features. Mark 3:9–12 contains six items that paraphrase activities in 1:21—3:6:

1. his disciples (2:15, 16, 18, 23);
2. the crowd (2:4);
3. he had healed many (1:34; 3:2);
4. the unclean spirits (1:23, 26, 27);
5. cried out (1:23, 26);
6. he charged them not to make him known (1:25, 34).

In this unit Jesus addresses his disciples as a result of the action of the large crowds that gather around him. People seek healing by touching Jesus, and unclean spirits fall down in obedience to Jesus, crying out that he is the Son of God (3:11). The first two units dramatize an aspect of Jesus' role that was not evident in the progression that introduced Jesus' teaching activity (1:14–20). Jesus is an authoritative teacher-healer who attracts large crowds and receives special laudation (that reiterates the honorific statements in 1:1, 11) from unclean spirits who cannot rebuff his power. Jesus' healing activity, an aspect of his role that was not evident at the time of his call of the four disciples (1:16–20) is now incorporated into the setting of discipleship.

In the third and final unit of the progression, 3:13–19, Jesus selects twelve disciples to whom he will transfer his abilities as a teacher-healer.[27] This unit parallels units two and three in the first progression (1:16–18, 19–20), and it establishes expectations that were not explicit for the first four disciples who had responded to Jesus' summons. The additional commission to the disciples is based on Jesus' social identity as a teacher-healer in the first two units of the progression (3:7–8, 9–12). The narration features Jesus "summoning" (*proskaleisthai*) those whom he himself wants (3:13) and introduces three dimensions of activity for those whom he summons:

1. to "be with" Jesus (3:14);
2. to be "sent out to preach" (3:14);
3. to "have authority to cast out demons" (3:15).

The expectation to "be with" Jesus was evident from 1:16–20 where the men were asked to leave everything and follow Jesus. The expectation to be "sent out to preach" was probably implicit in the promise that the disciples would be made "fishers of men" (1:17). In any case, the promise in 1:17 is now explicated in terms of preparation to perform the activity of preaching in which Jesus himself was engaged in 1:14–15. The assertion that the disciples would acquire "authority to cast out demons" (3:15) is new information. It seems appropriate, however, for this attribute of Jesus to be transferred to his disciples along with the attribute of preaching. As the attributes of Jesus unfold, so the activities, abilities, and responsibilities of discipleship will unfold. The three activities now enumerated for the Twelve are an elaboration of the encounters in the initial progression.

After the unit describes the purposes for which the Twelve were appointed, it contains a list that names the Twelve (3:16–19). This enumeration of the Twelve is an elaboration of 1:14–20 in which the first four disciples were called. As the list begins, the narrator presupposes the reader's knowledge that Simon was one of the disciples called in the first interval. As a result, he proceeds straight to an explanation that Jesus gave him a special name: "Simon whom he surnamed Peter" (3:16). Next he names James and John in a form that repeats 1:19: "James the son of Zebedee and John his brother" (3:17). After the repetition of Mark 1:19, he indicates that Jesus gave them a special name: "James the son of Zebedee and John the brother of James, whom he surnamed Boanerges, that is, sons of thunder" (3:17). This form of repetition elaborates Mark 1:16–20.

Next on the list is Andrew, the only disciple among the first four who was not given a surname by Jesus. Then the author presents a list that moves through a different James and Simon to Judas Iscariot: "Andrew, and Philip, and Bartholomew, and Matthew, and Thomas, and James the son of Alphaeus, and Thaddaeus, and Simon the Cananaean, and Judas Iscariot, who betrayed him [*paredōken*]" (3:18–19). As Mark 3:7–19 elaborates 1:14–20, it ends on a theme with which 1:14–20 began: the

termination of John's ministry through arrest, imprisonment, and execution. Much as Jesus began his ministry after the arrest (*paradidonai*) of
John the Baptist (1:14), so Jesus' ministry will end with the betrayal
(*paradidonai*) by Judas Iscariot that leads to trial and crucifixion.

The three-step progression in Mark 3:7–19, therefore, provides the
vehicle for recapitulating the activity of Jesus in the preceding narrative,
linking this activity with the title Son of God, and transferring this activity
to twelve disciple-companions. As the three units of action elaborate the
themes in the initial progression (1:14–20), they end with a reference to
Jesus' betrayal (*paradidonai*) by Judas Iscariot, a theme introduced in the
first line of the initial three-step progression (1:14).

The Rejected Prophet:
Mark 6:1–3, 4–6, 7–13

In the next three-step progression (Mark 6:1–13) Jesus encounters
public rejection in his homeland and transfers to his disciple-companions
the responsibility of working as teacher-healers in a context of rejection.[28]
Occurring between the raising of Jairus's daughter (5:35–43) and the death
of John the Baptist (6:14–29), the progression interrelates the powerful
ministry of Jesus with his future death and transfers these dimensions of
power and rejection to his followers. The framework of the progression is
as follows:

1. *He went away* from there and *came* to his own country; and *his disciples
   followed* him. And . . . he began to teach; . . . and many who heard him
   were astonished, saying . . . And they took offense at him (6:1–3);
2. And *Jesus said to them* . . . And he could do no mighty work there . . . And
   he marveled . . . and he went about . . . teaching (6:4–6);
3. And *he called to him* [*proskaleitai*] *the twelve*, and *began to send them out*
   two by two, and gave them . . . He charged them . . . And he said to them
   . . . (6:7–13).

This progression is an elaboration of 3:7–19 in a setting that incorporates
rejection into Jesus' powerful ministry and into the disciples' preparation
for a ministry constituted by many of the attributes of Jesus' activity.

Mark 6:1–3, the first unit of the progression, presents Jesus "in his
homeland" teaching in the synagogue on the Sabbath.[29] The disciples
receive special mention in the narration introducing the unit (6:1) even
though they do nothing in it. As Jesus teaches, the assembly reflects on
Jesus' abilities as a teacher and healer. The episode portrays no specific
action of Jesus but is a generalized scene composed on the basis of Jesus'
activity in the previous narrative. Four of the statements in the unit

elaborate themes from the two preceding progressions and the intervening scenes:

1. his disciples followed (1:18; 2:14–15; 3:7);
2. on the Sabbath he began to teach in the synagogue (1:21; 3:1);
3. many were astonished (1:22, 27, 2:12; 5:20, 42);
4. mother, brothers, and sisters (3:20, 31–35).

Jesus' return to his homeland with his disciples is a reiteration of Mark
1:14–20, the initial progression in the narrative. Jesus' entrance into a
synagogue on the Sabbath where people are astonished at his teaching is a
reiteration of Mark 1:21–28, where he first entered a synagogue and
taught. Then the statement by the people in the setting is a restatement of
the amazement at the end of the initial synagogue episode (1:27). The
interrogative form of the amazement in the initial setting is repeated in
the new setting, and the response to Jesus in the initial setting is elabo-
rated through the inclusion of information that has emerged in the intervening scenes. The question "What is this?" (1:27) is now stated as
"Where did this man get all this [his abilities]?" (6:2). The inquiry moves
beyond amazement at Jesus' action to an interest in the source of his
abilities. This is a natural restatement in light of the variety of acts Jesus
has performed in the intervening scenes. Then the statement "A new
teaching! With authority he commands even the unclean spirits, and they
obey him" (1:27) is now stated as: "What is the wisdom given to him?
What mighty works are wrought by his hands!" (6:2). The reformulation
includes healing miracles performed through the use of his hands (1:29–
31, 40–45; 5:21–24a, 35–43) as well as powerful teaching and exorcisms
revealing the wisdom present within him.

Then the reformulation takes an additional step. The people reflect on
his status as a hometown boy whose mother, brothers, and sisters are
present in their midst. As in the previous progressions, the technique of
enumeration is noticeable: "Is not this the carpenter, the son of Mary and
brother of James and Joses and Judas and Simon, and are not his sisters
here with us?" (6:3). This part of the response is an elaboration of the
reference to Jesus' family in Mark 3:21, 31–35. In rhetorical terms, this
scene is a recapitulation of previous scenes in which the inability of his
family to understand is interrelated with the queries of the people who
see his activity in the synagogue.

The second unit of the progression begins with Jesus' response to their
rejection of him. He responds with a proverb that a prophet is not without
honor except in his homeland, among his kinfolk, and in his house (6:4).
The series of three phrases makes the saying especially emphatic, and
none of the other gospels replicates this feature. The response of Jesus

dominates the second unit and introduces his public stance toward rejection of his role as a wonder-working teacher. Jesus reacts in the role of a rejected prophet. Because of his rejection, Jesus is unable to perform any powerful works in his homeland (6:5). Nevertheless, he maintains his role as healer and teacher by laying his hands on a few sick people to heal them and by traveling around to the surrounding villages to teach (6:5–6).

The third unit of action portrays Jesus "summoning" (*proskaleisthai*) the Twelve, sending them out two by two, and giving them authority over unclean spirits (6:7).[30] The first statement is a reformulation of the previous assertion that they would be "sent out to preach" (3:14), and the second statement reiterates that they would "have authority to cast out demons" (3:15). The succeeding material, then, is an elaboration of the statements in the third unit of the progression in Mark 3:7–19. In addition to sending them out and giving them authority, Jesus instructs them concerning the meager furnishings and supplies they should take. The technique of enumeration is again noticeable as the mode of Jesus' itinerant ministry is transferred to the disciples:

> He charged them to take nothing for their journey except a staff; no bread, no bag, no money in their belts; but to wear sandals, and not put on two tunics (6:8–9).

After the enumeration, Jesus gives the Twelve specific guidelines to follow when they encounter rejection on their mission:

> "Where you enter a house, stay there until you leave the place. And if any place will not receive you and they refuse to hear you, when you leave, shake off the dust that is on your feet for a testimony against them" (6:10–11).

Maintaining one's activity in the face of rejection, albeit in a different location, is a feature to be transferred from Jesus' action to the action of the followers of Jesus.

Perhaps the knowledge that supplies would be meager was implicit from Jesus' call to Peter, Andrew, James, and John to leave their work, kinfolk, and associates in order to follow him (1:14–20). Perhaps also it was implicit in the stories in chapter 2 that the disciples would face rejection along with Jesus (2:1—3:6). Yet Jesus' summons to the disciples contained no explicit statements concerning these aspects of their role as disciple-companions until this progression in the narrative. In 6:6b–13 it becomes clear that the disciples are to "be like their teacher" in yet one more way. They not only receive a specific commission to go out (6:7) but they also are told how to respond to rejection of their activity (6:11). They go forth preaching repentance, casting out demons, anointing sick people with oil, and healing (6:13)—the same activities their teacher continues even when he encounters public rejection. A qualitative progression in the portrayal of Jesus and of discipleship occurs in the setting of repetitive form. Jesus' acceptance of the role of teacher and healer in the face of rejection is systematically transferred to twelve disciples who are commissioned and given the ability to perform the basic services of teachers and healers in settings where the potential for rejection is always present.

The emphasis on rejection in 6:1–13 stands in stark contrast to the overwhelmingly positive response featured in 3:7–19. And if the reader expects Jesus to get more and more entangled with the scribes and Pharisees as a result of the meeting of the Pharisees with the Herodians to plan Jesus' destruction (3:6), it is not clear that the reader should expect the people in Jesus' hometown to reject him. Nevertheless, the progression is appropriate. The confusion and anger expressed by the scribes and Pharisees (2:1—3:6), the lack of understanding expressed by Jesus' mother and brothers (3:21, 31–35), and the request by the Gerasenes that Jesus go away from their neighborhood (5:17) prepare the reader for the negative reception of Jesus in his homeland (6:1–3). In the midst of a logical progression that arose from the plan to destroy Jesus, a qualitative progression occurs in which the negative responses to Jesus are accepted by Jesus as an important aspect of his identity. The new situation, therefore, reveals a new dimension of his identity. He is not only appropriately called Son of God but also appropriately called "a prophet without honor." Since new dimensions in the identity of Jesus mean new dimensions in discipleship, Jesus now sends the disciples out equipped with instructions for action when they are rejected (6:11).

The ambivalent context of success and rejection provides the setting for the disciples to accept their commission as apostles sent out to extend the activities characteristic of Jesus' ministry. They start their work between the most powerful healing of Jesus (bringing a young girl back to life) and the violent death of the preacher-baptizer who was the agent through whom Jesus' activity gained authority and sanction from God (Mark 1:4–11). The dynamics of the situation are exhibited especially well at the end of the account of the death of John the Baptist. John's disciples take the corpse of their teacher and bury it in a tomb as Jesus' disciples gather around Jesus and report all the things they have done and taught on their mission as apostles (6:29–30).

The Suffering, Dying, Rising Son of Man:
Mark 8:27–30; 8:31–33; 8:34—9:1

In the next three-step progression (Mark 8:27—9:1) the disciples wrestle with the central dimensions of Jesus' thought and action.[31] The progression occurs between the healing of a blind man at Bethsaida (8:22–26) and the Transfiguration of Jesus (9:2–13). Between the two events Jesus challenges his disciple-companions to incorporate suffering, death, and resurrection into his identity and to accept the ramifications of these additional aspects of his identity for their role as disciple-companions. The framework of the progression emerges as follows:

1. And *Jesus went on* with his *disciples* . . . and . . . he asked his disciples . . . And he asked them . . . And he charged [*epetimēsen*] them . . . (8:27–30);
2. And *he began to teach* them . . . And he said this plainly . . . he rebuked [*epetimēsen*] Peter, and said . . . (8:31–33);
3. And *he called* [*proskalesamenos*] to him the *multitude with his disciples*, and said to them . . . (8:34—9:1).

The first unit of the progression (8:27–30) features Jesus on the way to the villages of Caesarea Philippi with his disciples.[32] In this instance the movement is a conventional *peripatos* (stroll) in which dialogue occurs between Jesus and the disciples.[33] On the way, Jesus inquires about his identity vis-à-vis both "people" in general and "his disciples" in particular. The questions and answers reiterate the subject matter of Mark 6:14–16, which occurred immediately after the previous progression. The repetition gathers information from the preceding section into a setting where a three-step progression again interrelates Jesus' identity with the role of discipleship. When Jesus asks the disciples who people say he is, they answer: "John the Baptist, and others say, Elijah; and others one of the prophets" (8:28). The answer has the form of a series of three and is a shortened version of Mark 6:14–16, which contains the series of three within an expanded setting:[34]

King Herod heard of it; for Jesus' name had become known.
Some said, "John the baptizer has been raised from the dead; . . .
But others said, "It is Elijah."
And others said, "It is a prophet, like one of the prophets of old."
But when Herod heard of it he said, "John, whom I beheaded,
      has been raised" (6:14–16).

The first unit of the progression, like the first unit of the previous progressions, restates themes from the preceding material in a new setting. Again the information concerns the portrayal of Jesus in the narrative. But this time the disciples are asked to produce the information on the basis of their association with Jesus as disciple-companions. After the disciples' reiteration of other people's points of view, Jesus asks the disciples who they themselves say he is. Peter answers for the disciples, "You are the Christ [Messiah]" (8:29).

Peter's answer is a new step in the elaboration of Mark 1:1: "the gospel of Jesus *Christ*, the Son of God." In 1:14–20 Jesus came into Galilee, after the arrest of John the Baptist, preaching *the gospel* of God and calling disciple-companions. This was the first step in the formal elaboration of Mark 1:1. In 3:7–19 Jesus, having been followed by a huge multitude and acclaimed as *Son of God* by unclean spirits (3:11), appointed twelve disciples to be with him, to be sent out to preach, and to have authority to cast out demons (3:14–15). In the final line of the progression, the reader is told that the last disciple on the list would deliver Jesus over to people who would arrest him. This was the second step in the formal elaboration of Mark 1:1. In 6:1–13 Jesus is portrayed as a prophet who meets rejection in his hometown and transfers to his twelve disciples his powers to heal and his ability to deal with rejection. This third step in the formal elaboration prepares the way for the account of John the Baptist's death and burial (6:14–29).

Mark 8:27–30, the first unit of the progression at 8:27—9:1, introduces the title "Christ" into a setting that reiterates the discussion that preceded the recitation of John the Baptist's death. This title, which stands in Mark 1:1, does not occur once in the narrative between 1:1 and 8:30. Peter's answer, therefore, is a restatement of a feature of Mark 1:1 in a setting that gathers together the thought and action from the intervening scenes and asks the disciples to relate that thought and action to their understanding of the identity of Jesus.

The second unit of the progression (8:31–33) features Jesus teaching the disciples that the Son of man must suffer many things, be rejected, be killed, and after three days rise up (8:31). At this point the identity of Jesus becomes an item of instruction in Jesus' program of teaching. For the first time the disciples are asked to learn an aspect of Jesus' identity in anticipation of events that will happen to him rather than on the basis of events that they have already observed happen to him.[35] They must anticipate both for themselves and for their teacher the significance of an identity that arises out of rejection and leads to public humiliation and death.

In the second unit of the progression Peter takes issue with Jesus' teaching. He begins to rebuke Jesus after Jesus has taught that the Messiah must suffer, die, and rise as the Son of man (8:32). In turn, Jesus rebukes Peter in language that reflects exorcistic pronouncements. The repetitive form is the medium, once again, for qualitative progression in the portrayal of Jesus and the portrayal of the disciples. For the first time, Jesus thoroughly incorporates the concept of public humiliation and death into his prophet-teacher role. Also for the first time, a disciple counters an assertion made by Jesus. In this progression, therefore, the total scope of Jesus' identity is exhibited to the disciples, and in this setting a disciple is shown to have, for the first time, the courage to disagree with Jesus. The disagreement is short-lived, however. With Jesus' rebuke of Peter, the second unit ends, and the third unit begins.

The third unit of the progression (8:34—9:1) begins as Jesus "summons" (*proskaleisthai*) the crowd with his disciples.[36] This time the summons concerns the central cognitive dimension of Jesus' value system. Anyone who adopts Jesus' system of thought and action must understand that one saves one's life only by losing it (8:35). The cognitive base of this system of thought requires the willingness of a person to deny the usual concerns for him- or herself, family, and occupation in order to adopt the mode of Jesus' thought and action in the narrative. This basic premise has been evident since the first call to disciples in 1:16–20. But the cognitive system itself involves a much deeper form of reflection and response. The metaphor for describing the underlying value system is chosen from the context of death by crucifixion. A person must be willing to pick up a cross and follow Jesus (8:34). If obedience to God means kinship to Jesus (3:35), embodying the system of Jesus' thought and action means accepting loss of personal life in an ignominious form. Instead of accepting this role in life, a person may be ashamed of Jesus and his words (8:38). If a person is ashamed, he or she will not use the thought and action of Jesus as a guideline for his or her own words and deeds, and the result will be shame instead of acceptance when the kingdom of God comes with power (8:38—9:1).

Mark 8:27—9:1 harks back to the very first progression in which Jesus called disciples to follow him (1:14–20). In the second unit of that progression (1:16–18), Jesus issued a direct command to two men: "Follow me . . ." In contrast, Mark 8:34—9:1 features Jesus issuing a mandate in conditional form not only to the Twelve but to the crowd with the disciples: "*If* anyone would come after me, *let him* [or *her*] deny himself, and take up his cross and follow me" (8:34). The issue is what a person "wants" from Jesus and what a person "wills" to do about it.[37] The summons, issued to the crowd along with the disciples, continues with an explanation of the reasoning underlying the conditional mandate: "*For* whoever would save his life will lose it; and whoever loses his life for my sake and the gospel's will save it" (8:34).[38]

With an explanation of the reasoning underlying the teaching, Jesus returns to the term "gospel" which played a central role in 1:14–20. The elaboration of "the gospel of Jesus Christ, the Son of God" in 1:1 finally reaches a stage of qualitative progression where the personage of Jesus and the meaning of "the gospel" are so thoroughly intertwined that the direct speech of Jesus juxtaposes "me and the gospel" (8:35). This juxtaposition stands as another part of the answer to the question Jesus put to the disciples, "Who do men say that I am?" The disciples' first answer was

John the Baptist, and Mark 1:14–20 began by interrelating Jesus and the gospel with the arrest of John the Baptist. Through the interrelation of John the Baptist's arrest and death with the activities of Jesus and the disciples (1:14; 6:14–20), and through the plan of the Pharisees and Herodians to destroy Jesus (3:6), the reader has become aware that Jesus' activity may end in a violent public death. However, the disciples have not had to face the possibility of Jesus' death at the hands of hostile public officials. Jesus' rejection by his own people (6:1–3) introduced the necessity for them to understand how to respond when their own activity was rejected (6:11): when rejected they were to go to a town that welcomed them. Mark 8:27—9:1, however, takes the step that the reader, not the disciples, has anticipated. The disciples are asked to interrelate the fate of John the Baptist with the identity of Jesus and to accept an identity as disciples who are willing to gain life by losing it (8:35).

The Authoritative Son of David:
Mark 10:46–48, 49–52; 11:1–11

After the section in Mark 8:27—10:45, in which three three-step subsections exist around the passion predictions, the three-step repetitive form ending with a summons by Jesus is less evident. Yet two more three-step progressions appear to be present.[39] The first is Mark 10:46—11:11. This progression exhibits Jesus' willingness to serve others and transfers the task of serving others to two disciples whom he delegates to procure a young colt for him to ride into Jerusalem. It occurs between Jesus' teaching that the Son of man came not to be served but to serve and give his life as a ransom for many (10:32–45), and Jesus' cursing of the fig tree and cleansing of the Temple (11:12–26). The progression thus interrelates the central dimensions of Jesus' teaching with the public results of the system of thought and action manifested by Jesus in the narrative. The structure of the progression is established by the following framework:

1. And *they came* . . . and as *he was leaving* . . . with *his disciples* and a great multitude, Bartimaeus, a blind beggar, the son of Timaeus, was sitting . . . [and] he began to cry out and say . . . And many rebuked [*epetimēsen*] him . . . but he cried out all the more . . . (10:46–48);
2. And *Jesus stopped and said* . . . and Jesus said . . . and Jesus said . . . (10:49–52);
3. And when they drew near . . . *he sent* two of his disciples, and said to them . . . (11:1–11).

This interval takes Jesus and his disciples into Jerusalem, precisely where the disciples have not wanted to go.

The first unit of the progression (10:46–48) features Jesus and his disciples traveling in and out of Jericho. The specific reference to the disciples (10:46) even though they do nothing in the episode indicates once again the first part of a three-step progression.[40] The first unit of action features blind Bartimaeus twice crying out to Jesus, "Son of David, have mercy on me!" (10:47, 48). The title "Son of David" marks an additional step in the qualitative progression that unfolds the identity of Jesus. This title has not occurred thus far in the narrative, although Jesus cited an occasion with David and his companions as a precedent to defend his own disciples' plucking of grain on the Sabbath (2:25–26). In the present setting the repetitive plea to Jesus anticipates the cry of the crowd in the third unit: "Blessed is the kingdom of our father David that is coming" (11:10). Jesus is heading toward Jerusalem with the power and authority associated with David who originally captured Jerusalem and established it as the political and religious center of the nation of Israel.

The second unit of action begins when Jesus stops and speaks (10:49). As Jesus commands those around him, "Call him," he is transferring a function to others which he alone has performed in the narrative. In contrast to the other progressions in which Jesus calls the disciples in the final unit, this progression features a command from Jesus that counters the action of many around him to rebuke Bartimaeus. This unit of action brings themes and episodes in the preceding section to a dramatic conclusion. Jesus' willingness to serve others rather than to be served establishes the context for the story. When Bartimaeus cries out for help, Jesus responds despite the attempts of people around him to abort the efforts of Bartimaeus (10:48).[41] Instead of hindering and rebuking, those around Jesus should call people to Jesus. As those around Jesus accept the command, they call the blind man using words that only Jesus uses in other places throughout the narrative: "Take heart [cf. 6:50]; rise [cf. 2:9; 3:3], he is calling you" (10:49). In the second and third units of the initial progression (1:16–18, 19–20), Jesus exercised his authority by calling four men to follow him. In the second unit of 10:46—11:11, Jesus uses his authority to command others to call a person to him. This unit of action reaches a high point when Jesus asks blind Bartimaeus, "What do you want me to do for you?" (10:51). With this question, the theme from the preceding narrative—concerning what a person wants from Jesus and what a person wills to do about it—receives paradigmatic resolution.[42] In contrast to the disciples who show confusion as they attempt to reconcile their desires and expectations with the concepts and responsibilities which they receive as part of their role as disciples, blind Bartimaeus has an accurate perception of what he has the right to expect from Jesus on the basis of his role as an afflicted person in society. In contrast to requests for special honors, Bartimaeus asks that his blindness be healed. When Jesus grants him his wish on the basis of his faith, he "follows" Jesus on the way toward Jerusalem (10:52) in the manner in which the disciples are expected to follow.[43]

In the third and final unit of the progression (11:1–11) Jesus' function as Son of David and Bartimaeus's acceptance of discipleship reach their conclusion. In analogy with 6:7 when Jesus sent the disciples out two by two, Jesus sends two of his disciples to procure the animal on which he immediately rides into Jerusalem. Mark 11:1–11 features Jesus requesting that they fulfill a task that will transport him and them into Jerusalem. Just as the authority of the Son of David resides within Jesus who came to serve, so the two disciples take a specific authoritative statement with them when they go to take a young beast of burden away from its owner long enough for Jesus to use it to enter Jerusalem (11:3).[44] Since Jerusalem and the Temple represent the center of Jewish heritage and authority, Jesus' dramatic entry into Jerusalem and the Temple, as well as the disciples' full participation in the entry, introduces the role of both Jesus and his followers in replacing Jewish heritage with a new point of view and a new mode of action.[45] Authority within rejection and service characterizes this new stance. While in 6:7–13 the disciples are sent out into villages and towns where rejection is always a possibility, 11:1–11 portrays Jesus sending them to fulfill duties that result in their presence in Jerusalem itself—the city that holds the power of Jewish salvation and brings rejection, suffering, and death.

The Future Son of Man and the Dying Messiah-King: Mark 13:1–2, 3–4, 5–37

The final three-step progression in the Markan narrative (13:1–37) emerges out of the activity of Jesus and his disciples in the Jerusalem Temple (10:46—12:44). When Jesus leaves the Temple, his disciples ask him questions that create a period of interchange before the final events begin to transpire (14:1–15:47).[46] In this progression Jesus inaugurates the final program of activities that will prepare the disciples for his separation from them. The framework that establishes the three-step progression emerges as follows:

1. And *as he came out of the temple, one of his disciples said* to him . . . And *Jesus said* to him . . . (13:1–2);
2. And as *he sat . . . Peter and James and John and Andrew* asked him privately . . . (13:3–4);
3. And *Jesus began to say to them,* "Take heed . . . But take heed . . . for they will deliver . . . and when they bring you to trial and deliver you up . . . And brother will deliver up brother . . . (13:9–13); Take heed . . . (13:5–23); But in those days after that tribulation . . . And then . . . And then . . .

(13:24–27); But of that day or that hour . . . Take heed, watch . . . Watch therefore . . . Watch (13:32–37).[47]

The first unit of action (13:1–2) occurs as Jesus is coming out of the Temple. One of the disciples addresses Jesus as teacher and remarks that the stones and building of the Temple are magnificent (13:1). In response, Jesus asks them to look at the great buildings and predicts that these buildings will all be leveled to the ground (13:2). This unit is a remarkable inversion of the first unit of action in the three-step progression that inaugurates the narrative program of the gospel (1:14–15), and it parallels that unit in length and poignancy. In 1:14–15, Jesus comes into Galilee and announces the coming of the kingdom of God; in 13:1–2, Jesus comes out of the Jerusalem Temple and announces the destruction of its magnificent structure. In other words, the kingdom of God that attends Jesus' activity is accompanied by the demise of the Temple as the center of religious activity for those who do the will of God.[48]

On the one hand, Mark 13:1–2 concludes the previous section when Jesus teaches in the Temple, and it interrelates Jesus' message about the kingdom of God with his teaching activity in the Jerusalem Temple. On the other hand, this unit of action introduces the issue that opens the trial which consequently brings a death sentence upon Jesus (14:58).[49] Jesus' prediction of the destruction of the Temple establishes an identity for Jesus that completes his rivalry with Jewish leaders from the outset of his teaching activity. Jesus' authoritative teaching is meant to replace the leadership of the Temple institution with its pervasive instructional outreach. Both scribes and Pharisees are perceived as teachers who come from Jerusalem (3:22; 7:1). They represent the teaching staff of the Temple and its activities. While the kingdom of God stands behind Jesus' teaching, the Temple stands behind the teaching of the scribes and Pharisees. In 13:1–2 the kingdom of God that establishes the context for Jesus' teaching brings the destruction of the Temple, which provides the context for the teaching of the scribes and Pharisees.

The second unit of action (13:3–4) occurs when Jesus sits down on the Mount of Olives opposite the Temple.[50] Peter, James, John, and Andrew ask Jesus about the destruction of the Temple and the consummation of all things. As 13:1–2 is an inversion of Mark 1:14–15, so 13:3–4 is an inversion of 1:16–18, 19–20. In contrast to the first three-step progression where Jesus summons these four men to follow him, in 13:3–4 these four men call forth from Jesus a discourse about the future when he will no longer be with them. In 1:16–20 these four men willingly responded to the summons of Jesus. Now Jesus willingly responds to their request for information about the future. With Jesus' acceptance of their initiative as appropriate, a new phase begins in the relationship between Jesus and the disciples. Prior to this setting, their initiatives always contain a problematic or inappropriate dimension. In contrast, Mark 13:3–4 presents the inner circle of Jesus' disciple-companions taking an appropriate initiative by asking about the future: "Tell us, when will this be, and what will be the sign when these things are all to be accomplished?"

The third unit of action is filled with direct speech by Jesus. He opens with, "Take heed that no one leads you astray" (13:5). After warning the four disciples to avoid being led astray by self-announced leaders and by events that appear to be the consummation of all things (13:5–8), he renews his warning with, "But take heed to yourselves" (13:9). At this point Jesus begins to apply the actions and events of his own ministry to the actions and events of the future ministry of his disciples. As Jesus will be delivered up to courts (14:53–65; 15:1–5), so the disciples will be delivered up (13:9). As Jesus will be beaten before his crucifixion (15:15), so the disciples will be beaten in synagogues (13:9). As Jesus has proclaimed the gospel of God (1:14–15), so the disciples must preach the gospel to all nations (13:10). In this setting, the startling announcement is made to the four disciples: "You will be hated by all for my name's sake" (13:13).[51] Jesus' predictions of his own arrest, trial, abuse, and death are transferred to the setting of discipleship. The fate of the teacher is not simply a set of occurrences that Jesus alone must face. Those who adopt his value system and mode of life must be prepared to accept the same fate. More than this, however, they must be on guard against false messiahs and false prophets who will attempt to lead them away from this form of commitment. The remarkable aspect of the situation is that these four disciples could not imagine what kind of composite role they were being called into when they first responded (1:16–20). While the disciples are willing to accept the social stigma of people who had forsaken their vocations, families, and associates to accompany a wandering preacher-teacher, there is little indication that they could expect to "be hated by all" (13:13) either during or after the lifetime of their teacher. Nevertheless, they must remain true to their commission to preach the gospel to all nations (13:10). In other words, an additional aspect of Jesus' role as teacher is to transmit information about the future when he will be absent from his followers. What Jesus predicts in this unit, which is dominated by his direct speech, he manifests in his own suffering and death in the last section of the narrative. Both his word and his action, therefore, leave a future mandate for anyone who chooses to be a follower of Jesus.

THE OUTLINE OF MARK

The three-step progressions that end with a summons by Jesus unfold the identity of Jesus and reveal the means by which Jesus' system of thought and action is transmitted to disciple-companions. This analysis is

offered as a solution to a basic dispute over the outline of Mark. Some
have thought that most sections in Mark begin with a scene in which Jesus
interacts with his disciples.[52] In contrast, others have argued that a
combination of thematic features—other than Jesus' interaction with his
disciples—makes a scene the introduction to a new section of material.[53]
Analysis on the basis of compositional and rhetorical structure reveals that
three-step progressions ending with a formal call to discipleship inaugurate sections of material that programmatically transmit to the disciples
attributes of thought and action that Jesus embodies in the narrative. The
three-step progressions act as transitions in the narrative to the next stage
of interaction between Jesus and his disciples. The first unit of action
features Jesus as the center of attention. The second unit features interaction between Jesus and others that sets the stage for the final unit. The
third unit of action places the disciples under the summons and instruction of Jesus. In this way, Jesus' action sets the stage for the dimensions of
discipleship that are displayed in the overall framework of the narrative.

Each three-step progression inaugurates a section of material that explores new attributes in the identity of Jesus and new dimensions in the
responsibilities of discipleship. When Jesus first arrives in Galilee and
announces the arrival of the kingdom of God, the responsibility of the
disciple is simply to respond by leaving his present circumstances and
following Jesus (1:14–15). After a section which features Jesus in situations
of teaching, healing, and conflict (1:21—3:6), Jesus' ability to heal is
identified with the title "Son of God," and his abilities are slated for
transferal to twelve disciples whom he selects out of the multitude of
people following him (3:7–19). When Jesus' teaching and healing in the
succeeding section (3:20—5:43) bring rejection in his hometown, Jesus
describes himself as a rejected prophet and sends the Twelve out with
instructions concerning their action when they themselves are rejected
(6:1–13). After a section that recounts the death of John the Baptist and
introduces the inability of the disciples to understand the significance of
the feedings in the wilderness (6:14—8:26), Jesus discusses with his
disciples his identity as a suffering, dying, rising Son of man and summons
them to a type of discipleship that accepts loss of life as a means of gaining
life (8:27—9:1). After Jesus repeatedly attempts to explain his role as a
suffering, dying, and rising Son of man to his disciples (9:2—10:45), he—
as the authoritative Son of David who raises expectations of the kingdom
of David—elicits the participation of his disciples in his approach of the
Jerusalem Temple (10:46—11:11). After teaching daily in the Temple for a
number of days (11:12—12:43), Jesus predicts the destruction of the
Temple and prepares Peter, Andrew, James, and John for the future when
they must perpetuate the system of thought and action that Jesus embod-

ies in the narrative (13:1–37). They must perpetuate this system, described as "gospel," at a time when Jesus is absent from them and when they face the same kind of circumstances that Jesus will face in the final events of the narrative. Immediately after Jesus' lengthy discussion with the disciples about the future, Jesus and his disciples face the events that fulfill the expectations that have been raised concerning Jesus' arrest, trial, crucifixion, burial, and resurrection (14:1—16:8).

This outline, emphasizing three-step progressions that inaugurate new sections of the narrative, is based on both repetitive and progressive forms in the Gospel of Mark. The outline highlights the portrayal of Jesus and the portrayal of the disciples in the framework that programmatically integrates the thought and action of Jesus with the thought and action of discipleship. When Jesus repeats the same pattern of behavior in new situations where a major shift occurs in the narrative, his basic identity as a disciple-gathering teacher remains intact. When new attributes of Jesus emerge in the new situations, a qualitative progression occurs that unfolds attributes of Jesus' thought and activity which the reader may not have anticipated at the beginning but which the reader accepts as appropriate when they emerge. In this manner, the author molds the folklore of early Christian groups into a unified presentation of "the gospel of Jesus Christ, the Son of God." In Mark, the "gospel of God" is transformed into a biographical account of a prophet-teacher who embodies wisdom and power and transmits his mode of thought and action to a select group of disciple-companions who associate with him.

CONCLUSION

In this chapter repetitive style in Mark led us to the three-step progressions that provide the framework for the passion predictions in 8:31; 9:31; and 10:32–34. The regular occurrence of a summons by Jesus in the third unit of action led us in turn to three-step progressions with a similar rhetorical form that occur at points where a major shift occurs in the narrative. Analysis of the three-step progressions associated with a major shift in the narrative reveals that the three-step progressions programmatically elaborate the topic of "the gospel of Jesus Christ, the Son of God," which stands in the first verse of the narrative. Through the technique of elaboration, previous statements are reformulated in new situations, and attributes of Jesus' thought and action programmatically unfold in qualitative progressions that appear appropriate to the reader. The technique of elaboration builds upon a repetitive form that exhibits Jesus repeating a pattern of behavior through which he places the disciples under a summons that transfers dimensions of his thought, behavior, and plight to the role of discipleship.

The pattern of behavior exhibited by Jesus in the three-step progressions identifies him as a teacher whose goal is to transmit his system of thought and action to a group of disciple-companions who will perpetuate the system after his death. The death of the teacher tests the success of the effort. After this time there is no possibility for the disciple to return to the teacher in order to receive further instruction and encouragement. The disciple-companion goes on his own to embody the system of thought and action that his teacher attempted to transmit to him. Therefore, the three-step progressions build to Mark 13 where Jesus instructs the disciples about the future when he will be absent from them and when they will be expected to manifest his system of thought and action in the world. The anticipatory teaching that Jesus inaugurates in the three-step progression in 8:27—9:1 reaches its fruition in the three units of action in 13:1–37 that inaugurate the final section of the narrative. In 13:9–13 Jesus asks Peter, Andrew, James, and John to anticipate a nearly parallel replication of his activities in their own future activities. During this period of time they cannot return to him for instructions but should "say whatever is given you [them] in that hour" (13:11).

The repetitive form in the three-step progressions therefore provides the vehicle for exhibiting Jesus' basic identity in changing situations. Jesus' attributes as a healer, a rejected prophet, a public servant who undergoes public humiliation and death, an authoritative Son of David, and a rising, returning Son of man programmatically unfold before the reader at points where the reader is prepared to accept these attributes as appropriate for Jesus. The reader thus knows that the new attributes are simply additional features of Jesus' basic role as a teacher-Messiah who transmits a system of thought and action to a group of disciple-companions that he gathers around him.

NOTES

1. E. Vivas, "Literary Classes," 103.

2. The phrase "planned framework" and the term "structure" are used in this essay in the sense in which they are defined by C. H. Holman, et al. See "Structure," in *A Handbook to Literature*. The term "formal structure" is used in the sense of the general plan or outline of Mark's gospel in contrast to various structural features within it.

3. B. M. Metzger, *The Text of the New Testament*, 21–25. For the chapter divisions (*kephalaia*) and titles (*titloi*) for Mark in Codex Alexandrinus and many other later manuscripts, see H. F. von Soden, *Die Schriften des Neuen Testaments* I.1, 407–9. For interpretations of the *kephalaia* in the early manuscripts as early lectionary divisions, see P. Carrington, *The Primitive Christian Calendar*; M. D. Goulder, *Midrash and Lection in Matthew*; idem, *The Evangelist's Calendar*.

4. Metzger, *Text of the New Testament*, 104.

5. See the careful work on the outline of Mark: E. Wendling, *Die Entstehung des Marcus-Evangeliums;* G. Wohlenberg, *Das Evangelium des Markus;* K. L. Schmidt, *Der Rahmen der Geschichte Jesu;* G. Hartmann, *Der Aufbau des Markusevangeliums mit einem Anhang.*

6. The consensus within the context of the specific disagreements is helpfully outlined by E. Trocmé (*The Formation of the Gospel According to Mark*, 80): Section 1: 1:1 or 1:14 to 3:6 or 3:19; Section 2: 3:7 or 3:20 to 6:6, 6:13, or 6:29; Section 3: 6:7, 6:14, or 6:30 to 8:21, 8:26, or 8:30; Section 4: 8:22, 8:27, or 8:31 to 10:45 or 10:52; Section 5: 10:46 or 11:1 to 13:37; Section 6: 14:1 to 16:8. For a review of many outlines of Mark, see R. Pesch's study of Mark 13, *Naherwartungen*, 48–73. For recent work on the outline, see D. Blatherwick, "The Markan Silhouette?" See also F. G. Lang, "Kompositionsanalyse des Markusevangeliums."

7. K. Burke, *Counter-Statement*, 25.

8. F. Neirynck, *Duality in Mark*, 110–12; idem, "L'Evangile de Marc (II)." A threefold pattern in storytelling is so widespread that it has been referred to as the "Law of Three." See. A. Olrik, "Epische Gesetze der Volksdichtung"; E. Tavenner, "Three as a Magic Number in Latin Literature"; E. B. Lease, "The Number Three, Mysterious, Mystic, Magic." For a more recent discussion, see R. Alter, *The Art of Biblical Narrative*, 95–96.

9. See V. K. Robbins, "Summons and Outline in Mark," 98–100.

10. "And your sisters" (*kai ai adelphai sou*) is present in A D 700 etc. but absent from ℵ B C K L W Δ Θ II, etc. It is quite possible that *kai ai adelphai sou* was added in later manuscripts by means of mechanical expansion; see B. M. Metzger, *A Textual Commentary on the Greek New Testament*, 82.

11. Robbins, "Summons and Outline," 98–99.

12. For a detailed discussion of the story of Peter's denial, see K. E. Dewey, "Peter's Curse and Cursed Peter"; idem, "Peter's Denial Reexamined"; W. Schenk, *Der Passionsbericht nach Markus*, 215–23; D. Dormeyer, *Die Passion Jesu als Verhaltensmodell*, 150–57.

13. For recent discussions of the Gethsemane pericope, see W. H. Kelber, "The Hour of the Son of Man and the Temptation of the Disciples (Mk 14:32–42)"; idem, "Mark 14:32–42"; G. Szarek, "A Critique of Kelber's 'The Hour of the Son of Man and the Temptation of the Disciples: Mark 14:32–42.' "

14. For a recent discussion of the passion predictions, including a survey of past discussions, see N. Perrin, "Towards an Interpretation of the Gospel of Mark," 14–30.

15. Robbins, "Summons and Outline," 102–5.

16. D. Rhoads and D. Michie, *Mark as Story*, 54–55.

17. Robbins, "Summons and Outline," 105–12.

18. Burke, *Counter-Statement*, 125.

19. For an analysis of Mark 1:14–20, see V. K. Robbins, "Mark I.14–20"; E. Best, *Following Jesus*, 166–74.

20. For a discussion of the omission of "Son of God" (*huiou theou*) in some manuscripts, see Metzger, *Textual Commentary*, 73.

21. This conclusion was reached during my recent work with data from the Chreia Project, Claremont, California. For an account of the origins, scope, and goals of this project, see E. N. O'Neil, "The Chreia in Greco-Roman Literature and Education." On the program of training through which people learned to compose in Greek or Latin, see S. F. Bonner, *Education in Ancient Rome*, 250–76.

22. My initial insights into the elaboration procedure in antiquity were gained from B. L. Mack, "The Elaboration of the Chreia in the Classroom."

23. This technique has provided the basis for L. E. Keck's proposal that 1:14–15 represents the conclusion to the introduction of the Gospel of Mark. See Keck, "The Introduction to Mark's Gospel."

24. Cf. Robbins, "Mark I.14–20," 220–31.

25. For programmatic discussions of these verses, see L. E. Keck, "Mark 3:7–12 and Mark's Christology," 345–46; K. G. Reploh, *Markus—Lehrer der Gemeinde*, 35–50; J. Gnilka, *Das Evangelium nach Markus (Mk 8,27–16,20)*, 132–43.

26. For the status of "they followed" (*ēkolouthēsan*) in the text, see Keck, "Mark 3:7–12," 345–48; Metzger, *Textual Commentary*, 79–80.

27. Reploh, *Markus*, 43–50; Gnilka, *Markus*, 135–43; Best, *Following Jesus*, 180–89.

28. For programmatic analyses of this verse, see Gnilka, *Markus*, 226–42, with references.

29. For a comprehensive analysis of Mark 6:1–6, see E. Grässer, "Jesus in Nazareth (Mark VI.1–6a)."

30. For a redactional analysis of Mark 6:6b–13, see Reploh, *Markus*, 50–58; Best, *Following Jesus*, 190–98.

31. For detailed analyses of Mark 8:27—9:1, see Best, *Following Jesus*, 19–54; N. Perrin, *What is Redaction Criticism?* 40–57.

32. The construction of the verse with a third singular verb and the multiple subject *ho Iēsous kai hoi mathētai autou* exhibits Mark's attempt both to keep the focus on Jesus and to make special mention of the presence of the disciples. See especially W. L. Lane, *Commentary on the Gospel According to Mark*, 287–92.

33. See D. Aune, *Prophecy in Early Christianity*, 399 n.93: "The peripatos and the dialogue were first combined by Epicurus (R. Hirzel, *Der Dialog*, I [Leipzig: S. Hirzel, 1895], 364 n. 2). Diogenes Laertius frequently refers to a certain Athenodoros as the author of a literary work entitled *Peripatoi* (iii.3; v.36; vi.81; ix.42). In the Greco-Roman period the term peripatetic was applied to Epicurean philosophers (Cicero, *Letters to Atticus*, vii.1.1: 'ut philosophi ambulant'; cf. Hirzel, *Der Dialog*, I:364 n. 1). By the second century A.D., when Plutarch and Lucian had revived the dialogue as a literary form suitable for ethical, religious, and philosophical discussion, the *peripatos* had become, to judge by Plutarch's fourteen surviving dialogues, an essential feature (Plutarch, *Amatorius*, 771d; idem, *De facie* 937c; idem, *Non posse suav.* 1086d, etc.)." Cf. W. Mundle, "Die Geschichtlichkeit des messianischen Bewusstseins Jesu," 309. Unfortunately, Mundle used the observation to argue for the messianic consciousness of Jesus rather than to understand the Gospel of Mark.

34. See Robbins, "Summons and Outline," 99–100.

35. This kind of learning may be called "anticipatory enculturation." Anticipatory "socialization" concerns a person's attempt to attain membership in another social group; see R. K. Merton, *Social Theory and Social Structure*, 319–22. Anticipatory "enculturation" refers to learning designed to prepare a person for performance in a particular achieved role in society. See T. R. Sarbin and V. L. Allen on "Role Theory," 547.

36. For helpful analyses of 8:34—9:1, see Lane, *Mark*, 304–14; E. Schweizer, *Good News According to Mark*, 174–80.

37. The Greek word used for both "want" and "will" in this section is *thelō*. For an analysis of *thelō* in 8:27—10:45, see V. K. Robbins, "The Healing of Blind Bartimaeus (Mark 10:46–52) in the Marcan Theology," 239.

38. On the antithetical aphorism in this verse, see R. C. Tannehill, *The Sword of His Mouth*, 98–101.

39. Robbins, "Summons and Outline," 108–12.

40. See Robbins, "Blind Bartimaeus," 228–30.

41. Those around Jesus are described by means of the language of exorcism. They "rebuke" *(epitimaō)* him to "be silent" *(siōpaō)*, while Bartimaeus in turn "cries out" *(krazō)*. Cf. Mark 1:23–25; 5:7; 9:24–26.

42. Robbins, "Blind Bartimaeus," 239.

43. See esp. P. J. Achtemeier, "And He Followed Him"; also E. S. Johnson, "Mark 10:46–52," 203.

44. In order to understand the saying, "The Lord has need of it" (11:3), it must be correlated with 12:36–37 where it is asserted that David calls the Messiah "Lord." Cf. F. Hahn, *The Titles of Jesus in Christology*, 82–86.

45. Cf. W. Kelber, *The Kingdom in Mark*, 102–5, where the positive role of the disciples is ignored in order to concentrate on the new place for the kingdom.

46. See Pesch, *Naherwartungen*, 70–73; cf. Kelber, *Kingdom in Mark*, 109–11.

47. Robbins, "Summons and Outline," 110–12.

48. Cf. Kelber, *Kingdom in Mark*, 111–12.

49. See J. R. Donahue, *Are You the Christ?* 103–13.

50. Cf. Kelber, in *Kingdom in Mark*, 112–13, who sees the importance of the division of the scenes but wrongly construes the four disciples to function as opponents of Jesus in this setting.

51. The extreme social implications of this verse were first brought to my attention by J. A. Wilde in "The Social World of Mark's Gospel," 56–61.

52. Cf. Keck, "Mark 3:7–12"; idem, "Introduction to Mark's Gospel."

53. See, e.g., Blatherwick, "Markan Silhouette?" 184–92.

3

Conventional Repetitive Forms in Mark

Whereas the anticipations and gratifications of progressive and repetitive form arise during the process of reading, the expectations of conventional form may be anterior to the reading.[1]

An author communicates not only through a system of shared conventions (a genre), but also through modifications of those conventions.[2]

While the preceding chapter contains an analysis of repetitive and progressive forms that provide a formal structure for the Gospel of Mark, this chapter and the next three contain an analysis of repetitive and progressive forms from the perspective of conventional form. A conventional form, as we recall from chapter one, is a "categorical expectancy," an expectation that may be anterior to the process of reading itself.[3] We must also be aware that "categorical expectations are very unstable"[4] and that an author can, "if his use of repetitive and progressive principles is authoritative enough," succeed in gaining acceptance of the forms he creates through modification of existing conventional forms.[5] The success of the revision of conventional forms is highly dependent on the situation in which the new forms are launched:

If the changes in conventional form are introduced to obtain a new stressing, to produce a kind of effect which the violated convention was not well able to produce, but which happens to be more apropos to the contemporary scene, the changes may very rapidly become "canonized" in popular acceptance.[6]

This chapter and the next three present evidence that suggests that the author of the Gospel of Mark modified conventional repetitive and progressive forms in prophetic biblical literature. He accomplished this by adopting a socio-rhetorical pattern in contemporary culture associated with Greco-Roman religio-ethical teachers who gathered disciple-companions.

The present chapter concerns conventional repetitive forms that existed prior to the writing and reading of the Gospel of Mark. On the side of biblical and Jewish tradition, verbatim repetitive forms in prophetic documents programmatically remind the reader of the socio-rhetorical pattern of the prophet of the Lord, who is the major actor in the document. The social dimension of the pattern concerns the role of the prophet in society. The rhetorical dimension of the pattern concerns the action and speech that challenge kings, priests, and individuals to live according to the ways of the Lord. Through repetition of phrases like "and the word of the Lord came to . . ." and "so he went and did . . ." and "he said, 'Thus says the Lord'. . ." the document transmits a socio-rhetorical pattern for the prophet of the Lord. This pattern establishes and confirms the perpetual activity of God in human events and the perpetual selection of certain people to function as his spokespersons in the setting of those events. The Elijah/Elisha narrative and the book of Jeremiah have special importance for analysis of conventional repetitive forms that existed as "categorical expectations" prior to the Gospel of Mark. These two documents contain strings of traditions integrated by narrative prose that creates a biography depicting the adult career and death of a prophet without including birth or childhood stories. The selection of the Elijah/Elisha narrative is encouraged by explicit references to Elijah in Mark[7] and by the parallels between the miracles of Jesus and the miracles of Elijah and Elisha.[8] The selection of Jeremiah is encouraged by the presence of repetitive forms characteristic of the Elijah/Elisha narrative in a biographical account that organizes poetic oracles into a sequence "that begins with the call of the prophet and ends with his suffering and virtual martyrdom (the so-called Passion of Jeremiah)."[9] Verbatim repetitive forms in the Elijah/Elisha narrative and the book of Jeremiah are conventional repetitive forms that represent a significant precedent to the repetitive forms in the Gospel of Mark.

On the side of Greek and Greco-Roman tradition, Xenophon's *Memorabilia* is perhaps the only extant document able to reveal repetitive forms that transmitted the socio-rhetorical pattern of the disciple-gathering teacher in popular Mediterranean culture prior to the Gospel of Mark. Xenophon's *Memorabilia* is important for this analysis because of the following: the existence of this loosely connected account of Socrates' actions and conversations for four hundred years prior to the composition of the Gospel of Mark; the popularity of Socrates within Greco-Roman society; the loss of other accounts of religio-ethical teachers written prior to or contemporary with the Gospel of Mark; the prominence of disciple-companions in the setting of Socrates' teaching and action; and the conclusion of the document with an account of the trial and death of Socrates.[10] The repetitive forms in Xenophon's *Memorabilia* reveal the role of the religio-ethical teacher who gathers disciple-companions in order to transmit to them the system of thought and action that he himself embodies. Through repetition of phrases like "by what he said and what he himself did he benefited his companions . . ." and "he encouraged them to do . . . and restrained them from doing . . ." and " 'Tell me,' he said . . ." the author establishes and confirms the consistent embodiment and transmittal of the system of thought and action by the disciple-gathering teacher.

Conventional repetitive forms represent only one kind of conventional form in the Gospel of Mark. Succeeding chapters contain analysis of conventional progressive forms, the interrelation of repetitive and progressive forms, and categorical expectations other than repetitive and progressive forms. Our initial goal, however, is to analyze conventional repetitive forms that accompany the portrayal of the prophet of the Lord and the disciple-gathering teacher and to observe the intermingling and adaptation of these repetitive conventions in the Gospel of Mark.

CONVENTIONAL REPETITIVE FORMS IN PROPHETIC BIBLICAL DOCUMENTS

When an interpreter begins to probe conventional forms in Mark, the literary accounts of great men in the Hebrew Bible must be the first natural candidates for influence. References to Abraham, Isaac, Jacob, Moses, David, and Elijah in the Markan narrative make it certain that the author's heritage includes information about major personages in biblical tradition.[11] Many interpreters have looked only within biblical and Jewish traditions for conventional forms relevant to analysis of the Gospel of Mark. In fact, a widespread point of view appears to exist that "the only place where there is anything that approaches a Gospel form is . . . the Old Testament."[12] Our investigation suggests that influence from conventional forms in biblical literature represents only part of the picture, but the analysis is incomplete until it includes influences from the Hebrew Bible. Let us turn, therefore, to analysis of conventional repetitive forms in the Elijah/Elisha narrative and the book of Jeremiah.

Our analysis of the Elijah/Elisha narrative and the book of Jeremiah concerns the role of repetitive forms in the narrative's socio-rhetorical pattern. The socio-rhetorical pattern for the Elijah/Elisha narrative is summarized in a letter by Jehu to the seventy sons of Ahab in Samaria:

> "Know then that there shall fall to the earth nothing of the word of the Lord, which the Lord spoke concerning the house of Ahab; for the Lord has done what he said by his servant Elijah" (2 Kings 10:10).

The central concern of the socio-rhetorical pattern exhibited in the Elijah/ Elisha narrative is the transmission of the word of the Lord to various people. The word of the Lord is pronounced by means of a prophet who serves as an agent of the word of the Lord. The position of the prophet vis-à-vis kings, priests, and individuals reveals the social dimensions of the pattern.[13] The action and speech that challenge kings, priests, and individuals to live according to the ways of the Lord reveal the rhetorical dimensions of the pattern.[14] The prophet is legitimated as a man of God when the things he asserts prove to be true. The socio-rhetorical pattern contains three essential elements:

1. the word of the Lord comes to Elijah and Elisha;
2. Elijah and Elisha do and say the word of the Lord;
3. events occur according to the word of the Lord as pronounced by Elijah and Elisha.

The principal repetitive forms in the Elijah/Elisha narrative reiterate the elements of this socio-rhetorical pattern. The first element of the form emerges in the programmatic repetitions that "the word of the Lord came upon Elijah."[15] When the actual words of the Lord come to Elijah, they contain imperatives that command the prophet, with some variation, as follows: go and do and say.[16] As a result of the commands, Elijah or Elisha go and do what the Lord commands.[17]

In addition to whatever actions Elijah or Elisha are asked to perform, they are usually asked to deliver a word of the Lord to someone. As they begin, it is common for them to say, "Thus says the Lord (God of Israel) . . ."[18] Twice a word of the Lord begins with "Hear the word of the Lord (1 Kings 22:19; 2 Kings 7:1). Frequently the statement contains "As the Lord (the God of Israel, your God) lives . . ."[19] Twice Elijah adds "before whom I stand" (1 Kings 17:1; 18:15), and twice Elisha adds "whom I serve" (2 Kings 3:14; 5:16). The final element in the pattern is the assertion by the narrator that things occurred "according to the word of the Lord (which he spoke by Elijah [or Elisha])."[20]

Within this socio-rhetorical pattern, the prophet of the Lord frequently makes commands to individuals on the basis of the word of the Lord to him.[21] Most often the individuals do as the prophet commands, and always the things occur as the prophet says they will.[22] Three times the narrator asserts that when people did what the prophet commanded them to do, the events occurred "according to the word of the Lord" (2 Kings 5:14; 7:16; 10:17).

The style of repetition in the Elijah/Elisha narrative provides the legitimation for the prophets who speak words of the Lord. Events within the chronology of Israel's history create new situations for words of the Lord to be pronounced whereby prophets of the Lord are legitimated as true representatives of God's plan and will on the plane of human history.

The same socio-rhetorical pattern evident in the Elijah/Elisha narrative is exhibited by the book of Jeremiah. The major elements of the pattern are presented in the opening verses: "The words of Jeremiah, the Son of Hilkiah, of the priests who were in Anathoth in the land of Benjamin, to whom the word of the Lord came . . ." (Jer. 1:1–2). The account of Jeremiah concerns the words of the Lord that were pronounced by Jeremiah during the succession of kings from Josiah to Zedekiah, under whom the captivity of Jerusalem by the Babylonians occurred.[23] The repetitive forms associated with the prophet of the Lord in the Elijah/Elisha narrative also occur in Jeremiah, with some additions. The assertion that the word of the Lord came to Jeremiah occurs throughout the book in some variation of the following form: This is the word of the Lord which came to Jeremiah the prophet (concerning) . . .[24] Ten times this assertion is put in first-person form on the lips of Jeremiah: "the word of the Lord came to me (saying)."[25] In addition, the book of Jeremiah contains an alternative formulation that "the Lord spoke to Jeremiah."[26] Also, a first-person form of this occurs: "The Lord said to me."[27]

After the comment of the narrator that introduces the word of the Lord, a command comes to Jeremiah to go somewhere and proclaim the word that is given to him. After this command, the Lord frequently says, "You shall say to them . . ."[28] Then the familiar "thus says the Lord (of hosts/the God of Israel) . . ." occurs, beginning the oracle—approximately one hundred fifty times in the entire document. Frequently the exhortation "hear the word of the Lord" is added.[29] Seven times the phrase "as the Lord lives" occurs as part of the oracle,[30] and fifteen times the phrase "behold the days are coming says the Lord" occurs.[31]

These repetitive forms are conventional forms throughout biblical literature. The statement that "the word of the Lord came to . . ." occurs in Ezekiel, Hosea, Joel, Jonah, Micah, Zephaniah, Haggai, and Zechariah.[32] The personal form, "the word of the Lord came to me," is frequent in Ezekiel and Zechariah,[33] and "the Lord (he) said to me" is present in Isaiah, Ezekiel, Hosea, Amos, Habakkuk, and Zechariah.[34] Also "thus says the Lord,"[35] and, somewhat less frequently, "hear the word of the Lord"[36] occurs throughout prophetic biblical literature. With a frequency far too numerous to cite, this literature also contains "says the Lord (God of Hosts)." Much less frequently, phrases like "in/on that day,"[37] "behold the days are coming says the Lord,"[38] and "as I live (says the Lord)"[39] occur. Through these conventions, the socio-rhetorical pattern of the prophet of the Lord is perpetuated within Israelite and Jewish literature, society, and culture.

When repetitive forms in the Gospel of Mark are compared to the repetitive forms in prophetic biblical literature, a modification appears that reflects a shift in the socio-rhetorical pattern used to portray the

action and speech of Jesus. In prophetic biblical narrative, the action and
speech of the prophet exhibit the action and speech of the Lord. The
action and speech of the prophet are both the Lord's word to the people
("word *of the Lord*" as subjective genitive) and the prophet's word to the
people (e.g., "word *of Jeremiah*" as subjective genitive). But the terminology in prophetic biblical narrative does not easily suggest that the
"word" is a word about the prophet (e.g., "word *of Jeremiah*" as objective
genitive). In other words, the use of the phrase "word of the Lord"
dissuades the reader from concluding that the prophet embodies a word of
the Lord apart from the transmission of that word from the Lord to the
prophet in each new situation that emerges.

A shift in the prophetic pattern is subtly reflected in the use of the term
"gospel" rather than "word" in Mark. The opening verse in Mark, like the
opening verse in prophetic books, focuses its attention on an individual
who is identified by name. Also, when Jesus begins to speak and act, he
presents God's gospel to people ("gospel *of God*" as subjective genitive:
1:14). Yet, the reader never sees God tell the gospel to Jesus, and God
never tells Jesus to go and tell the gospel to others. As a result, the
"gospel of God" becomes both Jesus Christ's gospel ("gospel *of Jesus
Christ*" as subjective genitive) and the gospel about Jesus Christ ("gospel
of Jesus Christ" as objective genitive).[40] In other words, the action and
speech of God are remote enough that the action and speech of Jesus
become the essential content of the gospel. Indeed, the centrality of
Jesus' speech and action in Mark leads the author to make virtually no
distinction between "Jesus" and "the gospel" (8:35; 10:29).

Therefore, the shift in terminology from "word" to "gospel" in Mark is
part of a shift in the socio-rhetorical pattern contained in the document.
The three-step rhetorical pattern that exists in prophetic biblical narrative
is as follows:

1. the word of the Lord comes to the prophet;
2. the prophet announces the word of the Lord;
3. events occur according to the words of the Lord that the prophet
   announces.

In Mark the three-step pattern that dominates the narrative is as follows:
1. Jesus comes into a place accompanied by his disciples;
2. people interact both positively and negatively with the action and
   speech of Jesus;
3. Jesus summons his disciple-companions to transmit features of his
   action and thought that he has enacted before them.

The major difference in the socio-rhetorical pattern occurs in the first step. There are no repetitive forms in Mark insisting that the word of the Lord comes to Jesus. Instead, the action and speech of Jesus himself gains center stage. With this shift in emphasis, the reader presupposes that Jesus embodies within himself the understanding and initiative that produce the action and speech that flow from him. There is, to be sure, no uncertainty on behalf of the reader concerning whether the action and speech of Jesus occur "in accordance with the will of the Lord." Yet the socio-rhetorical pattern of the document is different from the pattern contained in prophetic biblical narrative. The social dimension of the pattern concerns the role of a prophet-teacher who transmits a system of thought and action that he himself embodies. The rhetorical dimension of the pattern concerns the action and speech of the prophet-teacher who establishes the integrity of his activity through consistency between what he says and what he does. In Mark, in other words, Jesus is legitimated not only through a pattern whereby events occur according to the will of the Lord but also through a pattern where Jesus enacts what he teaches. The system of thought and action enacted by Jesus is a system that he himself embodies and transmits to others by a consistent interrelating of thought and action in his own life.

Minor repetitive forms in the Gospel of Mark reveal the shift from the socio-rhetorical pattern of the prophet of the Lord to the socio-rhetorical pattern of a disciple-gathering prophet-teacher. Although the Gospel of Mark contains six verbatim quotations from prophetic biblical books[41] and two references to the prophet Isaiah (Mark 1:2; 7:6), it perpetuates virtually none of the verbatim repetitive forms of the Elijah/Elisha narrative, the book of Jeremiah, or any other prophetic biblical book. Never once in the Gospel of Mark, for example, does Jesus say, "thus says the Lord," "hear the word of the Lord," "the Lord said to me," or "behold the days are coming says the Lord." Since the conventions of prophetic biblical speech have influenced the style of Jesus' speech in the narrative, however, phrases that perpetuate much of the rhetorical authority of prophetic speech do appear. But none of the repetitive phrases in Jesus' speech claim authority for Jesus' speech by reference to "the Lord." Rather, the phrases perpetuate the authority of Jesus' speech and action in a manner that continually points to Jesus himself. Instead of "thus says the Lord" or "the Lord said to me," Jesus says, "truly, I say to you."[42] Instead of "hear the word of the Lord," he says "hear," or "he who has ears to hear, let him hear."[43] Instead of "behold the days are coming says the Lord," he says "take heed" or "watch."[44] The prophetic speech of Jesus does not perpetuate a repetitive reference to the Lord as the source of the speech. Rather, the speech of Jesus reflects the influence of a socio-rhetorical pattern that emphasizes the teacher's self-embodiment of the system of thought and action he teaches.

Thus, the Gospel of Mark exhibits a modification of conventional forms associated with the socio-rhetorical pattern of a prophet of the Lord. The presence of verbatim repetitive phrases in Jesus' speech reveals a heritage of conventional repetitive forms in prophetic biblical narrative. But the forms have been changed so that Jesus repeatedly points to himself as an authority without referring to the Lord as the source of his speech and action. Since the change is likely to have occurred as a result of a first-century socio-rhetorical pattern in Mediterranean culture, it is necessary for us to look for a major socio-rhetorical pattern within Greco-Roman literature that represents an alternative to the socio-rhetorical pattern of the prophet of the Lord.

MINOR REPETITIVE FORMS IN
XENOPHON'S *MEMORABILIA*

The search for the alternative socio-rhetorical pattern that has influenced the Gospel of Mark leads to portrayals of disciple-gathering teachers in Greco-Roman literature. Xenophon's *Memorabilia* emerges as the most informative document, since it alone—within Greco-Roman literature prior to the Gospel of Mark—exhibits the socio-rhetorical pattern of the disciple-gathering teacher by means of minor repetitive forms throughout the document. The loss of Greco-Roman documents that transmitted the stories about disciple-gathering teachers makes it impossible for the interpreter to exhibit repetitive forms that may have become conventional in the manner in which conventional forms are observable in prophetic biblical literature. In order to understand the importance of Xenophon's *Memorabilia* for an analysis of repetitive forms associated with the disciple-gathering teacher, and to understand the lack of analysis of other Greco-Roman documents in this chapter, I will briefly outline the history of the memorabilia form.

Xenophon's *Memorabilia* is the earliest known document of the memorabilia form, written ca. 390–355 B.C.E., and it is the only complete example of the form known from Mediterranean antiquity. Xenophon's *Memorabilia* was one of the experiments in biographical writing during the fourth century B.C.E.[45] It gives no information about the birth or youth of Socrates, but offers a defense of Socrates by recounting scenes from his adult career until his death. Clearly, it became a model for later compilations,[46] and interest in it was revived during the first and second centuries especially among Cynics and Stoics.

The actual title for the Greek memorabilia form is *apomnē-moneumata*.[47] Besides Xenophon's *Apomnēmoneumata* (Latin: *Memo-*

rabilia), various works with this title were used as sources by second- and third-century C.E. authors. Our evidence suggests that *apomnē-moneumata* tended to be written about people known for possessing wisdom or at least possessing the ability for witty retorts. For this reason references to various *apomnēmoneumata* surface in Athenaeus's *The Deipnosophists* (ca. C.E. 200) and Diogenes Laertius's *Lives of Eminent Philosophers* (third cent. C.E.).

Our evidence suggests that Lynceus of Samos, a contemporary of Menander (342/341–293/289 B.C.E.), was one of the first to write an *apomnēmoneumata* after Xenophon. Though Xenophon's work by this title has one person as its main subject, it is possible that Lynceus's *Apomnēmoneumata* had more. In any case, Athenaeus quotes four passages from this work, and all the stories bear the form of an aphoristic or apophthegmatic narrative.[48] Only when Athenaeus transmits a piece of information from Lynceus without quoting him is the aphoristic dimension lacking.[49] When Athenaeus seeks material containing witty retorts by wise men and women, he is able to find material that serves his purpose in this and other *apomnēmoneumata*.

According to Athenaeus (4.162B), both Stilpo (ca. 380–300 B.C.E.) and Zeno (335–263 B.C.E.) wrote documents entitled *Apomnēmoneumata*. Diogenes Laertius does not list a document with this title under Stilpo's works (2.120), but he gives a specific title for Zeno's document—*Apomnēmoneumata Kratētos* (of Crates). No direct quotations appear to be made from these works in extant literature. Persaeus (ca. 306–ca. 243 B.C.E.) used excerpts from the works of Stilpo and Zeno to write a document entitled *Convivial Dialogues (Sympotikoi Dialogoi)*.[50] Diogenes Laertius knows this work by Persaeus (7.1.1), and he lists a work entitled *Apomnēmoneumata* by him (7.1.36).[51] According to Diogenes Laertius (7.163), a man named Ariston (ca. 320–250 B.C.E.) wrote a three-book work entitled *Apomnēmoneumata*. We know nothing of its content; indeed its existence was already doubted in antiquity.[52]

During the first century B.C.E., Dioscurides wrote a work entitled *Apomnēmoneumata*. Only two accounts from it are preserved.[53] Diodorus, probably of Tyre (b. ca. 110 B.C.E.), also wrote an *apomnēmoneumata* from which Diogenes Laertius presents a paraphrase in 4.1.2. Also, an otherwise unknown Empodus wrote an *apomnēmoneumata* which is cited in Athenaeus 9.370C. Again, when quotations are made from *apomnēmoneumata*, the material tends to be aphoristic. Also, the people featured in these documents are known for their wisdom—Solon,[54] Plato, Speusippus, Zeno, and Socrates.

Favorinus (b. ca. C.E. 81) wrote an *apomnēmoneumata*, no longer extant, which Diogenes Laertius cites twenty-one times. Sometimes

Diogenes simply relates an item of information which he gathered from the work; in other instances he quotes portions of it. Diogenes cites the first book of the work eight times, the second book four times, the third book twice, the fifth book twice, and the work without specific reference four more times.[55] Diogenes' citations of Favorinus's *Apomnēmoneumata* indicate that this document, nearly contemporary with Mark, featured philosophers and teachers. Various material was contained in it about Socrates, Plato, Aristotle, Xenophanes, Speusippus, Crates, Pythagoras, Parmenides, Zeno the Eleatic, Empedocles, and Eudoxos. Moreover, Diogenes explicitly states that eight of the eleven had *mathētai* (disciples).[56] In two instances (3.1.62; 8.8.90) Diogenes retrieved information about the death of philosophers from Favorinus's *Apomnēmoneumata*, but never does he cite information about anyone's birth from it. Diogenes found information about Plato's birth in Favorinus's *Miscellaneous History*,[57] but for this kind of information he regularly depends on Apollodorus's *Chronology* and occasionally other works.[58] The evidence from these citations suggests that *apomnēmoneumata* contemporary with Mark perpetuated scenes from the adult life of philosopher/teachers in order to recount major tenets of their teaching, to narrate interactions they had with people around them, to present events which included the *mathētai* who were attracted to them, and to relate the circumstances that brought about their deaths. Greco-Roman biographical literature featuring kings, generals, and statesmen tended to possess different impulses and call for different composition and arrangement of materials.

In order to place *apomnēmoneumata* in a proper literary perspective, it is helpful to distinguish memorabilia (*apomnēmoneumata*) from written notes (*hypomnēmata*), on the one hand, and from historical biography (*bios*), on the other hand. A document entitled *Apomnēmoneumata* was written for other people to read. It contained stories, sayings, apophthegms, speeches, and dialogues loosely connected by means of editorial comment that gave a semblance of overall coherence. In contrast, *hypomnēmata* were notes taken down in the context of lectures or of travel, and the notes were not intended for circulation or publication. *Hypomnēmata*, therefore, contain items of information in a format that may not include repetitive editorial comment that gives the reader the experience of an integrated account.[59] In contrast to both *apomnēmoneumata* and *hypomnēmata*, a *bios* is an account of a person from birth to death using information from historical narratives and other written documents. While the author knows and uses information from historical accounts, he produces an alternative to a historical account by exhibiting the character of the person through incidental acts, short statements, and jests.[60]

Apomnēmoneumata, therefore, feature a person of wisdom who interacts with others to transmit the wisdom he embodies. The account contains scenes from the adult life of the personage that exhibit the activities that established his legacy within the culture. The scenes present the person interacting with rival persons of wisdom, disciple-companions, and others to exhibit the system of thought and action with which he is associated by the author of the account. *Apomnēmoneumata* may contain scenes from the death of the personage, but show little or no interest in his birth or childhood.

The dominant scholarly view has been that Xenophon's *Apomnēmoneumata (Memorabilia)* is more unlike than like the NT gospels.[61] One of the main reasons appears to be the differences in the "literarity" of the documents. As Xenophon writes, he maintains a narrator's presence to inform the reader why he includes one kind of material and then another kind. Another reason appears to be the lengthy dialogues in Xenophon's *Memorabilia*. Socratic dialogues rather than short scenes dominate the content. These differences, however, may obscure the socio-rhetorical pattern in the arrangement, composition, and literary structure of the work. Any form of literature is likely to exhibit a range of literary sophistication. Often a greater degree of sophistication will result in a longer document. Also, the author's consciousness of his art will often be explicit when greater literary sophistication exists. A range of literary sophistication is manifest in the NT itself, and the manifestation of a greater range within the broader literary culture should not blind us to the socio-rhetorical features that NT literature shares with Greco-Roman literature.

The basic impulse that underlies Xenophon's *Memorabilia* and the Gospel of Mark is the portrayal of a religio-ethical teacher manifesting his adult role through interaction with those around him. Xenophon's *Memorabilia* portrays Socrates as a man of wisdom and virtue exhorting his companions and other people to learn wisdom and adopt a virtuous life. This portrayal furnishes the impulse for the form which came to be known as memorabilia. Since Socrates' embodiment of wisdom and virtue is the logical prerequisite for his proper influence on others, the literary procedure Xenophon followed was to introduce a dimension of Socrates' virtue in an opening narrational comment, then to recount various episodes or dialogues that display this dimension of Socrates' activity.

While the stated purpose of Xenophon's *Memorabilia* is to expose the indictment against Socrates at the trial as erroneous, the means of the exposé is an exhibition of the consistency between Socrates' deeds and words. Socrates embodied virtue, and virtue is especially apparent in deeds. Also, Socrates possessed wisdom, and wisdom is especially apparent in words. By alternating accounts of Socrates' deeds with accounts of Socrates' discussions with his companions and others, Xenophon integrated the literary document and demonstrated that virtue and wisdom pervaded Socrates' action and speech.

The socio-rhetorical pattern underlying the portrayal of Socrates in Xenophon's *Memorabilia* is stated by the narrator in 1.2.17: "all teachers themselves show their disciples how they themselves do what they teach, and lead them on by speech . . ." This socio-rhetorical pattern contains three essential elements: (1) the teacher himself does what he teaches others to do; (2) the teacher interacts with others through speech to teach the system of thought and action he embodies; and (3) through his teaching and action the teacher transmits a religio-ethical system of thought and action to later generations through his disciple-companions.

While it is characteristic of biblical narrative to perpetuate a socio-rhetorical pattern through verbatim repetitive forms,[62] Greco-Roman literature perpetuates a socio-rhetorical pattern through repetition that contains minor variations. We must remind ourselves, as we did above in chapter two, of the directive within Greco-Roman rhetorical literature:

> We shall not repeat the same thing precisely—for that, to be sure, would weary the hearer and not elaborate the idea—but with changes (*Rhetorica ad Herennium* 4.42.54).

For this reason, an author repeats a phrase with variation throughout his document, elaborating the idea by saying the same thing over and over again with slight modifications.

The socio-rhetorical pattern of the religio-ethical teacher is manifest in phrases that are repeated with variation in Xenophon's *Memorabilia*. First, the narrator repeatedly introduces and concludes scenes of dialogue by referring to "such things" (*toiauta/toiade*) said and done by Socrates.[63] This leads to repeated references to Socrates "himself" (*autos/heauton*) and to what he himself did and said (*epoiei/prattōn/ta erga; legōn*).[64] By this action and speech he was useful (*ōphelimos*), a special benefit, to others.[65] He exerted his influence on others especially through conversation (*dialegesthai*),[66] exhorting (*protrepein*) his companions and others toward good actions and thoughts,[67] and discouraging (*apotrepein*) them from bad actions and thoughts.[68] The opportunity for these conversations often emerges "when seeing . . . he said" (*idōn/horōn . . . ephē/ēreto*) or "when learning that . . . he said" (*aisthomenos . . . ephē*).[69] Frequently the conversation begins with Socrates' statement, "Tell me" (*eipe moi*).[70] The result of this activity is that Socrates was able (*hikanos*) to make his companions do what he directed them (*poiein* plus infinitive), making them better (*beltiōn*).[71]

As the Gospel of Mark does not contain assertions that "the word of the Lord came to Jesus," so it does not contain assertions that Jesus himself said and did those things which made him a special benefit to others. In other words, the editorial leverage attained by the first step in the pattern both in prophetic biblical literature and in Xenophon's *Memorabilia* is not given repetitive form in the Gospel of Mark. Rather, at the beginning of Jesus' ministry the narrator asserts that Jesus "preaches the gospel of God" (Mark 1:14) and "[teaches] them as one who ha[s] authority, and not as the scribes" (Mark 1:22). The socio-rhetorical pattern that receives repetitive form in Mark elaborates the second step in the pattern of prophetic biblical literature and Xenophon's *Memorabilia*, namely, going to a place where Jesus interacts with people. On his own initiative, Jesus goes to a place where he confronts people or they confront him. While the Gospel of Mark never contains a command of the Lord to Jesus, it expands the situation of confrontation into two parts: (1) As Jesus goes to a place accompanied by his disciple-companions, his presence is the occasion for exhibiting an attribute of identity by means of a statement by the narrator, by Jesus himself, or by some other person; (2) Jesus interacts with people in a manner that reveals one or more attributes of his identity. Then, the Gospel of Mark features a third step: (3) Jesus summons his disciple-companions to undertake activity similar to the action and speech that Jesus has enacted before them.

The repetition in the Gospel of Mark features Jesus repeatedly "going into" a village-town or other place accompanied by his disciples, interacting with one or more people there, then "going away" to another village-town or place.[72] The repetition of this movement emphasizes the itinerant dimension of Jesus' activity that presents the occasions where he interacts with other people. No "word of the Lord" is necessary to move Jesus into action. On his own initiative he goes to these places, engages people in conversation, and exhorts people to accept the system of thought and action he embodies as a valid approach to the world. The narrator presents the occasions for interaction with comments that "Jesus saw . . . and said,"[73] people "asked . . . and he said,"[74] or Jesus "asked."[75] In the midst of this activity the disciples of Jesus receive special attention. Much as Xenophon's *Memorabilia* repeatedly refers to Socrates' conversations and exhortations to his disciple-companions, so the Gospel of Mark persistently reminds the reader that Jesus is accompanied by disciples whom he regularly summons to participate in the system of thought and action he manifests in their presence.[76] Thus, while the Gospel of Mark claims a heritage that lies within prophetic biblical literature, it exhibits characteristics of the socio-rhetorical pattern present in Xenophon's *Memorabilia*.

Perhaps, therefore, it is not irrelevant that Christian writers during the second century referred to the gospels as *apomnēmoneumata*. In Papias's account of the gospels (ca. 110–115 C.E.), the verb *apomnēmoneuō* is used to describe Mark's composition of the first account of Jesus' life. It is quite possible that the verb, in this context, means "to write an *apomnēmoneumata*":

> Peter gave his teachings in chreia-form; he was not making a compilation *(syntaxis)* of the dominical oracles. Therefore Mark was not wrong when he wrote down single items as he composed in the form of an *apomnēmoneumata (hōs apemnēmoneusen)* (Euseb., *Hist. Eccl.* 3.39.15).[77]

In the middle of the century (between 150 and 160 C.E.), Justin refers to the gospels as *Apomnēmoneumata tōn Apostolōn* (of the apostles). In the *Dialogue with Trypho* (155–160 C.E.) Justin refers thirteen times to the Christian *Apomnēmoneumata*. Seven of these times he refers to them as *Apomnēmoneumata tōn Apostolōn [autou]*.[78] In another instance (103.8), when Justin is citing material from Luke, he refers to the *Apomnēmoneumata* "compiled by the apostles and those who followed" *(hypo tōn apostolōn autou kai tōn ekeinois parakolouthēsantōn syntetachthai)*. Here Justin has expanded the form of reference using the language in the Lukan prologue (1:3) where Luke says, "It seemed good also for me having followed . . ." *(edoxe kamoi parēkolouthēkoti . . .)*. Four other instances refer to "the *Apomnēmoneumata*,"[79] and 106.3, referring to Mark 3:16–17, says it is "written in His *Apomnēmoneumata*."[80]

In the *Dialogue with Trypho*, Justin, in spite of frequent reference to the *Apomnēmoneumata of the Apostles*, never once calls them gospels. He uses the term *euaggelion* twice in the dialogue. In the first instance (10.2) Trypho is discussing Paul's view about festivals, sabbaths, and circumcision (Gal. 4:10; 5:2–12), and he uses the term *euaggelion* in the sense that Paul uses it in Gal. 4:13. In the second instance (100.1) Justin refers to the tradition about Jesus contained in Matt. 11:27. He uses the term *euaggelion* in the sense in which it is also used in the *Didache*.[81] All the written traditions possessed by the Christians are "the gospel"; therefore, traditions from Pauline letters and the *apomnēmoneumata* about Jesus are the gospel.

Even the earliest titles of the accounts of Jesus' life indicate that the scribes were aware that "gospel" was not a description of the documents in terms of literary form. While they did not write *Apomnēmoneumata* in the title, this literary form was probably presupposed. So the accounts of Jesus' life were not entitled *Markou Euaggelion* (Mark's gospel), and so forth. With this title, *Euaggelion* would be a literary title like *Apomnēmoneumata, Dialogoi,* or *Historiai*. Instead, the term "gospel" referred to all the traditions about Jesus whether they were in letters or narrative accounts. Therefore, the official titles for the *Apomnēmoneumata about*

Jesus became "according to Mark" *(kata Markon)*, and the like. *Euaggelion* did not appear in the title. When the term did appear, it was derived from a description of the subject matter in the document rather than from "gospel" as an established literary form. Does this not mean, then, that we would have good reason to refer to Mark as a Christian form of *apomnēmoneumata*?

Around 140 C.E., Marcion proposed that a revised version of Luke be considered "the Gospel" and ten letters of Paul be "the Apostolikon."[82] No other writings should be considered Scripture by the Christian church. Marcion's actions evidently introduced the impulse that caused early Christians to refer to each *Apomnēmoneumata* as "a gospel."[83] Marcion considered only an account of Jesus' life to be "the Gospel." Paul's letters, in turn, were "the Apostolikon." The early church leaders countered with a broader selection—there must be four "gospels," and "the Apostolikon" must include the Acts of the Apostles and letters attributed to other apostles. The earliest occurrence of the plural term "gospels" with reference to Christian documents occurs in Justin's *First Apology* (between 152 and 154 C.E.) when he refers to "the *apomnēmoneumata* composed by the apostles, which are called Gospels" *(First Apology* 1.66.3). It had not been customary to refer to each narrative about Jesus as "a gospel"; Justin considers it necessary to inform his readers that the *apomnēmoneumata* to which he refers are called "gospels" within the Christian community.[84]

For almost two hundred years after Justin, early Christians could still refer to the gospels as *apomnēmoneumata*. Tatian's *Oration to the Greeks* (ca. 160 C.E.) appears to refer to the gospels as *apomnēmoneumata*,[85] and Eusebius in the fourth century (ca. 300–340 C.E.) calls them *apomnēmoneumata*.[86] Thus three pieces of evidence suggest that an analysis of the perpetuation and adaptation of conventional forms in the Gospel of Mark should include Xenophon's *Memorabilia* as well as prophetic biblical literature. First, repetitive forms in Mark suggest an intermingling of the socio-rhetorical pattern of the prophet of the Lord with the socio-rhetorical pattern of the disciple-gathering teacher. While repetitive forms in prophetic biblical literature exhibit the pattern of the prophet of the Lord, repetitive forms in Xenophon's *Memorabilia* exhibit the pattern of the disciple-gathering teacher. Secondly, Papias considered the Gospel of Mark to have both form and content like an *apomnēmoneumata*, and he described the process of composition and the final product in such terms. Thirdly, even after the Christian community began to call the accounts of Jesus gospels, Christian writers until the fourth century could refer to them as *apomnēmoneumata*. Detailed investigation of the perpetuation and adaptation of conventional forms in the Gospel of Mark, therefore, must glean comparative data at least from prophetic biblical literature and Xenophon's *Memorabilia*.

CONCLUSION

Analysis of minor repetitive forms is a beginning for analysis of conventional forms in Mark. Such analysis suggests that a basic pattern from prophetic literature has been adapted to a basic pattern from the portrayal of disciple-gathering teachers. In the adapted pattern, Jesus gathers disciples and transmits a system of thought and action that explains how a person's life is saved by losing it. The repetitive forms present Jesus "repeating his identity . . . under changing situations."[87] This identity is constituted by a blending of features characteristic of authoritative biblical prophets and autonomous disciple-gathering teachers.

Analysis of repetitive forms is, however, only a beginning. Additional analysis must include progressive forms, the interrelation of repetitive and progressive forms, and categorical expectations other than repetitive and progressive forms. Only such an expanded analysis can show the comprehensive nature of the intermingling of conventional forms in Mark's gospel.

The remainder of the analysis, therefore, will pursue the entire set of relationships that emerge around Jesus as a disciple-gathering prophet-teacher. These relationships begin when Jesus, on the basis of his knowledge of the gospel of God, calls individuals, crowds, and disciples to action. In turn, people follow Jesus to listen to his teachings and observe his actions. This activity is the means by which the system of thought and action manifest in Jesus is transmitted to people who gather around him. Jesus' summoning activity is most direct with those men whom he selects to be members of a small group of disciples who accompany him wherever he goes. Scenes in which Jesus summons these disciples and commissions them to certain activities occur throughout the narrative in a programmatic, repetitive manner. The scenes also, however, present a progression. After the legitimation of Jesus as an authoritative person, the progression begins with Jesus' appearance as a prophet-teacher who calls disciple-companions to follow him (1:14–20). The narrative ends when the death of Jesus creates the necessity for the disciples to establish an independent life of their own on the basis of the system of thought and action that Jesus teaches and enacts as recounted in the narrative.

Analysis of the perpetuation and adaptation of conventional forms in the Gospel of Mark therefore requires analysis of repetitive and progressive forms that present the full cycle of relationships which occur while a disciple-gathering teacher is alive. In the midst of the familiar repetitive forms, the progressive forms unfold the attributes of Jesus' identity and unveil the responsibilities of discipleship. Together, the forms present a cycle of relationships that begins when Jesus calls people into discipleship and ends when he dies, leaving them with a system of thought and action. The intermingling of conventional repetitive and progressive forms in the cycle reveals the nature of Mark's gospel as a biographical narrative written in the religious, social, cultural, and literary milieu of the first-century Mediterranean world. We must, therefore, analyze the entire cycle of relationships from the initial call to discipleship to the death of the teacher. Only such an analysis can exhibit the full implications of the phenomena we have uncovered in the analysis of minor repetitive forms in Mark.

NOTES

1. K. Burke, *Counter-Statement*, 126–27.

2. C. H. Talbert, *What Is a Gospel?* 11; cf. A. Fowler, "The Life and Death of Literary Forms."

3. Burke, *Counter-Statement,*126–27, 204–12.

4. Ibid., 204.

5. Ibid.

6. Ibid.

7. Mark 6:15; 8:28; 9:4, 5, 11, 12, 13; 15:35, 36.

8. G. Hartmann, *Der Aufbau des Markusevangeliums mit einem Anhang,* 147–51; B. Lindars, "Elijah, Elisha, and the Gospel Miracles"; R. E. Brown, "Jesus and Elisha."

9. Ibid., 99. Cf. Hartmann, *Der Aufbau des Markusevangeliums;* D. A. Baker, "Form and the Gospels," 24; and W. Roth, "The Biblical Matrix of Literary Structure and Narrative Execution of the Synoptic Gospel." For studies that have explored patterns within other portions of the Hebrew Bible to explain patterns within the Gospel of Mark, see E. C. Hobbs, "Norman Perrin on Methodology in the Interpretation of Mark," 85–87; and H. C. Kee, *Community of the New Age,* 27, 45–46. I have concluded that the repetitive and progressive forms in the Elijah/Elisha narrative and the book of Jeremiah are the most instructive for analysis of the overall form of the Gospel of Mark.

10. C. W. Votaw, *The Gospels and Contemporary Biographies in the Greco-Roman World,* 30–48, 53–62; M. Hadas and M. Smith, *Heroes and Gods,* 49–56. For Socratic literature, with special interest in its religious features, see J. Beckman, *The Religious Dimension of Socrates' Thought.*

11. Abraham, Isaac, and Jacob: Mark 12:26. Moses: Mark 1:44; 7:10; 9:4, 5; 10:3, 4; 12:19, 26. David: Mark 2:25; 10:47, 48; 11:10; 12:35, 36, 37. Elijah: Mark 6:15; 8:28; 9:4, 5, 11, 12, 13; 15:35, 36.

12. Baker, "Form and the Gospels," 24.

13. For a detailed analysis of the social role of prophets in the Hebrew Bible, see D. L. Petersen, *The Roles of Israel's Prophets.*

14. For rhetorical analyses of the Deuteronomic literature and prophetic biblical literature, see I. Broide, "The Speeches in Deuteronomy, Their Style and Rhetoric Devices"; M. Weinfeld, *Deuteronomy and the Deuteronomic School*, 171–78; G. Braulik, *Die Mittel deuteronomischer Rhetorik*; J. A. Thompson, "The Use of Repetition in the Prophecy of Joel"; J. R. Lundbom, *Jeremiah: A Study in Ancient Hebrew Rhetoric*; idem, "Poetic Structure and Prophetic Rhetoric in Hosea"; W. L. Holladay, *The Architecture of Jeremiah 1—20*; Y. Gitay, *Prophecy and Persuasion*.

15. 1 Kings 17:2, 8; 18:1; 19:9; 21:17, 28 (cf. 2 Kings 3:15 [power]).

16. Cf. 1 Kings 17:3, 9; 18:1; 19:11, 15; 21:18; 2 Kings 1:3, 15.

17. Cf. 1 Kings 17:5, 10; 18:2; 19:6, 8, 19; 2 Kings 1:4, 5.

18. The words in parentheses indicate words not always included in the basic form. 1 Kings 17:14; 20:13, 14, 28, 42; 21:19; 22:11, 19; 2 Kings 1:4, 6, 16; 2:21; 3:16, 17; 4:43; 7:1; 9:6, 12.

19. Cf. 1 Kings 17:1, 12; 18:10, 15; 22:14; 2 Kings 2:2, 4; 3:14; 4:20; 5:16, 20.

20. Cf. 1 Kings 17:16; 22:38; 2 Kings 1:17; 2:22; 4:17, 44; 7:20.

21. Cf. 1 Kings 17:11, 13; 18:41; 22:15; 2 Kings 2:2, 4; 8:1; 9:1, 26.

22. Cf. 1 Kings 17:15; 18:42; 19:21; 2 Kings 8:2; 9:4.

23. For studies attentive to repetitive forms in Jeremiah, see Lundbom, *Jeremiah*; Holladay, *Architecture of Jeremiah 1—20*; and B. Renaud, "Jér 1: Structure et théologie de la rédaction."

24. Cf. Jer. 1:1–2; 11:1; 14:1; 18:1; 21:1; 25:1; 26:1; 27:1; 28:12; 29:30; 30:1; 32:1, 26; 33:1, 19, 23; 34:1, 8, 12; 35:1, 12; 36:1, 27; 37:6; 39:15; 40:1; 42:7; 43:8; 44:1; 46:1; 47:1; 49:34.

25. Jer. 1:11, 13; 2:1; 13:3, 8; 16:1; 18:5; 24:4; 25:3; 32:6.

26. Cf. Jer. 30:4; (34:5); 36:4; 37:2; 46:13; 50:1.

27. Jer. 1:9, 14; 3:6, 11; 11:6, 9; 13:1, 6; 14:11, 14; 15:1; 17:19; 24:3; 25:15; 27:2.

28. Cf. Jer. 7:27, 28; 8:4; 10:11; 11:3; 13:12, 13; 14:17; 15:2; 16:11; 19:3, 11; 23:37, (38); 25:27, 30; 26:4; 34:2; 37:6; 43:10.

29. Cf. Jer. 2:4; 7:2; 9:20; (11:2); (13:15); 17:20; 19:3; 21:11; 22:2; 29:20; 31:10; 34:4; 42:15; 44:24, 26.

30. Jer. 12:16; 16:14, 15; 23:7, 8; 38:16; 44:26; cf. 22:24; 46:18.

31. Jer. 7:32; 9:25; 16:14; 19:16; 23:5, 7; 30:3; 31:27, 31, 38; 33:14; 48:12; 49:2; 51:47, 52; cf. 8:1; 12:16; 16:16; 21:7; 30:8; 31:6, 28; 48:47; 49:39; 50:4, 20.

32. Ezek. 1:3; Hos. 1:1; Joel 1:1; Jonah 1:1; 3:2; Mic. 1:1; Zeph. 1:1; Hag. 1:1, 3; 2:1, 10, 20; Zech. 1:1, 7; 7:1, 8.

33. Ezek. 3:16; 6:1; 7:1; 11:14; 12:1, 8, 17, 21, 26; 13:1; 14:2, 12; 15:1; 16:1; 17:1, 11; 18:1; 20:2, 45; 21:1, 8, 18; 22:1, 17, 23; 23:2; 24:1, 15, 20; 25:1; 26:1; 27:1; 28:1, 11, 20; 29:1, 17; 30:1; 31:1; 32:2; 33:1, 23; 34:1; 35:1; 36:16; 37:15; 38:1; Zech. 4:8; 6:9; 7:4; 8:1, 18.

34. Isa. 8:1, 3, 5, 11; 31:4; Ezek. 3:22; 23:26; Hos. 3:1; Amos 8:2; (Hab. 2:2); Zech. 11:13, 15.

35. Isa. 7:7; 10:24; 28:16; 29:22; 30:15; 37:21, 33; 38:1, 5; 43:1, 14, 16; 44:6, 24; 45:1, 11, 14, 18; 48:17; 49:7, 8, 22; 50:1; 52:3; 56:1, 4, 8; 64:8; 65:13; 66:1, 12; Ezek. 2:4; 3:11, 27; 5:7, 8; 6:3, 11; 7:5; 11:5, 7, 16, 17; 12:10, 19, 23, 28; 13:2, 8,

13, 18, 20; 14:4, 6, 21; 15:6; 16:3, 36, 59; 17:3, 19, 22; 20:3, 5, 30, 39, 47; *et passim.* Amos 1:3, 6, 9, 11, 13; 2:1, 4, 6; 3:11, 12; 5:3, 4, 16; 7:17. Obad. 1:1; Mic. 3:5; Nah. 1:12; Hag. 1:2, 5, 7; 2:6, 11; Zech. 1:2, 4, 14, 17; 2:8, 3:6; 6:12; 7:9; 8:1, 3, 4, 7, 9, 14, 19, 20, 23; 11:4; 12:1.

36. Isa. 1:10; (2:9); 28:14, (23); 39:5; (46:3; 49:1); 66:5; Ezek. 6:3; 13:2; 16:35; 20:47; 25:3; 33:30; 34:7; 36:1; Hos. 4:1; (5:1); Amos 3:1; 5:1; 7:16; Mic. 6:1; (Zech. 3:8).

37. Isa. 3:18; 4:2; 7:18, 20, 21, 23; 10:20, 27; 11:10, 11; 12:1, 4; 17:4, 7, 9; 19:16, 18, 19, 23, 24; 22:8, 12, 25; 27:1, 2, (6), 12, 13; 28:5; 30:23; 31:7; Hos. 1:5; Mic. 4:6; 5:10; Zeph. 1:10; Hag. 2:23; Zech. 12:3, 4, 6, 8, 11; 13:1, 2, 4; 14:6, 8, 9, 13, 20.

38. Isa. 39:6; Amos 8:11; 9:13.

39. Ezek. 16:48; 17:16; 18:3; 20:3, 31, 33; 33:11; 34:8; 35:6; Zech. 2:9.

40. J. Weiss, *Das älteste Evangelium*, 24–29; W. Marxsen, *Mark the Evangelist*, 117–19, 126–38.

41. Mark 1:3; 4:20; 7:6–7; 11:17; 13:26; 14:27.

42. Mark 2:11; 3:28; 8:12; 9:1, 41; 10:15, 29; 11:23; 12:43; 13:30; 14:9, 18, 25, 30.

43. Mark 4:9, (12), 23; 7:14; (8:18); (9:7).

44. Mark 4:24; 8:15; 13:5, 9, 23, 33, 35, 37; 14:34, 37, 38.

45. A. Momigliano, *The Development of Greek Biography*, 52.

46. Ibid., 53.

47. Ibid., 54.

48. Athenaeus, *The Deipnosophists* 6.248D–E (three passages featuring Cleisophus and Philip); 10:434D (Callisthenes and Alexander).

49. Ibid., 13.583F.

50. Ibid., 4.162B.

51. E. Köpke *(Über die Gattung der Apomnēmoneumata in der griechischen Literatur*, 14) considers them to be the same work.

52. Ibid., 16–17.

53. Diogenes Laertius, *Lives of the Eminent Philosophers* 1.2.63 (Solon); Athenaeus, *Deipnosophists* 11.507D (Plato).

54. Considered a philosopher by Diogenes Laertius.

55. Diogenes Laertius's *Lives* refers to Favorinus's *Apomnēmoneumata*, Book I: 1.4.79; 2.5.23, 39; 3.1.20, 25; 5.5.76; 9.2.20; Book II: 4.1.5; 5.1.21; 5.5.76, 89; Book III: 3.1.40; 8.1.12; Book V: 3.1.62; 9.3.23; without specific references: 3.1.48; 8.2.63, 73; 8.8.90.

56. In *Lives*, Diogenes Laertius refers to the following authors: Socrates (2.5.20); Plato (5.1.1); Aristotle (5.1.2–4); Speusippus (4.1.2); Crates (6.5.93); Pythagoras (8.1.3, 10); Empedocles (8.2.58); Eudoxos (8.8.87).

57. See 3.1.3.

58. Diogenes Laertius refers to Apollodorus, *Chronology (Lives* 2.3.7; 2.5.44; 5.1.9; 9.5.25; 9.8.50; 10.1.14); Plato, *Theaetetus (Lives* 2.5.18); Hermippus, *On Aristotle (Lives* 5.1.1); Dinon, *History of Persia,* Heracleides, *On Laws,* and Eupolis, *Flatterers (Lives* 9.8.50); Metrodorus, *On the Noble Birth (Lives* 10.1.1).

59. See G. Kennedy, "Classical and Christian Source Criticism," 136–37. See also the response by W. A. Meeks, "Hypomnēmata from an Untamed Sceptic."

60. Plutarch, Life of Alexander 1.1.

61. Cf. Weiss, Das älteste Evangelium, 6–11; K. L. Schmidt, "Die Stellung der Evangelien in der allgemeinen Literaturgeschichte," 51–62.

62. R. Alter, The Art of Biblical Narrative, 88–113.

63. toiauta legōn/prattōn: Memorabilia 1.1.16, 20; (1.2.9, [10]); 1.3.8; 1.5.6; 2.1.1; (2.5.5); 3.1.3; (4.2.8); 4.3.18; (4.4.4); 4.4.25; (4.8.11). toiade legōn/dialegomenos (dialechthenta): 1.2.40; 1.5.1; 1.7.5; 2.6.1; 2.10.1; 3.3.1; 3.6.2; 4.3.2; 4.4.5; 4.5.2. Occasionally these phrases are supplemented by reference to "such" (toioutos) a man Socrates was: Memorabilia 1.2.2, 3, 8, (50), 62; (2.6.37); 4.8.11.

64. Memorabilia 1.1.16; 1.2.2, 4, 8, 18, 28, 29, (52), 55, 59; 1.3.1, 4, 14; 1.5.6; 1.6.14, (15); 3.8.1; (3.10.15); 4.2.1; 4.3.18; 4.5.1, 2; 4.6.15; 4.7.1, 8.

65. Memorabilia 1.2.(52), 55, 59–60, 61; 1.3.1; (1.6.8, 14); (1.7.2); 2.4.1; (2.6.16, 25, 37); (2.7.7, 8, 9, 12); (2.9.8); (2.10.3, 6); 3.1.1; (3.3.15); (3.4.11); (3.6.2, 3); (3.7.9); 3.8.1; 3.10.1; 4.1.1, (4, 5); (4.2.11); (4.3.17); 4.4.1; (4.5.6, 7, 10); (4.7.3, 5); 4.7.8, (10); 4.8.11.

66. Cf. Memorabilia 1.1.16; 1.2.9; 1.5.6; 1.6.1; 1.7.5; 2.4.1; 2.6.1; 2.10.1; 3.3.1; 3.5.1; 3.10.1; 4.4.5; 4.5.1–2, 12; 4.6.15.

67. Memorabilia 1.2.64; 1.4.1; 1.7.1; 2.1.1; 2.5.1; 4.5.1; 4.8.11.

68. Memorabilia 1.1.4; 1.2.29, 30; 1.7.1, 5; 4.7.6.

69. Cf. Memorabilia 1.2.29; 2.2.1, 2.3.1; 2.5.1; 2.7.1; 2.8.1; 3.1.1; 3.4.1; 3.5.1; 3.7.1; 3.12.1; 3.14.5; 4.1.3; 4.2.1, 8.

70. Memorabilia 1.3.9; 1.4.2; 2.1.1; 2.2.1; 2.3.1; 2.6.1; 2.9.1; 2.10.1; 3.7.1; 4.2.8; 4.3.3; 4.5.2; 4.6.2.

71. Cf. Memorabilia 1.2.2, 3, 9, 27, 29, 61; 1.4.1, 19; 2.9.3; 3.2.3; 4.2.6, 37, 38; 4.4.25; 4.5.1, 3; 4.6.1; 4.7.3; 4.8.3, 10.

72. Mark 1:(7), 9, 14, 21, (24), 29, 35, 38, 39, (45); 2:1, 13, (17); 3:1, 20; 5:1, 2, (17), 20, (23), 24, 38, 39; 6:1, 32, 34, 36, 46, 48, 53, 54; 7:17, 24, 31; 8:10, 13, 22, 27; 9:28, 30, 38; 10:1, (45), 46; 11:(9), 11, 12, 13, 15, 27; 14:17, 32, 37, 39, 40, 41.

73. Mark 1:16–17, 19; 2:5, 14; 6:34; 8:33; 9:25; 10:14; 11:13–14; 12:(15), 34.

74. Mark 4:10; 7:5, 17, 26; 9:11, 28; 10:2, 10, 17; 12:18; 13:3; 14:60–61; 15:2, 4.

75. Mark 5:9; 8:5, 23, 27, 28; 9:16, 21, 33; 11:29.

76. Mark 3:13; 6:7; 8:1, 34; 10:42; 12:43.

77. For this translation, see R. M. Grant, The Earliest Lives of Jesus, 17–18. See also R. O. P. Taylor, The Groundwork of the Gospels, 75–90; W. R. Schoedel, Polycarp, Martyrdom of Polycarp, Fragments of Papas, 107–8. See also J. Kürzinger, "Die Aussage des Papias von Hierapolis zur literarischen Form des Markusevangeliums."

78. Justin, Dialogue with Trypho 100.4; 101.3; 102.5; 103.6; 104.1; 106.1, 4.

79. Justin, Dialogue with Trypho 105.1, 5, 6; 107.1.

80. Grant (Earliest Lives of Jesus, 20) considers this to mean the Apomnēmoneumata of Peter.

81. The Didache refers to teachings which are "in our Lord's gospel" (15.4), "in his gospel" (8:2), or "in the gospel" (15:3). The term "gospel" does not yet refer to a

specific narrative about Jesus. See H. Koester, *Synoptische Überlieferung bei den Apostolischen Vätern*, 10–11.

82. A. von Harnack, *Marcion*, 37–237.

83. N. R. Petersen, Jr., "So-called Gnostic Type Gospels and the Question of the Genre," 34–35.

84. This practice continued in Irenaeus and Clement of Alexandria; see ibid., 33.

85. Tatian, *Oration to the Greeks* 21.1. See Grant, *Earliest Lives of Jesus*, 22–28.

86. Eusebius, *Demonstration of the Gospels* 3.6 (See J. Migne, *Patrologia Graeca*, 22.224B)

87. Burke, *Counter-Statement*, 125.

4

The Introduction and the Initial Phase in the Teacher/Disciple Cycle in Mark 1:1—3:6

Judaism and Christianity demanded renunciation and a new start . . . the only context in which we find it (conversion) in ancient paganism is that of philosophy, which held a clear concept of two types of life, a higher and a lower, and which exhorted men to turn from one to the other.[1]

Up to this point I have analyzed progressive forms, repetitive forms, and conventional forms primarily at the level of minor forms in a piece of literature. The three-step progressions in the Gospel of Mark, the conventional repetitive forms in prophetic biblical literature, and the repetitive forms in Xenophon's *Memorabilia* and in Mark are brief rhetorical forms related to the kinds of forms with which biblical interpreters have considerable familiarity.

In this chapter and the next two chapters, I will treat rhetorical form that extends over an entire document, a form that has been explored only rarely in recent criticism of the gospels.[2] A primary example of an expanded rhetorical form is the speech, which may be so long that it takes two, three, or four hours to deliver orally or to read.[3] The long speech has rhetorical form in an expanse containing an introduction, body, and conclusion. Minor forms are present in every section of the speech, contributing to the rhetorical purpose of the overall composition. The long speech receives its rhetorical form by means of progression (which may be subtle and slow) that builds upon repetitive and conventional forms. These forms allow the new to emerge out of the familiar.

Since I focus on the Gospel of Mark, the rhetorical form of biographical accounts of disciple-gathering teachers must be taken into account. Based on my outline (chap. two), Mark contains an introduction (1:1–13), body of the account (1:14—15:47), and conclusion (16:1–8). Major challenges for the rhetorical critic are to describe the types of minor progressive forms that contribute to the overall progression of the story, and to describe the minor repetitive and conventional forms that allow the new to emerge out of the familiar.

As a rhetorical critic I have a special concern with conventional forms,

forms that bring "categorical expectancies" to the reading of the document.[4] The task is especially challenging, because Mark contains influences from both biblical tradition and Greek tradition; however, the kinds of influence from the two traditions are imbalanced. On the one hand, Mark's gospel intermingles sociocultural patterns whose heritage lies in both biblical and Greek traditions. These patterns had become commonplace within certain sectors of first-century Mediterranean society. The interpreter has access to these patterns of understanding and action through the literary documents from the biblical, Greek, and Hellenistic periods in which the sociocultural patterns exhibit themselves in rhetorical forms. On the other hand, Mark exhibits explicit literary influence from biblical literature but not from Greek and Hellenistic literature written outside Jewish circles. Therefore, as the interpreter seeks the sociocultural patterns in first-century Mediterranean society that support the portrayal of Jesus as a disciple-gathering teacher-Messiah, he or she must also seek conventional expectations that arise directly from reading biblical literature.

In the Gospel of Mark, the intermingling of conventional forms and patterns occurs in a biographical account that begins with an introductory stage in which the Messiah Jesus is presented to the reader as an adult personage sanctioned by God, Isaiah, and John the Baptist. The body of the account presents the Messiah Jesus as a disciple-gathering prophet-teacher who performs powerful acts, summons people to a particular system of thought and action, dies on a cross, and is buried in a tomb. The conclusion features the resurrection of the Messiah Jesus from the tomb with a promise to three women that the disciples will see him in Galilee. As the account progresses from the beginning verse to the final verse, rhetorical forms intermingle conventional forms and patterns from biblical and Greek heritages, allowing the new to emerge from the familiar in a manner that the reader considers to be appropriate.

This chapter contains an analysis of the intermingling of forms and patterns in the introduction (1:1–13) and in the initial phase of the body of Mark's gospel (1:14—3:6). While the introduction adapts minor forms and patterns from biblical heritage, the initial phase of the body of the story intermingles forms and patterns from biblical heritage with the sociocultural pattern of the disciple-gathering teacher, a pattern which has its heritage in Greek society and literature.

CONVENTIONAL PROGRESSIVE FORMS IN THE INTRODUCTION TO MARK: MARK 1:1–13

Rhetorical analysis of the introduction to Mark (1:1–13) calls for special attention to conventional progressive forms in biblical literature. Progressive forms, as we recall from chapter one, raise and fulfill expectations in an extended sequence. There are two basic kinds of progressive forms: (1) logical progressions and (2) qualitative progressions. Logical progressions are progressions within the plot that flow from one another in such a manner that the reader may anticipate the next turn of affairs. Qualitative progressions, in contrast, appear appropriate after they have occurred, since particular qualities of character, action, and speech have prepared the reader for the next situation. But there is no obvious indicator in the text that the next situation will arise.

Progressive forms, like repetitive forms, may be conventional forms. In other words, progressive patterns may exist as categorical expectations prior to the reading, because they are known from previous social, rhetorical, or literary conventions. A major conventional progressive form in the Gospel of Mark presents the occurrence of events that have been either predicted or authoritatively asserted. This progressive form is logical since the events flow logically from the predictions or assertions, and it is conventional since it provides the warp and woof of much literature in the Hebrew Bible. The first logical progression occurs in Mark when God speaks through Isaiah to Jesus, "Behold I send my messenger before thy face" (1:2), and John appears in the wilderness, preaching a baptism of repentance for the forgiveness of sins (1:4). Subsequent logical progressions occur as Jesus, the narrator, or others make promises that begin to be fulfilled, or when they make assertions or give explanations that anticipate or suggest later events.

Qualitative progressions occur in the midst of logical progressions in Mark. Qualitative progressions emerge with the unfolding of the attributes of a person's character, action, and speech in the narrative. Qualitative progressions in the portrayal of Jesus begin with the narrator's assertion that Jesus is the Messiah, Son of God (1:1). They unfold the attributes of Jesus as the narrator speaks, as God speaks, as Jesus himself speaks and acts, and as various people and spiritual forces speak and act throughout the narrative.

Analysis of qualitative progressive form has occupied Markan scholarship since at least the middle of the nineteenth century when scholars began to analyze the sequence of events in Mark in relation to the messianic nature of Jesus' activity. Christian H. Weiss's analysis (1838) began a trend of reliance on progressive patterns in Mark to describe the development of the messianic attributes of Jesus' ministry.[5] William Wrede's analysis of the messianic secret (1901), however, contained a full-scale attack on the perception of progressive form in Mark's gospel. In a section on "Mark as Author" ("Markus als Schriftsteller") he asserted:

If one considers together the different portions of the account one discovers
that in general no internal sequence is provided . . . on the whole one portion
stands next to the other with a piecemeal effect. There is naturally a connection, but it is the connection of ideas and not of historical developments. . . .
Not by a single syllable does he indicate that he desires to see two facts
brought into connection which he happens to tell one after the other.[6]

Wrede's assertion wielded extensive influence, supporting the presupposition that the only forms of importance in Mark were minor forms. Two
observations brought slight revisions to Wrede's assertion: (1) agreement
that a chronological account of the passion events had existed very early
within the Christian community; and (2) movement from Galilee to Jerusalem (with a promise of appearing back in Galilee) in Mark. When
scholarly agreement arose that the author of Mark's gospel possessed a
chronological account of the passion events (but not the events of Jesus'
ministry) as a source, Martin Kähler's suggestion that the gospels are
"passion narratives with extended introductions"[7] became highly influen-
tial. References to later events in Mark (e.g., Mark 3:6; 8:31; 9:31; 10:32–
34) support an impression of progression from ministry to passion events.
Also, the geographical location of Jesus' ministry in Galilee and of Jesus'
crucifixion in Jerusalem creates geographical movement that provides a
general framework for the stories and sayings of Jesus. By integrating
geographical movement with movement toward the passion events, interpreters produced an outline of Mark that presupposed an overarching
form of progression. This progressive form did not conflict with the
presupposition that the minor forms in any one of the gospels were more
important than progressive forms that integrated the entire document.[8]

Theodore J. Weeden's analysis (1971)[9] can be considered an analysis of
progressive form in Mark, and a significant number of subsequent analyses have adopted Weeden's approach, or a revised version of his approach.[10] Detecting a progression in the portrayal of the disciples,
Weeden analyzed a startling movement from unperceptiveness to misconception and, finally, to rejection of Jesus.[11] From this observation,
Weeden developed a thesis of christological conflict in the portrayal of
Jesus. He proposed that Jesus' teaching in the second half of the narrative
shows the invalidity of a christology based on the thaumaturgic activity of
Jesus in the first half of the narrative.[12] While interpreters appear to grant
the presence of progressive form in the portrayal of the disciples, severe
criticism has been launched against the failure to observe that Peter,
James, John, and Andrew are the disciples given the responsibility for
transmitting the gospel to all nations (13:10). Criticism has also focused on
the unlikely possibility that the author devoted eight chapters to a type of

activity by Jesus that is the object of a full-scale attack in the final eight chapters.[13]

My analysis in this chapter and the next two chapters provides an alternative to the approaches of Weiss, Wrede, and Weeden. The analysis exhibits the intermingling of rhetorical forms associated with Yahweh, with prophets, and with disciple-gathering teachers. As the story begins, Jesus—but not the disciples—is introduced to the reader. The first verse of Mark begins a qualitative progression by associating "a message of good news" (cf. Isa. 52:7) with Jesus, who is given a special title: Messiah (Son of God). The words "the beginning of the gospel of Jesus Christ [the Son of God]" have their closest parallel in Hos. 1:2: "the beginning of the word of the Lord to Hosea" (*archē logou kuriou pros Hōsēe*).[14] Instead of simply naming Jesus in the opening verse and announcing the source of his speech and action in a word of the Lord, according to the convention of prophetic biblical literature, the verse calls attention to special qualities in both "the word" and "the person" of Jesus. With the first verse, therefore, the stage is set for a qualitative progression through the document. The reader begins to ask: What are the characteristics of this message of good news, and what are the attributes of the Messiah (Son of God) who is associated with this message? The reader expects that the qualities of Jesus' character, action, and speech will emerge to answer these questions as the narrative progresses.

While Mark 1:1 begins a qualitative progression through the story, Mark 1:2–3 begins a logical progression when it announces the coming of a messenger who will prepare the way for Jesus. The assertion raises the expectation that the next event will be the appearance of the messenger. The narrative fulfills the expectation when John the baptizer appears, preaching a baptism of repentance for the forgiveness of sins.

Much as Mark 1:1 modifies conventional qualitative form at the beginning of prophetic biblical literature to emphasize the quality of Jesus' character, action, and speech, so Mark 1:2–3 modifies conventional progressive form in the setting where a person is commissioned by God. On the one hand, Mark 1:2–3 fulfills a categorical expectation from biblical literature when it presents direct address by God to Jesus:

> Behold, I send my messenger before *thy* face,
> who shall prepare *thy* way;
> the voice of one crying in the wilderness:
> "Prepare the way of the Lord [Messiah],
> make his paths straight."[15]

This passage contains two parts that function according to the principle of *parallelismus membrorum*. The second part repeats in different words the assertion in the first part. "The voice of one crying in the wilderness" (1:3) is "my messenger" whom "I send . . . before thy face" (1:2). The cry, "Prepare the way of the Lord [Messiah], make his paths straight" (1:3), is the action of preparing the way (1:2). Through these words, God addresses Jesus much as he addressed Abraham, Moses, Samuel, Isaiah, Jeremiah, Ezekiel, Hosea, and Jonah in the past. On the other hand, the assertions by God are a combination of words he previously spoke to Moses (Exod. 23:20), words he spoke through Malachi (Mal. 3:1), and words he spoke through Isaiah (Isa. 40:3). This word of the Lord, now attributed solely to Isaiah, "updates" previous words of the Lord by joining previous words together in a new setting. While the updating technique is conventional within biblical literature (e.g., the updating of Exod. 23:20 in Mal. 3:1), it is unusual to begin the logical progression at the beginning of the document with a word of the Lord attributed to a prophet at an earlier time in Israel's history. This feature modifies conventional biblical form by identifying the beginning of the gospel of Jesus Christ in a word of the Lord attributed to Isaiah the prophet.[16]

As the Gospel of Mark continues beyond the first three verses, the account is told in third-person narration as the accounts of Abraham, Moses, Samuel, Hosea, and Jonah,[17] rather than in first-person narration like the accounts of Isaiah, Jeremiah, and Ezekiel.[18] After God announces to Jesus through Isaiah that a messenger is coming before him, John the Baptist announces that one mightier than he is coming (1:7). This announcement contributes both to logical and to qualitative progression in the narrative. The announcement's nature as logical progressive form raises an expectation that Jesus will appear after John. Its nature as qualitative progressive form raises expectations for the character, action, and speech of Jesus through comparison (*synkrisis*) with John the Baptist.[19] When Jesus comes and is baptized by John, God speaks directly to Jesus from heaven: "Thou art my beloved Son, with thee I am well pleased" (1:11). This is a qualitative assertion by God, absent of the features of logical progressive form. The statement by God contains no commands, directions, or explanations characteristic of the scenes at the beginning of the careers of the special men whom God has commissioned in the past. God's pronouncements to Abraham, Moses, Samuel, Isaiah, Jeremiah, and Ezekiel contained commands concerning what they were supposed to do, explanations concerning what God himself was going to do, and words they were supposed to say to the people to whom they were sent.[20] The statement in Mark simply announces qualities of Jesus to the reader through words that were previously addressed to David (Ps. 2:7); to Isaiah (Isa. 42:11); and to Abraham about Isaac (Gen. 22:2). These statements legitimate Jesus as a special man of God and make it clear that Jesus will be acting in accordance with the will of God. Noticeably absent, however, are commands, directions, and explanations from God.

The absence of the conventional commands, directions, and explanations from God in Mark signals a distinctive application of the progressive forms that exist in prophetic biblical literature. According to the conventions of prophetic biblical literature, the attributes of Yahweh's character, action, and speech unfold as he initiates the action in each section of the document through his commands, directions, and explanations. The reader watches with interest as the document unfolds the attributes of Yahweh's action and speech in a qualitative progression. The reader accepts the progression of Yahweh's actions and speech as appropriate since it is understood that Yahweh will do nothing that violates his character as a righteous God. The character, action, and speech of the prophet unfold in the setting of God's commands, directions, and explanations. In other words, a qualitative progression in the prophet's speech and action occurs in the setting of logical progressions introduced by Yahweh's commands, directions, and explanations. The reader knows the basic things the prophet will say and do next, since the prophet will do what Yahweh commands him to do. But the specific attributes of the prophet's character, action, and speech unfold as the prophet responds to Yahweh's actions and speech in his own peculiar way.

As a result of this absence in Mark, the attributes of Jesus' character, action, and speech unfold as he himself initiates the action in the next section of the narrative. The reader cannot be sure what Jesus will do next, but whatever he does will be appropriate since Jesus, the beloved Son of God, will do nothing displeasing to God (1:11). In other words, the absence of the conventional commands, directions, and explanations from God features a qualitative progression in the character, action, and speech of Jesus analogous to the qualitative progression in the character, action, and speech of Yahweh in prophetic biblical literature. No commands or directions come from God to introduce logical progressive form that directs the action and speech of Jesus. No words are given to Jesus to say to others so that the quality of his speech is grounded in the actual speech of God. Jesus does not enter into dialogue with God, as do Moses, Samuel, Isaiah, and Jeremiah. Therefore, the specific features of Jesus' task, and the accompanying characteristics of his speech and action, are undefined. From the introduction to Mark, the reader learns that Jesus is associated with a message of good news (1:1), that he is the Messiah (1:1), that he is the beloved Son of God (1:1, 11), that he is mightier than John the Baptist (1:7), that the Spirit of God has come upon him and can control him (1:10, 12), and that Satan is an adversary, the angels are allies, and wild beasts hold no power to destroy him (1:13). But the reader is unsure exactly what this Messiah will do, since no commands, explanations, or directions have come from God to Jesus. Basic qualities of Jesus have been introduced to the reader, but the precise role of Jesus the Messiah remains undefined in a manner that contrasts with the beginning of the accounts of the men of God in prophetic biblical literature. A wide range of possibilities arise from contemporary messianic expectations, and the particular attributes of the character, action, and speech of the Messiah will be of interest to the reader.

The action of the disciples, however, occurs in a setting of Jesus' commands, directions, and explanations. And here, as Weeden has pointed out, a curious tension arises.[21] On one level the disciples do what Jesus commands them to do: procure a boat for him (4:1); preach repentance, cast out demons, and heal (6:13); distribute and gather bread and fish (6:41–43; 8:6–9); procure a colt upon which Jesus can enter into Jerusalem (11:2–7); and prepare the Passover meal (14:13–16). On another level, the disciples respond to Jesus' speech and action in their own peculiar way, similar in some respects to responses of prophets to Yahweh. In other words, a qualitative progression in the speech and action of the disciples occurs in the setting of logical progressions introduced by Jesus' commands, directions, and explanations.

THE INITIAL PHASE IN THE STORY OF
JESUS AND HIS DISCIPLES

After the introduction to the Gospel of Mark (1:1–13), the story contains a "second introduction" that begins with Mark 1:14.[22] As the narrative progresses, prophetic speech by Jesus intermingles with speech and action that characterizes Jesus as a disciple-gathering teacher. From this point on, the narrative progresses through phases that are best described as a teacher/disciple cycle. The progression unfolds the attributes of the teacher, the tenets of the teacher's system of thought and action, and the responsibilities of the disciple. The progression is qualitative where it introduces attributes of character, action, and speech that prepare the reader for the next situation but do not provide the means to anticipate the next situation in the sequence. The progression is logical where Jesus and the narrator make assertions that give the reader knowledge of events that will occur in the future. The interrelation of conventional qualitative and logical progressions within the cycle creates the distinctive nature of the Markan narrative among Mediterranean documents written before it, contemporary with it, and after it.

The portrayal of Jesus and the disciples in Mark contains three primary phases: a phase which initiates discipleship (1:14—3:6); a teaching/learning phase (3:7—12:44); and a phase of farewell and separation from the teacher (14:1—15:47). The initial phase exhibits the beginning of the teacher/disciple relationship as Jesus confronts men who have the potential for becoming his disciple-companions, and they agree to accompany him as he travels around to various places. This phase in the teacher/ disciple cycle is like the occasion of birth in the life cycle and the occasion of launching a ship in the sea-voyage cycle. While the preparation for the teacher/disciple cycle occurs in Mark 1:1–13, the preparation for a life cycle could begin with circumstances around conception and pregnancy, and the preparation for a sea voyage could begin with procuring supplies and planning an itinerary for the voyage. Mark 1:14—3:6 presents the initial phase of the teacher/disciple cycle in which the teacher and the disciple-companions accept the complementary roles of communicator and students.[23] The middle phase features a programmatic introduction of the teacher's system of thought and action to the disciple-companions. Since this is the most extensive phase, it provides the setting for the portrayal of the teacher's interaction with: curious onlookers; people who seek special favors; people who try but do not succeed in becoming faithful disciple-companions; and hostile peers. The final phase of the teacher/disciple cycle features the separation of the teacher from his disciple-companions when the teacher accepts a death penalty that the disciple-companions consider to be unjust and unnecessary to accept. The teacher must not flee from the death sentence, or he will violate a central feature within the system of thought and action that he has transmitted to his disciple-companions.

This chapter contains analysis only of the initial phase of the relation between a teacher and his disciple-companions. This phase is filled with actions by the teacher to attract disciple-companions and responses by people that create the occasion for association and interchange with the teacher. The first phase exhibits the role of the disciple-companions as a role complementary to Jesus the traveling prophet-teacher. While the initiation of a teacher/disciple relation reflects a practice common in Mediterranean culture during the first century C.E., the specific dynamics used to establish the relation reflect various forms of social, philosophical, and religious heritage. The purpose of this analysis is to explain the particular dimensions of Markan summons and response that initiate the teacher/disciple relation.

Jesus' coming forth after the arrest of John the Baptist (Mark 1:14) fulfills a logical expectation raised by Mark 1:2–3, 7–8 that Jesus' ministry should begin when John's ministry ends. Once Jesus steps forth, the reader expects (from 1:7–8) that his speech and action will exhibit more powerful attributes than the speech and action of John. The nature of Jesus' speech in Mark 1:15 is consistent with this expectation: "The time is fulfilled, and the kingdom of God is at hand; repent, and believe in the gospel." The call for repentance in Jesus' speech provides a base for comparison of Jesus' speech with John's action and speech, since John preached a baptism of repentance in the wilderness (Mark 1:4). The narrator's assertion that Jesus was "preaching the gospel of God" (Mark 1:14) and Jesus' assertion that people should "believe in the gospel" (Mark 1:15) fulfill qualitative expectations for Jesus' speech raised by the first verse of the document. The announcements concerning the fulfillment of time and the approach of the kingdom of God introduce new features appropriate in the speech of a person associated with a message of good news and characterized as mightier than John the Baptist. The action and speech are thoroughly consistent with expectations raised by the prophetic speech of Isaiah and the prophetic action and speech of John the Baptist.

When Jesus' activity moves to a setting where he is confronted by a man with an unclean spirit (Mark 1:21–28), Jesus successfully expels the unclean spirit from the man. With the initial confrontation, the unclean spirit says:

> "What have you against us, Jesus of Nazareth? Have you come to destroy us? I know who you are, the Holy One of God" (Mark 1:24).

When Jesus successfully casts out the unclean spirit, the people are amazed and call Jesus' powerful speech "a new teaching" which even the unclean spirits obey (Mark 1:27). In contrast to the people, the reader is not amazed, since the scene is a natural fulfillment of the claims about the special nature of Jesus from the beginning of the document. Moreover, the progression from Mark 1:14–15 to 1:21–28 is a conventional progression in biblical literature. One of the closest parallels is in 1 Kings 17:1–24 where the opening pronouncement of Elijah progresses to a scene in which Elijah heals the son of the woman at Zarephath.[24] The opening scene of the Elijah/Elisha narrative contains a comment by the narrator and direct speech by Elijah as follows:

> Now Elijah the Tishbite, of Tishbe in Gilead, said to Ahab, "As the Lord the God of Israel lives, before whom I stand, there shall be neither dew nor rain these years, except by my word" (1 Kings 17:1).

This pronouncement by Elijah sets the stage for the events in 1 Kings 17 in which Elijah is fed by ravens by the brook Cherith (1 Kings 17:2–7), and his words have the power to produce an abundance of oil and meal and to heal the son of the woman at Zarephath (1 Kings 17:8–24). When the son of the woman becomes ill, the woman addresses Elijah with the following words:

"What have you against me, O man of God? You have come to me to bring my sin to remembrance, and to cause the death of my son!" (1 Kings 17:18)

The conclusion to the story, when Elijah successfully restores her son, is the statement to the woman:

"Now I know that you are a man of God, and that the word of the Lord in your mouth is truth" (1 Kings 17:24).

The sequence from the opening scene of Elijah's declaration to Ahab to the scene of the healing of the woman's son represents a qualitative progression in the setting of logical progression introduced through words of the Lord containing commands, directions, and explanations. The existence of such a progression from prophetic speech to healing speech is a conventional form in biblical literature. In Mark, therefore, the qualitative progression from prophetic speech to healing speech not only fulfills the expectation that Jesus will be "stronger" than John the Baptist (Mark 1:7) but also fulfills conventional expectations from prophetic biblical literature.

In the midst of this progression in Mark, however, Jesus calls four disciples to accompany him, and there is no way the reader could have known that Jesus would manifest his character, action, and speech in this manner. This is a qualitative progression that is acceptable but which the reader has little reason to anticipate on the basis of conventional biblical form. To be sure, Elijah had a successor in Elisha, whom he commissioned as a result of God's instructions to him (1 Kings 19:16, 19–21). For this reason, the Jewish reader should have no difficulty accepting the progression as appropriate. Yet the movement directly from prophetic speech to speech that calls four men into the role of disciple-companion is unusual for biblical literature. When Jesus tells the first two fishermen that he will make them "become fishers of men" (Mark 1:17), he introduces logical progressive form into the narrative. The reader now expects Jesus to engage in the interaction necessary to equip these disciple-companions with the ability to "fish men." The reader may or may not know exactly what such a function will entail, although it is likely that a member of first-century Mediterranean culture would recognize the use of fishing imagery to describe the dynamics of teaching people a special system of thought and action.[25] The assertion by Jesus raises the conventional expectation, from Greek heritage, that the disciples will be "made into" people who are able to gain other people's attention and teach them the system of thought and action that the teacher transmits to them.[26]

While the qualitative progression from Jesus' prophetic action and speech (Mark 1:14–15) to his confrontation of four men with a command to become his disciple-companions (Mark 1:16–20) is acceptable to any reader on the basis of the previous assertions about Jesus in the narrative, the progression is more conventional in Greco-Roman literature than in biblical literature. The progression in Xenophon's *Memorabilia* 4.1.5 to 4.2.1–40 presents a good example.[27] Like Jesus' speech in Mark 1:14–15, the direct speech of Socrates in *Memorabilia* 4.1.5 provides a summary of the teacher's message before his activity begins.[28] Socrates' speech is as follows:

> Only a fool can think it possible to distinguish between things useful and things harmful without learning;
>
> only a fool can think that without distinguishing these he will get all he wants by means of his wealth and be able to do what is expedient;
>
> only a simpleton can think that without the power to do what is expedient he is doing well and has made good or sufficient provision for his life;
>
> only a simpleton can think that by his wealth alone without knowledge he will be reputed good at something, or will enjoy a good reputation without being reputed good at anything in particular (*Memorabilia* 4.1.5).

After this summary, the narrator introduces logical progression through the remark:

> I will now show his method of dealing with those who thought they had received the best education, and prided themselves on wisdom (*Memorabilia* 4.2.1).

The ensuing scene features Socrates confronting Euthydemus with exhortation and enticement until he decides to become Socrates' disciple-companion. At the end the narrator tells us:

> Euthydemus guessed that he would never be of much account unless he spent as much time as possible with Socrates. Henceforward, unless obliged to absent himself, he never left him, and even began to adopt some of his practices. Socrates, for his part, seeing how it was with him, avoided worrying him, and began to expound very plainly and clearly the knowledge that he thought most needful and the practices that he held to be most excellent (4.2.40).

The encounters between Socrates and Euthydemus result in Euthydemus's decision to spend as much time as possible with Socrates. In fact, "unless obliged to absent himself, he never left him." In return, Socrates began to expound things to him most plainly and clearly.

The progression from the summary of Socrates' teaching to his encounters with Euthydemus emphasizes the initial moments in the relation between a teacher and a disciple-companion. The dialogue after the successful efforts of Socrates extends the initial confrontations into an entire phase of preliminary interaction between Socrates and a disciple-companion. Similarly, the progression in Mark from the summary of Jesus' teaching (1:14–15) to his call of four disciples (1:16–20) to his ministry in Capernaum and the surrounding region (1:21—3:6) extends the initial moments of Jesus' ministry into an entire phase of preliminary interaction with his disciple-companions. The initial moment of confrontation between Jesus and his disciple-companions features immediate response to Jesus' summons, and the events that build on the initial moment portray the willingness of a select group to associate with Jesus on a sustained basis.

SUMMONS AND RESPONSE IN GREEK LITERATURE

In order to exhibit the intermingling of conventional patterns in the initial phase of the teacher/disciple cycle in Mark 1:14—3:6, we will turn our attention first to Greek literature outside the sphere of Judaism and Christianity. Israelite tradition prior to the Hellenistic period did not possess a fully developed social pattern of a teacher and his disciple-companions, even though it did contain the pattern of a prophet and his disciple-successor.[29] The major reason for the lack of a fully developed pattern in Israelite tradition appears to be the role of Yahweh as a summoner and teacher. Yahweh calls, commissions, and teaches wisdom and virtue in Israelite tradition. Any human teacher is simply an intermediary. For this reason the Hebrew Bible contains only infrequent references either to teachers or to disciple-companions. The term *talmîd*, the Hebrew equivalent of *mathētēs* (disciple-companion), occurs only in 1 Chron. 25:8 in the Old Testament; and the terms *môreh*, *mēbîn*, and *mĕlamēd*, possible Hebrew equivalents of *didaskalos* (teacher), occur a total of six times.[30] Even these instances, however, are not translated as *mathētēs* or *didaskalos* in the LXX. In fact, there is no certain occurrence of *mathētēs* (disciple-companion) and only one certain occurrence of *didaskalos* (teacher) in the LXX text of books in the Hebrew canon. The established occurrence of *didaskalos* is found in Esther 6:1,[31] a book written in Hebrew between 300 and 150 B.C.E. and translated into Greek soon after the latter date.[32] In this verse King Ahasuerus, when he cannot sleep during the night, tells "his teacher" to bring the daily records and read them to him. This occurrence reflects the Hellenistic custom of a king having his personal teacher.[33] Second Macc. 1:10, the only other LXX passage containing *didaskalos*, also reflects this custom when it refers to Aristobulus, the Jewish teacher of King Ptolemy. Even in the books of Esther and 2 Maccabees, however, there is no portrayal of the dynamics of a teacher/disciple relation. In the tradition of kings who are able leaders because of their possession of hard-earned wisdom, King Ahasuerus and King Ptolemy each maintain a teacher for the purpose of keeping the records of the king and nurturing the king's learning.

By the end of the first century C.E., the terminology and pattern of a teacher and his disciple-companions are well established in the writings of Flavius Josephus, tannaitic rabbinic traditions, and the gospels. The Gospel of Mark is representative of this shift in pattern and terminology, containing seventeen occurrences of the verb *didaskein* (to teach), twelve occurrences of the noun *didaskalos* (teacher), and forty-five occurrences of the noun *mathētēs* (disciple-companion).[34]

The source of the teacher/disciple pattern and of summons and response as a means of initiating a teacher/disciple relationship in Mediterranean culture is not difficult to uncover. The dynamics of summons and response accompanied the social identity of a teacher from the fifth century B.C.E. onwards in Greco-Roman literature and culture. The sophist tradition of the teacher and his disciples provides the base for development of the cultural and literary traditions. The impetus for the teacher/disciple relation is summarized in Plato's *Apology* 19E when Socrates describes the sophists' habit of seeking young men to join up with them:

> This also seems to me to be a fine thing, if one might be able to teach people, as Gorgias of Leontini and Prodicus of Ceos and Hippias of Elis are. For each of these men, gentlemen, is able to go into any one of the cities and persuade the young men, who can associate for nothing with whomsoever they wish among their own fellow citizens, to give up the association with those men and to associate with them and pay them money and be grateful besides.[35]

It was a common practice of sophists to travel from city to city in order to gather disciples who would seek to embody wisdom and virtue by associating with them, receiving instruction from them, and imitating them.[36] From the fifth century B.C.E. through the second century C.E., a wide variety of itinerant teachers was active throughout the Mediterranean world, producing a well-established cultural tradition of the traveling preacher-teacher who gathered disciples.[37] Cynics figure prominently among these itinerant teachers, traveling from city to city with personal furnishings of a short cloak, a wallet, and a staff, often gathering disciples who followed them around.[38] Often itinerants were more representative of a form of life in the culture than of a particular philosophy, and their message was syncretistic in content, blending philosophical and rhetorical streams of tradition.[39]

After the sophists had been active for a short time, the philosopher-teacher named Socrates (469–399 B.C.E.) began his activities in and around Athens. Socrates did not travel from city to city to gather disciple-companions, but his teaching activity gave rise to literature that portrayed him attracting young men into his company for the purpose of leading them to understand important truths about life and the world. Socrates' summons is found in the section of the dialogues customarily designated the *protrepticus*.[40] In the *protrepticus*, imperative mood is frequent on the lips of Socrates as he urges, and even compels, young men to respond to him.

One of the finest examples of Socrates' summons to a young man stands in the *Theaetetus* of Plato. Socrates, while talking with the geometrician Theodorus, hears that the young Athenian Theaetetus is one of Theodorus's most promising students. Once Socrates knows about Theaetetus, he wants to talk with him. In order to have the opportunity, he bids Theodorus: "Now please tell him to come here and sit by us" (144D). Theodorus calls him in a manner similar to the language of the gospels: "Theaetetus, come here (*deuro*) to Socrates" (144D). When, after an initial discussion, Theaetetus becomes afraid to continue, Socrates encourages him by saying:

> "Take courage (*tharrei*—Attic for *tharsei*);[41] and believe that Theodorus is right, and try earnestly in every way to gain an understanding of the nature of knowledge as well as of other things" (148C–D).

Near the end of Socrates' explanation of how he teaches like a midwife, Socrates says:

> "Come then to me (*prospherou oun pros me*), remembering that I am the son of a midwife and have myself a midwife's gifts, and do your best to answer the questions I ask as I ask them" (151B–C).

Theaetetus decides to accept Socrates' summons to enter into a relationship whereby he can gain the understanding which only Socrates is able to assist in bringing forth. In the words of Theaetetus: ". . . since you are so urgent it would be disgraceful for anyone not to exert himself in every way to say what he can" (151D). When Theaetetus accepts the summons, the initial step in the relationship is sealed. Theaetetus has agreed to spend enough time with Socrates to learn from him through observation, participation, and reflection.

A similar scene stands at the beginning of Plato's *Charmides*. When Socrates is told about Charmides, he asks Critias:

> "But why not call the young man here and show him to me?" (*alla ti ouk epedeixas moi ton neanian kalesas deuro*) (155A).

Critias agrees:

> "You are quite right, he said, and we will call him (*kai kaloumen auton*).
> Thereupon he said to his attendant,—Boy, call Charmides" (*kalei Charmidēn*)
> (155 A–B).

When Critias asks Socrates if it is all right that the young man be told that
he is coming to see a doctor who can cure his headache, Socrates agrees.
When Charmides responds readily to the summons, Socrates recounts a
Thracian physician's principle that any healing requires cure of the entire
body, including the soul (156E). Therefore, Charmides must make a
decision to accept the role of disciple-companion to Socrates:

> "If you agree to submit your soul first to the effect of the Thracian charms,
> according to the stranger's injunctions, I will apply the remedy to your head"
> (157C).

After explaining the situation more fully, Socrates states:

> "So if it is agreeable to you, I am ready to inquire with you; but, if it is not, to
> let it alone" (158E).

To this injunction, Charmides responds:

> "Why, nothing, he said, could be more agreeable to me: . . . therefore,
> inquire in whatever way you think we had better proceed" (158E).

The summoning process is successful; Charmides tells Socrates that he is
pleased to accept the role necessary for bringing his entire body, including his soul, into a state of health.[42]

One entire dialogue, the *Alcibiades Major*, is constituted by a summons
that receives a successful response at the end. This dialogue is unusual for
its detailed exploration of the need to enter into a learning relationship
and for its portrayal of the change that brings a person to an acceptance of
the role of disciple-companion.[43] The dialogue features only the teacher
Socrates and the Athenian Alcibiades. Socrates approaches Alcibiades and
tells him that he has been observing him for some time and now considers
it to be the proper time to confront him. When Alcibiades indicates a
willingness to enter into conversation, Socrates proceeds with the subject
matter of the dialogue.

In Socrates' opening statement (104E–105E), he asks Alcibiades what
he would say "if some god should ask him" (*ei tis soi eipoi theōn*) if he
prefer to live with his present possessions or to die immediately if he no
longer has the opportunity to acquire greater things (105A). Establishing
this framework for the question, Socrates challenges Alcibiades to think
about his goals in life in relation to what the gods do and do not permit a

person to achieve. Socrates' purpose is to convince Alcibiades that he must become a disciple-companion to him, and that he must understand that the god has directed Socrates in the matter. Only if Alcibiades allows Socrates to teach him, may he attain the knowledge to teach the representatives in the Athenian Assembly such things as the meaning of Justice, the time and place for war, and the means to establish peace.

The fascinating part of this dialogue, in contrast to others, is the total commitment of the interchange to the goal of persuading Alcibiades to associate continually with Socrates so that he may learn virtue for the purpose of teaching it to the citizens he will govern. While Alcibiades thinks he knows better than the Athenians what is useful to them (106C–109A), Socrates proposes that Alcibiades must attain knowledge of the just and the unjust, the good, the beautiful, and the useful. When Alcibiades' pride finally begins to collapse, Socrates discusses the art of "caring for oneself" (118B–124B) which leads to the "royal speech" (121A–124B) central to the dialogue.[44] Prior to the final statements in the dialogue, Socrates leads Alcibiades to perceive "caring for oneself" as self-knowledge (124B–135C). The dialogue ends when Socrates asks Alcibiades if he now knows how he may escape the condition of ignorance in which he finds himself (135C). Alcibiades says that it is possible only if it be the wish (*boulē*) of Socrates. Socrates corrects Alcibiades with the assertion: "If it be God's will" (*hoti ean theos ethelē*) (135D). Accepting this correction with enthusiasm, Alcibiades declares: "From this day onward it must be the case that I am your attendant, and that you have me always in attendance on you" (135D). When Socrates accepts Alcibiades' response as appropriate, Alcibiades resolves to "begin here and now" with interaction between Socrates and himself that will enable him to attain the knowledge necessary to be an outstanding leader of the people.

The *Theaetetus*, the *Charmides*, and the *Alcibiades Major* emphasize the importance of the resolve to accept the lengthy process of association and interchange necessary to attain the wisdom and virtue that provide the foundation for realizing the full potential of life. In all three dialogues, Socrates gains this response through an explanation of the purpose for which they are being summoned to enter a teacher/disciple relationship. Socrates explains to Theaetetus that he will assist him in bringing forth ideas that are ready to be born in him. Correspondingly, Socrates explains to Charmides that "curing the soul" is part of the process by which well-being is brought to the entire person. In the *Alcibiades Major* Socrates devotes the entire discussion to an explanation that self-knowledge is the basis of virtuous leadership. In each instance the explanation results in a decision on behalf of the young man to interact with Socrates as student-disciple to teacher. With this decision, the initial phase in the teacher/

disciple relation is complete. The summoning, urging, and explaining evoke a response to accept the role of student-disciple with the teacher.

Throughout most of Plato's dialogues the dynamics of teacher and disciple-companion are evident. Since, however, the corpus of dialogues presupposes the social identity of Socrates as a philosopher-teacher who gathers disciple-companions, some of the dialogues simply begin with a conversation between Socrates and a disciple-companion.[45] Also, sometimes a young man is so eager to enter into dialogue with Socrates that a simple question initiates the relationship. In the *Lysis,* for example, Socrates simply directs a question to Lysis which Lysis readily answers (207D). Lysis's willingness to answer removes the necessity for any summons. Socrates simply adopts the role of teacher by asking the question, and Lysis reciprocates in the role of disciple-companion by unhesitatingly answering the first question and the series of questions that follows (207E–210D).

Analogous features in the literary portrayal of the initial phase in the teacher/disciple relation appear in Aristophanes' *The Clouds.* In *The Clouds,* produced at the Great Dionysia in 423 B.C.E. and later revised, Aristophanes parodies the instructional activity of the sophists. He features Socrates in the role of the leading Athenian sophist, even though other literary evidence suggests that Socrates did not want to be considered a sophist and maintained persistent criticism of the sophists and their ways.[46] In the play, a wealthy farmer named Strepsiades has become a debtor through the extravagance of his son. He decides to attain from Socrates the skill of reasoning and arguing whereby he may protect himself against his creditors in court. In the play, Strepsiades twice and his son once refer to Socrates as a *didaskalos* (teacher).[47] In accord with Socrates' role as a *didaskalos* in *The Clouds,* Strepsiades comes to him desiring to become a *mathētēs* (student-disciple). Since the scene caricatures the sophists and their student-disciples, it contains harshness, rudeness, and foolishness uncharacteristic of a teacher's summons to a student-disciple. Nevertheless, various dimensions of the language and interaction are analogous to the settings throughout Greco-Roman literature where teachers summon young men into the role of student-disciple:

Socrates: Put off your cloak.

Strepsiades: Why, what have I done wrong?

Socrates: O, nothing, nothing: all go in here naked.

Strepsiades: Well, but I have not come with a search-warrant.

Socrates: Fool! Throw it off.

Strepsiades:	Well, tell me this one thing;
	If I'm extremely careful and attentive,
	Which one of your *mathētai* shall I resemble?
Socrates:	Why Chaerephon. You'll be his very image.
Strepsiades:	What! I shall be half-dead! O luckless me!
Socrates:	Don't chatter there, but follow me (*akoloutheseis emoi*).
	Make haste now (*deuri*), quicker, here.
Strepsiades:	O, but do first give me a honied cake:
	Zeus! how I tremble,
	To go down there, as if to see Trophonius.
Socrates:	Go on! why keep you pottering round the door.
Chorus:	Yes! go, and farewell; as your courage is great,
	So bright be your fate.
	May all good fortune his steps pursue,
	Who now, in his life's dim twilight haze,
	Is game such venturesome things to do,
	To steep his mind in discoveries new,
	To walk, a novice, in wisdom's ways.[48]

In this scene, imperative mood on the lips of Socrates and the occurrence of *akolouthein* (to follow) and *deuri* (to come) reflect the dynamics of the first encounter between teacher and student-disciple. To become a student-disciple is to submit to the will and goals of the teacher. One may expect to find words of encouragement and compulsion on the lips of the teacher. Acceptance of the role of student-disciple naturally evokes the image of following someone on a venture which leads down new, unknown paths.

In *The Clouds*, the initial phase of the teacher/disciple relation is captured in a dramatic moment. The teacher summons a young man; the young man responds; and the venture begins whereby the young man follows the teacher into unknown areas of life and knowledge. From the fifth century B.C.E. to the third century C.E., the rehearsal of the initial moment functions as a means of characterizing the entire relationship that develops between a teacher and a student-disciple. When Diogenes Laertius (ca. 200–250 C.E.) wishes to characterize Xenophon as a loyal disciple who defended the reputation of his teacher Socrates by composing the *Memorabilia*, he considers the essence of that relationship to be present in Socrates' summons of Xenophon. After introducing only a few details about Xenophon, therefore, he begins the section on Xenophon in the *Lives of the Eminent Philosophers* with:

The story goes that Socrates met him (Xenophon) in a narrow passage, and that he stretched out his stick to bar the way, while he inquired where every kind of food was sold. Upon receiving a reply, he put another question, "And where do men become good and honourable?" Xenophon was fairly puzzled; "Then follow me (*hepou toinun*)," said Socrates, "and learn." From that time onward he was a disciple (*akroatēs*) of Socrates (2.48).

The importance of the initial moment in the relationship between a teacher and a disciple is reflected in this story.[49] This moment may be the means by which an author portrays the influence of a teacher upon a young man for the rest of his life. Still, however, as in the *Alcibiades Major* the initial moment may be the beginning of a phase that continues for some time before the young man resolves to establish a prolonged teacher/disciple relationship with the teacher.

SUMMONS AND RESPONSE IN
HELLENISTIC JEWISH LITERATURE

When Israelite tradition began to be transmitted within Hellenistic culture, it was natural for the teacher/disciple pattern to make inroads into Jewish thought. Some of the earliest evidence for this infiltration resides in the Alexandrine recension of the LXX. In text A, *mathētēs* (disciple) is found for *mathēmata* (lessons) in Jer. 13:21 and for *machētēs* (warrior) in 20:11.[50] Then text A[1] contains *mathētēs* for *machētēs* (warrior) in Jer. 26:9 and *didaskalos* (teacher) is added in Dan. 1:3 and 2:14.[51] Scribal activity during the Hellenistic period, therefore, reveals a progressive incursion of teacher/disciple language into the LXX text.

Just as scribes were inclined to add the term *mathētēs* (disciple) to the text of the LXX, so Philo of Alexandria used the teacher/disciple pattern to explicate Israelite tradition. For him, Abraham, Isaac, Jacob, Moses, and Rebecca, in particular, are people around whom to incorporate the teacher/disciple pattern. Philo refers to Abraham as the one, above all, who was "taught by God" (*On Abraham* 52; *Life of Moses* 1:76). However, all three patriarchs—Abraham, Isaac, and Jacob—are symbols of virtue acquired by teaching, nature, and practice (*On Abraham* 52–53). They teach others by their embodiment of virtue. People learn from them as they are extolled by Moses in his books about them (cf. *On Abraham* 4–5).

In the essay on *The Sacrifice of Cain and Abel* reflection on the life of Jacob reveals the nature of God as the perfect teacher of wisdom and virtue:

Long experience had taught him (Jacob) that what the world of creation gives to the soul it makes secure only after long time, as it is with those who impart the arts and their rules to their pupils (*tois manthanousi*). They cannot at once fill to the brim the mind of the beginners (*tōn eisagomenōn*), as one fills a vessel. But when the fountain of wisdom, God, imparts each form of knowledge to the mortal race, he needs not time for the work. Such persons become apt disciples of the only wise Being (*tou monou sophou mathētai*) and discover quickly what they seek . . . (64).

As Philo continues with discussion of a person's attainment of wisdom from God, he assigns the instruction of human teachers to an inferior position that makes it unnatural for him to portray famous Israelites as teachers:

> When God causes the young shoots of self-inspired wisdom to spring up within the soul, the knowledge that comes from teaching must straightway be abolished and swept off. Ay, even of itself it will subside and ebb away. God's scholar (*phoitētēn*), God's pupil (*gnōrimon*), God's disciple (*mathētēn*), call him by whatever name you will, cannot any more suffer the guidance of men (79).

In the writings of Philo at the beginning of the first century C.E., therefore, the Greek philosophical tradition of teacher and disciple plays a significant role. Philo is careful, however, in his application of the teacher/disciple pattern, because of the vigorous criticism of human teachers he knows from Socratic tradition. His care is exhibited, for example, in his unwillingness to call Joshua a disciple of Moses. Philo uses the terminology and concepts of the Greek teacher/disciple tradition most freely to formulate his mystical view of a person's attainment of wisdom from God. By focusing one's gaze above, the mind becomes fixed on the things of God; wisdom pours freely from God to the eager student; and the person becomes a disciple (*mathētēs*) of God himself.[52] Yahweh is the primary teacher of wisdom and virtue, and Israelite leaders do not easily substitute for God in that role.

The care that Philo exercises in his description of famous Israelites as teachers is exemplified in his *Life of Moses*. During the early stages of Moses' life, he received lessons: ". . . when he and God were alone together, like pupil and teacher" (*hōs para didaskalōi gnōrimos*) (*Life of Moses* 1.80). When Moses learned his lessons thoroughly he became a perfect embodiment of the law rather than an extraordinary teacher. God himself retains the function of teacher as it becomes necessary for him to teach lesson after lesson to the people of Egypt and the people of Israel (*Life of Moses* 1.102, 134, 146, 325). In accord with the action of God, the perfect teacher, Moses, exhibits his perfect embodiment of the law through his religious and political leadership as law-giver, high priest, and prophet.[53]

Philo's use of the teacher/disciple pattern is probably most clearly exhibited in the essay on *The Posterity of Cain and His Exile* as he

describes Rebecca as an extraordinary teacher. In the essay, in which
Philo allegorizes Gen. 24:16–20, he describes Rebecca as a true disciple
of God who, because of her relationship to God, could be a teacher of
wisdom and virtue to men. The account is based on Rebecca's drawing of
water for Abraham's servant and the camels of the servant. Philo interprets the drawing and pouring of the water as an allegory for a teacher's
attainment and teaching of wisdom and virtue. Unlike Hagar who taught
slowly and gradually, Rebecca taught quickly, directly, and freely:

> Rebecca, it says, went down to the spring to fill her pitcher, and came up
> again. For from where is it likely that a mind thirsting for sound sense should
> be filled save from the wisdom of God, that neverfailing spring, its descent to
> which is an ascent in accordance with some innate characteristic of a true
> *mathētēs?* For the teaching of virtue awaits those who come down from empty
> self-conceit, and taking them in its arms carries them to the heights with fair
> fame (136).

As he continues, Philo praises Rebecca for her willingness to teach
wisdom and virtue so freely:

> Rebecca is therefore to be commended for following the ordinances of the
> Father (of all) and letting down from a higher position the vessel which
> contains wisdom, called the pitcher, on her arm, and for holding out to the
> *mathētēs* the teaching (*didaskalias*) which he is able to receive (146). . . .
> When she saw how readily receptive of virtue the servant's nature was, she
> emptied all the contents of her pitcher into the drinking-trough, that is to say,
> she poured all the teacher's knowledge (*epistēmēn*) into the soul of the learner
> (*tou manthanontos*). For, whereas sophists, impelled at once by mercenary
> motives and by a grudging spirit, stunt the natures of their pupils (*gnōrimōn*)
> by withholding much that they ought to tell them, carefully reserving for
> themselves against another day the opportunity of making money; virtue is an
> ungrudging thing, fond of making gifts, never hesitating to do good, as the
> saying is, with hand and foot and all her might (151).

In this passage, Philo shows direct influence from Socratic tradition. In
Plato's dialogues, Socrates takes the same stance as Philo when he argues
that the sophists, motivated by financial gain, are unable to teach wisdom
and virtue. For Plato, only Socrates' dialectical method, designed to bring
the realm of ideas to birth in human thought, could achieve this goal.
Philo substitutes Socrates' method with attainment of wisdom through
mystical ascent to God. With the ascent of the eager disciple's mind to
God, wisdom is given as a gift.

Throughout Philo's writings, therefore, the Greek philosophical tradition of teacher and disciple influences the presentation of famous Israelites as paradigms of wisdom and virtue for all nations and peoples. God,

however, is the perfect teacher of wisdom and virtue, and famous Israelites must first become eager disciples of God. Abraham, the one taught by God par excellence, is a teacher as his story is used to instruct others about the perfect trust embodied in his actions. Likewise, Moses, the perfect philosopher-king, stands as a paragon of wisdom and virtue, transcending human teachers through the perfect embodiment of God's law. Rebecca, through an allegorical ploy, becomes a perfect teacher of wisdom and virtue as she draws water and pours it for Abraham's servant. For Philo, the Israelite tradition of Yahweh as the one who summons, teaches, and commissions remains intact. Human teachers can transmit wisdom and virtue only if they have attained wisdom and virtue from God. Even then, their major function as teachers occurs as their perfect embodiment of virtue is recounted to others.

In contrast to the writings of Philo, the writings of Josephus contain teacher/disciple language that pervades the narration of biblical stories themselves and shows no concern about the inferiority of human teaching. Therefore, the writings of Josephus contain language and point of view highly similar to the gospels. Josephus uses the *didaskalos/mathētēs* terminology from the Greek philosophical tradition to describe ancient philosophers and their followers. Accordingly, in *Against Apion* 1.176 he indicates that Clearchus was "a *mathētēs* of Aristotle, and in the very first rank of peripatetic philosophers." Also, he calls Pherecydes, Pythagoras, and Thales *mathētai* of the Egyptians and Chaldeans (*Against Apion* 1.14). This perception of teacher and disciple in the Greek philosophical tradition provides the matrix for Josephus's understanding and portrayal of the relation of important Israelite leaders to their successors.

In *Antiquities*, Moses is presented as the *didaskalos* (teacher) of Joshua. The reference to Moses as Joshua's teacher occurs in the setting where Moses commands Joshua to choose some men and go to battle against Amalek and his army. As Josephus recounts the episode (*Antiquities* 3.49), he refers to Moses as the teacher of piety to Joshua:

> Moses then, having selected from the multitude all of military efficiency, put at the head Joshua, son of Nauekos, of the tribe of Ephraim, a man of extreme courage, valiant in endurance of toil, highly gifted in intellect and speech, and withal one who worshipped God with piety as Moses his teacher (*didaskalos*) nurtured it, and who was held in esteem by the Hebrews.

This passage reveals the influence of the teacher/disciple tradition in the writings of Josephus. There is nothing in Exod. 17:9–10 that could be considered a stimulus for his description of Moses as the teacher of Joshua. The first time Joshua is mentioned in the biblical text, he is asked to function strictly as a warrior at the head of a select group to fight against

Amalek. Josephus, however, through influence from the teacher/disciple tradition, presupposes a preparatory time in which Moses tutored Joshua in the religious traditions and practices essential for his role as leader of the people of Israel.

In *Antiquities* 6.84 Joshua is called a *mathētēs* (disciple) of Moses, and in 4.165 Josephus reflects on the succession of Moses by Joshua as though Joshua had received his appointment through official study with the philosopher-teacher Moses:

> Moses, already advanced in years, now appointed (*kathistēsin*) Joshua as his successor (*diadochon heautou*) both in his prophetical functions and as com²-mander-in-chief, whensoever the need should arise, under orders from God himself to entrust the direction of affairs to him. Joshua had already received a thorough training (*epepaideuto*) in the laws and in divine lore under the tutelage of Moses (*Mōuseos ekdidaxantos*).

Josephus's account of Moses' transfer of leadership to Joshua is especially informative when compared to the Hebrew Bible. There are two accounts of the commissioning of Joshua, Num. 27.18–23 and Deut. 31:14–15. In the account in Numbers, Yahweh instructs Moses to commission Joshua. When, in the account above, Josephus is following the text of Numbers, he seizes the opportunity to reflect on Moses' appointment (*kathistanai*) of Joshua after Joshua had received thorough instruction from him. In contrast, Deut. 31:14–15 recounts the commissioning by God himself:

> And the Lord said to Moses, "Behold the days approach when you must die; call Joshua, and present yourselves in the tent of meeting, that I may commission him." And Moses and Joshua went and presented themselves in the tent of meeting. And the Lord appeared in the tent in a pillar of cloud; and the pillar of cloud stood by the door of the tent.

In this account, Yahweh himself issues the summons and commissions Joshua to his task. When Josephus recounts tradition parallel to Deuteronomy (*Antiquities* 4.315–19), he makes no mention of God's special commissioning of Joshua. The result in Josephus's narrative is an adoption and adaptation of the teacher/disciple pattern for the presentation of Joshua's succession of Moses.[54] Moses commissions Joshua under instruction from Yahweh, of course, but, for Josephus, Moses calls, instructs, and commissions Joshua according to his role as the *didaskalos* of Joshua.

Josephus's portrayal of Elijah and Elisha as prophet and disciple displays the remolding of Jewish tradition even more vividly than his depiction of Moses and Joshua. Intermittently, Josephus uses the terms *gnōrimos* (student or acquaintance), *diadochos* (successor), and *mathētēs* (disciple) to describe Elisha's relation to Elijah. Undoubtedly the most important passage for comparison with the Socratic tradition and the Gospel of Mark is *Antiquities* 8.354 where Elijah summons Elisha to be his disciple:

> Elijah . . . returned to the country of the Hebrews and came upon Elisha, the son of Saphatēs, as he was ploughing and some others with him who were driving twelve yoke of oxen, and going up to him he threw his own mantle over him. Thereupon Elisha immediately began to prophesy and, leaving his oxen followed Elijah (*ēkolouthēsen Ēlia*). But he asked to be allowed to take leave of his parents, and when Elijah bade him do this, he parted from them and then went with the prophet; and so long as Elijah was alive he was his disciple (*mathētēs*) and attendant (*diakonos*).

The language of this passage calls forth the dynamics in the traditions about the sophists, Socrates, and Jesus. In Josephus's account, Elijah's travels bring him to Elisha whom he successfully attracts as a disciple. Elijah's action of casting his mantle over Elisha produces an immediate change in Elisha. Not only does Elisha begin to prophesy, but he also leaves his oxen and follows Elijah as a disciple and attendant.

When Josephus's story of Elijah's call of Elisha is compared with the biblical account, the influence of the Greco-Roman teacher/disciple tradition on Josephus's portrayal of the incident is highly evident. The Hebrew text of this episode acquires its meaning in the setting of the anointing of a prophet. Yahweh tells Elijah to go and anoint Elisha to be a prophet in his place (1 Kings 19:16). When Elijah finds Elisha and anoints him by casting his mantel upon him, Elisha leaves the oxen with which he is plowing and runs after Elijah. When Elisha tells Elijah that he will follow him after he has kissed his father and mother, Elijah tells him to go back to his work, because his intent was not to solicit Elisha's following of him but to confer upon him the ability to function as a prophet according to Yahweh's instructions. Whatever was Elijah's intention, however, Elisha returns to the oxen, slays them, and feeds them to the people; then, he arises, goes after Elijah, and waits upon him as a servant (1 Kings 19:19–21).

As interpreters have recognized, the Elijah/Elisha stories represent the closest parallel in the Hebrew Bible to the teacher/disciple relation in the gospels.[55] Nevertheless, essential features of the summoning teacher tradition are absent from the Hebrew account. Elisha accompanies Elijah as a servant, not a student-disciple, and Elijah is not portrayed teaching Elisha a particular system of understanding and action. In the Hebrew account, the prophet tradition includes a servant-successor tradition that is ready to be interpreted by means of the itinerant teacher/disciple tradition in Greco-Roman culture. Even the LXX account of the story, however, does not impose teacher/disciple language upon the relation of

Elijah and Elisha. The few alterations in the LXX account maintain the
Israelite tradition of the prophet/servant relation as it is recounted in the
Hebrew text.

In accord with Greco-Roman accounts of teachers with disciples,
Josephus's first-century account of Elijah's call of Elisha presupposes that
Elijah is taking the action necessary to convince Elisha to become his
disciple. As Josephus condenses the story, he portrays Elisha simply
leaving his oxen and his parents and following Elijah. Josephus omits the
biblical statement, "Go back again; for what have I done to you?" (1 Kings
19:20), because the entire account now presupposes that the action is
designed to attain the response of following as a disciple-companion. Still,
in contrast to the Socratic traditions and the Gospel of Mark, Josephus's
account of Elijah's call of Elisha does not contain a direct command to
come to him. Josephus retains the biblical feature whereby Elijah casts
the mantle over Elisha to confer the office of prophet upon him. Like
Mark's gospel, however, the Josephus account contains the structure and
terminology of the teacher who comes to a man who is engaged in his
daily labor, and of the disciple who leaves his work and parents to follow
his itinerant teacher.

The texts of both Philo and Josephus, therefore, reflect the incursion of
the teacher/disciple tradition into the framework of biblical tradition.
Philo reflects direct influence from the Socratic tradition when he discusses discipleship to God and portrays Rebecca as a teacher of wisdom
and virtue. In contrast, Josephus's *Antiquities* contains the kind of cultural
influence from the teacher/disciple tradition that is analogous to the
Gospel of Mark. Certain people are summoned by God to function as
teachers who call, teach, and commission disciples. These disciples are
summoned, taught, and commissioned for the purpose of accompanying
the teacher on his travels and of carrying the work forward both during the
ministry of the teacher and after his death.

In summary, neither the Hebrew Bible nor the LXX contains the
terminology and dynamics of teacher and disciple. The teacher/disciple
pattern and tradition are simply not characteristic of Israelite culture as it
is manifested in the biblical tradition. The language, concept, and tradition begin to appear in books of the LXX written during Hellenistic times,
and Hellenistic copyists add *didaskalos* and *mathētēs* to a few passages.
The modifications reflect a gradual imposition of Hellenistic teacher/
disciple conventions on the biblical texts. Since a king or a general
influenced by Hellenistic culture customarily took a teacher with him on
his travels, so must the kings in the LXX accounts have their own personal
teachers. Also, those who accompany important sages of Jewish tradition
must be disciples rather than warriors. The writings of Philo show the

distinction between human and divine teaching when the teacher/disciple tradition intermingled with the tradition of Yahweh as the one who calls, teaches, and commissions. Later in the first century C.E., the writings of Josephus illustrate how the teacher/disciple tradition began to find a comfortable place in narrative accounts of biblical stories. Josephus recasts the stories of Moses and Elijah from the perspective of Greco-Roman conventions: both are teachers who summon a disciple whom they appoint as a successor.

THE TEACHER/DISCIPLE RELATION
IN RABBINIC LITERATURE AND
PHILOSTRATUS'S *LIFE OF APOLLONIUS OF TYANA*

It is customary to presuppose that the teacher/disciple relation in Mark derives from the rabbi/disciple relation in first-century C.E. Judaism.[56] In four stories in Mark, Jesus is addressed either as *rabbi* or *rabbouni* (9:5; 10:51; 11:21; 14:45), and in many other stories Jesus' dialogue with his disciples follows patterns akin to patterns in rabbinic accounts.[57] Moreover, the phrases *akolouthein opisō* and *erchesthai opisō* (to follow after or to come after) are to be compared not only with the biblical phrases but with rabbinic accounts where disciples are featured in a position of following behind.[58] In addition, in four settings in Mark Jesus sits as he teaches (4:1; 9:35; 12:41; 13:3), and this position is characteristic of the rabbinic teacher.[59]

Analysis of the initiation of the teacher/disciple relation, however, suggests that the portrayal of the teacher/disciple relation in Mark is a distinctive adaptation of aspects from both Jewish and Greco-Roman traditions. In rabbinic literature, rabbis are not depicted traveling around as Jesus does to find people who will respond to his summons to become disciple-companions.[60] Instead, the tradition emphasizes the initiative by individual people to receive permission from a rabbi to become one of his student-disciples. The stories that characterize the beginning of a teacher/disciple relationship, therefore, receive their plot from the struggle of a young man to gain acceptance by a rabbi rather than the action and summons of a rabbi to attain a response from a person whom he wants as a disciple-companion. The stories tend to feature student-disciples who later become well-known rabbis themselves.

Perhaps the most dramatic story, existent only in Talmudic times, concerns Eliezer's desire to study with Yohanan Ben Zakkai. The story, as recounted in chapter 13 of *Abot de Rabbi Nathan B.*, reads as follows:

> They said concerning Eliezer that when he sought to study Torah, he was ploughing in difficult ground. He wept. Father gave him easier land, he still

wept. He told Father he wanted to study Torah. Father: You are 28, too late;
have children and send them. He was sad for three weeks. Elijah appeared to
him, "Go up to Ben Zakkai in Jerusalem." He went, kept weeping, finally said
he wanted to study Torah. Yohanan taught him Prayer, Shema', and Grace.
Taught him Mishnah, two a day, reviewed on Sabbath . . .[61]

In this story, Yohanan's fame is the basis for the desire of Eliezer to study
with him. As a well-known rabbi, Yohanan has no need to seek student-
disciples who will study with him. This story features the necessity of
Eliezer to receive permission from God himself to study with Yohanan. At
first God refuses to grant him permission, but after Eliezer persists in
weeping, Elijah appears and tells him to go and study. The dynamics, as
one can easily see, are quite different from those in the Gospel of Mark.
The rabbinic account presupposes a school tradition rather than an itinerant tradition. The student travels, but the teacher does not travel. Moreover, the account presupposes that the teacher/disciple relation is established by means of request rather than summons. The student-disciple,
by means of his initiative, confronts the teacher, instead of the teacher
summoning the disciple as in Socratic literature and in Mark. The rhetorical form of the story is different, therefore, showing a progression from the
disciple to the teacher, rather than from the teacher to the disciple.

Another story that shows the contrast between Mark and the rabbinic
tradition is the account of hardships Hillel faced in order to study Torah
with Shema'iah and Abtalion. While this story does not portray the initial
event in Hillel's relation with these two teachers, it shows the struggle of
the disciple to gain access to the teaching of the famous rabbi:

They said about Hillel the Elder that every day he used to work and earn one
tropaic, half of which he would give to the guard of the house of learning, the
other half (he spent) for his food and for that of his family.

One day he found nothing to earn, and the guard at the house of learning
did not permit him to enter. He climbed up and sat upon the window, to hear
the words of the living God from the mouth of Shema'iah and Abtalion.

They said: That day was the eve of the Sabbath in the winter solstice, and
snow fell down upon him from heaven. When the dawn rose, Shema'iah said
to Abtalion, "Brother Abtalion, on every day this house is light, and today it is
dark. Is it perhaps a cloudy day?"

They looked up and saw the figure of a man in the window. They went up
and found him covered by three cubits of snow. They removed him, bathed
and anointed him, and placed him opposite the fire, and they said, "This man
is worthy that the Sabbath be profaned on his behalf."[62]

Again the story features initiative on behalf of the individual who wants to
be the student-disciple. The progressive form of the stories in the Gospel

of Mark is quite different as they feature Jesus going out to find men who will accept his summons to become disciple-companions to him.

Finally, the progressive form of the tradition is poignantly illustrated by the story about Jesus (evidently, Jesus of Nazareth)[63] and Rabbi Joshua ben Perahiah in the Babylonian Talmud. This story shows how even a person who is already a disciple may suddenly find the relationship at an end through the rabbi's initiative:

> One of his (R. Joshua b. Perahiah's) disciples [MSS: Jesus] said to him, "Rabbi, her (your sister's) eyes are narrow." He (Joshua) replied, "Wicked person! Do you occupy yourself with such (a thought)?" He sounded four hundred horns (= shofar-blasts) and excommunicated him. He (Jesus) came before him many times. He said, "Receive me." But he (Joshua) refused to take notice. One day while he (Joshua) was reciting the Shema', he (Jesus) came before him. He (Joshua) said to him, "Repent." He answered him, "Thus have I learned from you: Whoever sinned and caused others to sin is deprived of the power of doing penitence."[64]

In this story again the issue is the acceptance of a student-disciple by a rabbi. In the midst of the story, Rabbi Joshua commands Jesus to repent, just as Jesus in Mark issues the command to repent in his opening statement in 1:15. Yet the teacher/disciple relationship is characterized by Jesus' request "Receive me," indicating again the direction of the initiative in order to begin and maintain a teacher/disciple relation. Persistently in rabbinic tradition, students struggle to initiate and maintain a student-disciple relation with a rabbi. In turn, rabbis do not go out to seek and summon people to become disciple-companions to them.

The focus of Mark on Jesus' summoning of disciple-companions rather than on people's requests to become disciples creates a different use of language in Mark than in the rabbinic tradition. In Mark, Jesus goes to Simon and Andrew and tells them he will make them fishers of men. In contrast, the rabbis say, "You make yourself into . . ." Therefore, instead of "Follow me and I will make you fishers of men" (Mark 1:17), Joshua ben Perahiah says, "Make for yourself a rabbi, and get a fellow disciple . . ." (*M. Abot* 1:6). The first part of the saying, "Make for yourself a rabbi," is also attributed to Rabbi Gamaliel in *M. Abot* 1:16. In accord with this kind of language, Rabbi Hillel is attributed with, "Be of the disciples of Aaron, loving peace, and pursuing peace, loving mankind, and bringing them near to the Torah" (*M. Abot* 1:12). In other words, the characteristic of the rabbinic tradition is to place the initiative on the person himself to seek a rabbi and to attempt to become a student-disciple to him.

Language about "being made into" is found in a collection of traditions about Shammai and Hillel in the Babylonian Talmud. Again, the rabbis do not go to someone with a promise to make them into something different. Instead, different people are portrayed coming to them with a special request. In these stories, the people request to be made a proselyte:

> A certain heathen once came before Shammai and asked him, ". . . Make me a proselyte on condition that you teach me the Written Torah (only)." He scolded and repulsed him in anger. (When) he went before Hillel, he accepted him as a proselyte . . .
>
> On another occasion it happened that a certain heathen once came before Shammai and said to him, "Make me a proselyte, on condition that you teach me the whole Torah while I stand on one foot." Thereupon he repulsed him with the builder's cubit which was in his hand. (When) he went before Hillel, he converted him . . .
>
> On another occasion it happened that a certain heathen was passing behind a school and heard the voice of a scribe reciting, 'And these are the garments which they shall make: a breastplate, and an ephod.' Said he, "For whom are these?" "For the High Priest," they said. Then said that heathen to himself, "I will go and become a proselyte, that I may be appointed a High Priest." So he went to Shammai and said to him, "Make me a proselyte on condition that you appoint me a High Priest." But he repulsed him with the builder's cubit which was in his hand. He then went before Hillel. He made him a proselyte.[65]

In each instance, after Hillel makes the heathen a proselyte he teaches the new proselyte something that requires him to reevaluate the reason that had motivated him to become a proselyte. Within the context of our study, the significant feature again is the progressive form of the tradition. Neither Hillel or Shammai go to a person with a promise to "make them become" something they are not. Rather, a person initiates a special relationship by coming to a famous teacher and asking him to make him into a proselyte.

When the Markan portrayal of the teacher/disciple relation is analyzed from a perspective of the intermingling of Jewish and Greco-Roman traditions, even some of the characteristics considered to be undeniably rabbinic call for reconsideration. While Jesus sits as he teaches in four contexts in Mark, nowhere does Markan narration assert that the disciples "sat before him."[66] In rabbinic literature the phrase "sat before him" is equivalent to "studied as a student-disciple with him."[67] Only in one teaching context in Mark does the narration refer to a sitting posture for those being taught, and in this story the people "sit around him" in a circle (Mark 3:32, 34), rather than "before him" in the standard rabbinic manner. Only in Gethsemane does Jesus tell the disciples to sit down (14:32), and the purpose is not to teach them but to have them wait for him while he prays. In contrast, Hillel says, "Sit down and I will tell you something . . ."[68] For the most part, Jesus teaches his disciples as he walks along with them. This feature, characteristic of the peripatetic philosophers, is also present in rabbinic tradition.[69] The centrality of travel in Mark, however, and the activity of teaching while en route indicate influence from itinerant tradition rather than school tradition as it is found in rabbinic literature.

In summary, while the Gospel of Mark and rabbinic literature both contain scenes in which disciples are following after the teacher, the rhetorical form of the stories which initiate the teacher/disciple relation are different. Underlying the difference in rhetorical form is a difference in social pattern. Mark presupposes an itinerant tradition, while rabbinic literature presupposes a school tradition. Social pattern and rhetorical form unite in different ways in the two types of literature, creating the summoning and promise form in Mark in contrast to the request form in rabbinic literature.

If the socio-rhetorical form of the teacher/disciple tradition in Mark resulted from the direct adoption of a tradition other than rabbinic tradition, a description of its features would be a simple matter. Instead, the teacher/disciple relation in Mark is an independent adaptation of itinerant tradition. As a result, aspects of the itinerant activity of prophets like Elijah and Elisha intermingle with aspects of the itinerant activity of a figure like Apollonius of Tyana. In Philostratus's *Life of Apollonius of Tyana*, discipleship presupposes itinerancy. The disciple must be willing to accompany Apollonius as he travels from village to village and country to country. Yet, Apollonius attracts disciples like the rabbis do, without summoning them. Damis, the leading disciple and the one responsible for much source material used by Philostratus, was never summoned by Apollonius. Rather, Damis came to Apollonius and exhorted him saying:

> "Let us depart, Apollonius, you following God, and I you (*su men theōi hepomenos, ego de soi*); for I think you will find that I can serve you . . ." (1.19).

In this scene the language of following emerges as the teacher/disciple relation is initiated. In accordance with his verbal preference, Philostratus uses *hepesthai* rather than *akolouthein* to refer to this following in the sense of discipleship.[70] In similarity with the rabbinic traditions, the initiative lies with the person who wants to become a student-disciple. In similarity with Mark's gospel, however, the concept of following presupposes itinerancy. As Damis continues, he recommends himself to Apollonius on the basis of his knowledge of the villages which Apollonius plans to visit on his travels:

"I know all about Babylon, and I know all the cities that there are, because I
have been up there not long ago, and also the villages in which there is much
good to be found; and moreover, I know the languages of the various barba-
rous races" (1.19).

When Apollonius responds that he himself knows all languages, though
he has never learned a single one, and, moreover, he understands all the
secrets of human silence:

> Thereupon the Assyrian (Damis) worshipped him (*prosēuxato auton*), when
> he heard this, and regarded him as a *daimōn*; and he stayed with him (*synēn
> te autōi*) increasing in wisdom and committing to memory whatever he learnt
> (1.19).

In this scene, Damis confronts Apollonius much like Peter and those with
him pursue Jesus to seek permission to be with him after their initial call
(Mark 1:35–39). When Damis shows the appropriate determination,
amazement, and awe, Apollonius allows him to remain with him. This
encounter results in a teacher/disciple relationship that continues until
the death of Apollonius.

As the initial encounter between Apollonius and Damis refers specifically to "following" Apollonius, so the description of Demetrius's relation
to Apollonius is couched in terms of the following:

> Now there was in Corinth at that time a man named Demetrius, . . . and his
> attitude towards Apollonius was exactly that which they say Antisthenes took
> up towards the system of Socrates; for he followed him and was anxious to be
> his disciple (*heipeto autōi mathētiōn*), and was devoted to his doctrines . . .
> (4.25).

Again, the dimension is missing whereby the teacher summons the man
into a teacher/disciple relation. By traveling to Corinth, however, Apollonius gains the response of Demetrius, and the response is characterized
in terms of following Apollonius as a student-disciple.

As the plot of *Apollonius* develops, the test of discipleship becomes
the ability to accompany Apollonius on his travels. Timasion (6.3) and
Nilus (6.12) become disciples of Apollonius by requesting permission to
accompany him on his travels. Apollonius grants both of them permission
on the basis of their wisdom. Timasion's wisdom is displayed through his
account of his boyhood relations with his mother (6.3), while Nilus's
wisdom is tested at great length by Apollonius to ascertain the clarity of
his resolve to leave the naked sages of Egypt and follow him (6.12–17).
Preparation for travel presents a special time to evaluate the teacher/
disciple relationship. Apollonius tests the commitment of those who have
joined him before he allows them to accompany him to Egypt and

Ethiopia (5.43). He leaves Menippus behind to watch Euphrates, and he asks Dioscurides not to journey with them because he appears not to have a strong inclination to travel. In another setting he issues a challenge to his disciple-companions through imagery of the athletic games in order to test them (5.43). The challenge to them ends with the statement the Eleans make to their athletes on their way to Olympia:

> "If you have laboured so hard as to be entitled to go to Olympia and have banished all sloth and cowardice from your lives, then march boldly on; but as for those who have not so trained themselves, let them depart whithersoever they like" (5.43).

Like the rabbis, therefore, Apollonius does not summon people into a teacher/disciple relationship. However, the teacher/disciple relationship in *Apollonius* is similar to Mark because it features teaching and learning in the context of an itinerant life. For the most worthy disciples, acceptance of discipleship means acceptance of the hardships and uncertainty of travel through unfamiliar villages and uninhabited areas. Following Apollonius means accepting the challenges he places before them as he works his way through the cities, villages, settlements, and desolate areas that he has established as the itinerary of his adult career until his death.

In summary, the teacher/disciple tradition in Mark represents an adaptation of biblical and Greek traditions that is not entirely paralleled either in rabbinic literature or in Philostratus's *Apollonius* in which a potential disciple seeks out a teacher and attempts to convince the teacher to accept him as a student-disciple. In other words, the scenes progress in the form of request stories rather than summoning stories. In rabbinic literature, the process may be a matter of gaining the consent of God as well as the consent of the rabbi. If the rabbi (and God) consent, the student-disciple begins to sit before the rabbi to learn from him, a relationship influenced by the institution of the schoolhouse in Pharisaic circles. In Philostratus's *Apollonius,* the disciple may perceive the teacher to be godlike and may perform obeisance before him. Since the dynamics of discipleship are influenced by the rigors of itinerant activity, Apollonius tests the potential disciple to see if his commitment is strong enough to carry him through the strain and stress that is analogous to the rigors of the athletic competition at Olympia. In Mark the teacher seeks, summons, and commissions people to be his disciple-companions, promising to make them into people who are able to seek, summon, and commission people in a manner similar to himself. Jesus' activity is itinerant activity, like Apollonius's activity. But the rhetorical form of the stories that initiate the teacher/disciple relation results from an adaptation of conventional forms

and patterns in circles independent from the direct influence of either
rabbinic traditions or Greek philosophical traditions. The rhetorical form
of these stories intermingles conventional patterns and forms from biblical
and Greek heritages in a manner that requires the interpreter to investigate the early literature as intensively as the literature contemporary with
Mark's gospel.

THE INITIAL PHASE OF
THE TEACHER/DISCIPLE RELATIONSHIP:
MARK 1:14—3:6

In the Gospel of Mark, the initial moment of the teacher/disciple
relation is expanded into an entire phase in which the disciples accompany Jesus, imitate him, and are defended by him. Throughout the
section inaugurated by the progression in Mark 1:14–20, Jesus attracts
people to his point of view and mode of action. The basic social identity of
Jesus' role is established in 1:21–28 when Jesus teaches in the synagogue
on the Sabbath.[71] In the midst of Jesus' teaching, he is confronted by a
man with an unclean spirit who calls him the holy one of God (1:24). On
the basis of Jesus' exorcism of the unclean spirit, the assembled crowd
perceives his exorcistic activity in the setting of the social identity of a
religious teacher. For this reason, they call his command to the unclean
spirit "new teaching" (1:27), and they compare him to scribes whose social
identity is established on the basis of their teaching (1:22; cf. 9:11;
12:35).[72]

After Jesus calls four men, they spend the rest of the day with him
(1:21–34). The next morning when Jesus goes off by himself to pray,
Simon and those with him pursue and find him (1:34–39). This scene
completes the resolve of the four men to leave their occupation and family
to accompany Jesus. On the previous day, Jesus had sought them out. On
this day, they seek Jesus and indicate that "all" are seeking him (1:37).
Because of their initiative, they receive an invitation from Jesus to accompany him on a traveling mission throughout the village-towns of Galilee
(1:38).[73] We cannot be sure that "Simon and those with him" refers only to
the four men, although this surely includes at least these four.[74] The scene
features Simon in a position of leadership, and it leaves open the possibility that more than three other men have come along. This is characteristic of the narrative, never limiting the followers to four, until, at the
beginning of the next phase, Jesus selects twelve "whom he desired"
(3:13).

Soon after the response of "Simon and those with him" (1:36–37), the
action of Jesus underscores the interest in the initial moment in the
teacher/disciple relation in this section. In Mark 2:13–17 Jesus goes out to

the sea again, and when he walks along the shore and sees a tax collector named Levi, he calls him, and Levi arises from his tax booth and follows Jesus (2:14). While the call of the first four disciples introduces the basic dynamics of leaving vocation, family, and associates to adopt an itinerant mode of life, this second scene of calling emphasizes the adoption of activities that reflect the special characteristics of Jesus' activity. The initial moment in the relation between Jesus and the tax collector extends into a scene where Jesus and his disciples eat with a group of tax collectors and sinners (2:15–17). This activity is immediately criticized by scribes of the Pharisees as deviating from the norm. Much as Socrates was accused of corrupting the youth and rejecting the gods acknowledged by the state, so Jesus is accused of inappropriate action when he forgives sins (Mark 2:1–12) and when he ignores the eating customs of the scribes and Pharisees. Jesus defends himself by saying:

> "Those who are well have no need of a physician, but those who are sick; I came not to call the righteous, but sinners" (Mark 2:17).

Jesus' defense is appropriate for the initial phase in the teacher/disciple cycle. The purpose for calling people into discipleship is analogous to the purpose for healing a person who is sick. A person calls an individual who needs an alternative mode of thought and action just as a person heals an individual who needs an alternative state of mental and physiological being.

The deviant form of the activity in which Jesus and his disciple-companions engage is emphasized by two additional episodes in which Jesus defends his disciples when they ignore laws about fasting and laws about gathering food on the Sabbath (2:15–28). When Jesus defends the disciples, his identity as a teacher who gathers and maintains disciple-companions is complete. Not only does Jesus summon individuals to join a small band of associates who accompany him as he travels, but he also defends them when they apply principles in accord with his mode of action.

The initial phase of Jesus' ministry, therefore, establishes the social identity of Jesus as a teacher who gathers disciples and gains their willingness to adopt his mode of activity. In the portrayal of a teacher, however, action and response transpire at two levels. While the teacher is approaching individuals, groups of people gather, and these groups are constituted by people who have the potential also to respond to the teacher's summons. In the context of the initiation of the teacher/disciple relation, large crowds gather around Jesus. The crowds fulfill a dimension complementary to the activity of the disciple-companions. Jesus is not a teacher in a school setting where only people who want a specific program of education will receive attention. Rather, Jesus is a public teacher who offers a range of services like many other wandering preacher-teachers in the Mediterranean world around the turn of the era. This activity is accompanied by a social identity that threatens the position of a specific group of teachers in the setting but gains the accolades of the multitudes. When Jesus exorcises an unclean spirit (1:21–28), he is declared to be a teacher whose message is authoritative and new. After this episode, Jesus' fame spreads throughout the entire region of Galilee (1:28), and in the evening large groups gather to have him heal the sick and cast out demons (1:32–34). After he cleanses a leper, he preaches and spreads his message, and people come to him from everywhere (1:45). After healing a paralytic and forgiving his sins (2:1–12), Jesus goes back to the sea, calls the entire crowd to him and teaches them (2:13). These activities portray the wide range of activities on which Jesus' social identity is based.[75] Jesus' primary role is that of a traveling teacher, and that role includes a range of services that attracts a large number of people into his sphere of influence.

The general result of Jesus' activity is summarized in the final sentence of the section (3:6) and in the beginning of the next section (3:7–19). Two contrasting relations are shown here. The Pharisees meet in council with the Herodians to plan the destruction of Jesus (3:6) while at the same time, a great multitude of people from Galilee, Judea, Jerusalem, Idumaea, beyond the Jordan, and from about Tyre and Sidon gather around Jesus (3:7–8), and Jesus chooses twelve disciples from these people (3:13–19). The two poles of response reveal the dynamics of a preacher-teacher whose words and deeds are designed to attract people to a special system of thought and action. On the one hand, the teaching deviates from the norms operative in society. Therefore, people in established positions of power conspire to bring the activity of the teacher to an end. On the other hand, the emphases in the system of thought and action offer an alternative mode for approaching the problems and frustrations of daily life. If a person wishes to adopt the alternative presented, he or she can respond in the form of either a primary or secondary relationship to the teacher. A small band of people adopt a primary relationship whereby they spend the majority of their time with the teacher. The interaction of these disciple-companions with the teacher goes through a series of phases until the teacher dies. Another group, much larger, follows by means of a secondary teacher/disciple relationship. Instead of committing all their time to itinerant activity with Jesus, they respond favorably to the basic attributes of Jesus' thought and action. Their response, by necessity, is based on partial knowledge of Jesus' thought and action. The reader, however, has the opportunity to respond on the basis of a comprehensive account of the activity of Jesus. His or her relationship to Jesus may be like Socrates' discipleship to Homer, as discussed in Dio Chrysostom,

Oration 55.2–4; and Pythagoras's discipleship to the Egyptians and Chaldeans, as discussed in Isocrates, *Busiris* 28–29 and Josephus, *Against Apion* 1.14. The reader sees the entire system of thought and action as it was manifested by Jesus during his adult life. Like the multitudes that follow, the reader has the opportunity to respond favorably to Jesus' thought and action. Instead of partial knowledge, however, the reader has a comprehensive account on which to base a response.

In the initial phase of the story, Jesus does not instruct his disciples in the details of his system of understanding. In fact, only three verses contain statements by Jesus to the disciples (1:17, 38; 2:14). He announces the kingdom of God to all, summons people to repentance and belief, and responds to specific situations on the basis of his social position as an authoritative teacher. Every statement he makes in this section is extremely brief[76] until he defends his disciples before scribes and Pharisees who question the propriety of their actions. In these situations Jesus responds with statements ninety-three and sixty-nine words long in the Greek text (2:19–22, 25–28).

The primary mode of speech and action in the initial phase is established by commands of Jesus. These commands introduce logical progressive form into both individual scenes of healing and the teacher/disciple cycle. Jesus issues the following commands in Mark 1:14—3:6:

1. "Repent and believe in the gospel" (1:15);
2. "Follow me and I will make you become fishers of men" (1:17);
3. "Let us go on to the next towns, that I may preach there also; for that is why I came out" (1:38);
4. "I will; be clean" (1:41);
5. "See that you say nothing to any one; but go, show yourself to the priest, and offer for your cleansing what Moses commanded, for a proof to the people" (1:44);
6. "I say to you, rise, take up your pallet and go home" (2:11);
7. "Follow me" (2:14);
8. "Come here" (3:3);
9. "Stretch out your hand" (3:5).

Commands 2, 3, and 7 provide the reader with clues to major future events in the relation between Jesus and his disciple-companions. These commands, therefore, give logical progressive form to Jesus' relationship to his disciples. The reader expects: the disciple-companions to learn through observation of Jesus' activities as they travel throughout the surrounding village-towns; Jesus to give special instructions to the disciples that will enable them to become "fishers of men"; and Jesus to give tasks to the disciples that will involve them in the kind of activity Jesus himself engages. The remaining commands establish the basic qualities of Jesus' character, action, and speech as they intermingle Jesus' healing activity[77] with his exhortations to respond to the system of thought and action he teaches and performs. Through these commands, progressive forms unfolding the qualities of Jesus' character, action, and speech occur in the midst of logical progressions that provide the reader with clues to the major events in the teacher/disciple cycle.

In Mark 2:6 scribes are introduced for the first time in the narrative, and in their presence Jesus' speech begins to contain aggressive proverbial wisdom. The narrator prepares the reader for resistance to the speech of Jesus when he says that the people were astonished at Jesus' teaching, for he taught as one who had authority, "and not as the scribes" (1:22). Now the negative mode of "not as the scribes" is manifested by the scribes' adoption of a role counter to Jesus' speech and action.[78] In turn, Jesus no longer simply commands people to do things. He encounters the scribes with aggressive speech. Three times his statements begin with rhetorical questions:

1. "Why do you question thus in your hearts?" (2:8);
2. "The wedding guests cannot fast while the bridegroom is with them, can they?" (au. trans., 2:19);
3. "Have you never read what David did . . .?" (2:26).

Twice the questions contain an either/or choice that creates an advantage for Jesus by limiting the alternative answers:[79]

4. "Which is easier, to say to the paralytic, 'Your sins are forgiven,' or to say, 'Rise, take up your pallet and walk'?" (2:9);
5. "Is it lawful on the sabbath to do good *or* to do harm, to save life *or* to kill?" (3:4).

Overall, Jesus' speech attains an aggressive quality through the introduction of negative words and adversative conjunctions. Two of the rhetorical questions quoted above contain negatives: "Have you *never* read what David did . . .?" (2:26); and "The wedding guests *cannot* fast while the bridegroom is with them, can they?" (2:19). The proverbial speech of Jesus functions aggressively as a result of both negative and adversative features:

1. "Those who are well have *no* need of a physician, *but* those who are sick; I came *not* to call the righteous, *but* sinners" (2:17);
2. "*No one* sews a piece of unshrunk cloth on an old garment; *but* if he does *not* (heed this), the patch tears away from it, the new from the old, and a worse tear is made" (au. trans., 2:21);
3. "*No one* puts new wine into old wineskins; *but* if he does *not* (heed this),

the wine will burst the skins, and the wine is lost, and so are the skins; *but new wine is for fresh skins*" (au. trans., 2:22);

4. "The sabbath was made for man, *not* man for the sabbath; so the Son of man is lord even of the sabbath" (2:27–28).

The aggressive proverbial wisdom in the initial phase of the Markan narrative emerges out of the folklore in early Christianity that celebrated a system of thought and action that deviated from norms established by Jewish leaders. "Both Jesus' teaching and his wonderworking activities constituted alternate, though socially deviant, means of achieving acceptable goals."[80] The identity of the deviant group arises out of antagonism that is directed toward scribes and Pharisees. Therefore Jesus is placed in settings where scribes and Pharisees object to the actions either of him or of his disciples, and Jesus responds with proverbs that appear to be the result of careful reflection and appear to be morally right.[81] The rhetorical questions that precede the proverbial statements establish clear referents for the proverbs that allow the proverbs to function without any suspicion of being riddles.[82] The questions which are riddlelike are given direct proverbial answers.

As the author of Mark incorporates the folklore of a particular sector of the Christian movement into a literary setting influenced by the cycle of relationships associated with Greek philosophical sects or schools,[83] he presents a rhetorical defense of Jesus in a cultural setting where his wonderworking could be considered to be "magic."[84] Controversy over Jesus' activity begins when he forgives the sins of a paralytic whom he heals (2:1–12). The controversy reaches a crisis when Jesus heals a man with a withered hand on the Sabbath (3:6). Jesus' use of proverbial wisdom to defend himself and his disciples sets the stage for a defense of his entire system of thought and action. Further defense of Jesus' thought and action emerges as he teaches and enacts the dimensions of the system in the remainder of the narrative. During the initial phase, Jesus simply summons people and defends himself and his disciple-companions with poignant proverbial wisdom. A substantive defense of Jesus must await an introduction of the details of his system of thought and action. In this section he does not attempt to teach anyone the details of his system. Rather, he initiates the teacher/disciple relationship and defends those who adopt the mode of action and thought that he himself manifests.

MARKAN SUMMONS AND RESPONSE
AS AN INTERMINGLING OF
JEWISH AND GRECO-ROMAN TRADITIONS

A philosopher-teacher's call to a student-disciple represents the first moment in the relationship. This moment results in the resolve of the disciple to associate extensively with the teacher in order to learn through discussion and observation. The summons to adopt the thought and action exemplified by the protagonist in the narrative characterizes the particular kind of literature akin to the Gospel of Mark. Not only disciples but also named and unnamed people among the crowds are summoned to enter into a special relationship with Jesus and his teaching. This portrayal is meant to attract the reader to the understanding and action transmitted through the stories and teachings recounted about the teacher. The response of people to a personage, however, may or may not be based on the fundamental role of the person in the story. In any culture, a number of functions may be performed by people with various social identities.[85] In first-century Greco-Roman culture, not only physicians but also political leaders, prophets, magicians, and philosopher-teachers were known for healing people of physical ailments.[86] The important consideration was not whether a person performed healings but the social identity in which he performed them. In Mark, both exorcisms and healings are part of Jesus' role as a teacher. Jesus' teaching informs, defends, summons, and heals. Both his words and actions attack spiritual forces that afflict people and offer an alternative approach to life. The unity between Jesus' words and actions is fundamental to biographical portrayal in Greco-Roman culture.[87] Any person whose speech and action are not consistent with one another is open to the sharpest criticism possible. The first section of the Gospel of Mark correlates Jesus' authoritative teaching with the action of healing.[88] The scribes and Pharisees are horrified by the content of the teaching and the action, but there is no suggestion that Jesus' action is inconsistent with his teaching. Rather, Jesus' teaching and action are fully interrelated, and the expectation is raised that such a correlation will continue throughout the narrative.

The fundamental base for Jesus' identity, therefore, is his teaching activity. As a teacher, Jesus is able to attract, command, and influence other beings by means of his word and action. Any social identity, however, is established by means of a range of activities performed through interaction with various kinds of people. The range of activities that characterizes a particular social identity can be referred to as a composite role.[89] Just as the scribes do more than teach,[90] so Jesus is involved in a range of activities that are perceived as part of his teaching role. One aspect of this role is the healing activity that emerges from his ability to command unclean spirits. His commands, in other words, are not only powerful enough to gain an obedient response from people, but they also gain an obedient response from violent, spiritual beings that afflict and cripple unfortunate people.

Both the role of Jesus and the role of his followers are composite in

Mark. Jesus' role of attracting people simply sets the stage for the next section of the narrative in which Jesus' role as exorciser-healer is high- ⁄ lighted in relation to teaching that instructs the followers in Jesus' system of thought and action. Likewise, the disciples' role of following Jesus simply provides the base for them to learn the composite nature of their role. In the next section of the narrative, additional aspects of their role are introduced to them through Jesus' word and action. In the initial section the disciples are simply attracted to Jesus' mode of action, and Jesus defends them when their actions are questioned by the Pharisees.

Analysis of the initiation of the teacher/disciple relation in Mediterranean literature indicates that the portrayal of the teacher/disciple relation in Mark is an independent adaptation of aspects from both Jewish and Greco-Roman tradition. In the first section of the Gospel of Mark (1:14—3:6), the tradition of calling dominates the portrayal of Jesus. Neither the action nor the language of Jesus in these scenes of calling is typical of the action and language of the rabbis. Rather, the action and language of Jesus reflect a combination of Israelite and Hellenistic traditions in the context of the Greco-Roman cultural role of the itinerant teacher. On the one hand, Jesus' call to individuals is reminiscent of the action of Yahweh in the biblical tradition. Yahweh confronts Abraham (Gen. 12:1–3) much as Jesus confronts Simon, Andrew, James, and John (Mark 1:16–20).[91] As Jesus tells his disciples he will make them into fishers of men, so Yahweh tells Abraham: "I will make of you a great nation . . . and I will bless you, and make your name great" (Gen. 12:2). In the same manner in which James and John leave their father Zebedee with the hired servants and follow Jesus (1:20), Yahweh commands Abraham: "Go from your country and your kindred and your father's house to the land that I will show you" (Gen. 12:1). In the scene of calling Yahweh confronts Abraham with command and promise much like Jesus confronts Simon, Andrew, James, and John. In both the LXX and Mark the future form of *poiein* (to make) is used when the individuals are promised to be made into something they presently are not. In both Genesis and Mark the action of confrontation and the language of command and promise are similar.

Also, Yahweh's call of Moses shows similarity in action and language to Jesus in the Gospel of Mark. When Yahweh confronts Moses, he not only commands him, "Come (*deuro*)," but also tells him that he will send him to perform a particular task for him with the promise that he, Yahweh, will be with him (Exod. 3:10). In a similar manner, the Markan narration indicates that Jesus selected twelve not only to be with him but also to send them out to perform tasks that extend the action of Jesus to people other than those he is able to confront on his own itinerant ministry (3:14–15; 6:7; 13:10).

In Mark, however, the function of Yahweh as summoner is not transferred directly from Yahweh to Jesus. The Gospel of Mark presents Jesus
performing a combination of activities from Jewish and Greco-Roman
traditions. Jesus summons, instructs, transfers his abilities and authority,
and sends people out to perform tasks as a mortal who is limited by other
people's authority and by an adult career that ends in death. In contrast to
Yahweh, the autonomy of Jesus is not complete. Jesus enjoys the favor of
heaven, but as a mortal he faces limitations that arise from the realm of
human society and action. In Mark, Jesus' mortality is portrayed through
the Greco-Roman tradition of autonomous itinerant teachers who gather
disciple-companions for the purpose of transmitting a system of thought
and action to them. In this role, Jesus can by no means perform all the
functions of Yahweh. As a matter of fact, dimensions of the autonomous
Yahweh tradition itself provide the overarching framework whereby Jesus'
autonomy receives its limits. As Jesus performs functions of Yahweh that
are functions common to teachers in Mediterranean culture, the Yahweh
tradition stands above his mortality to sanction him, empower him, and
require that he accept mortal death. In other words, while Jesus, as
portrayed in Mark, has authority from heaven, he is a mortal who must
adopt a social role and accept the consequences of that role. In Mark,
action and response surrounding an itinerant teacher who gathers disciple-companions and programmatically transmits a system of thought and
action to them establish the context for Jesus' authority and limitations.
The role of the itinerant teacher in Mediterranean culture provides the
framework for possession of autonomous wisdom and power which is
limited by mortality in the realm of human action. As an autonomous
itinerant teacher sanctioned and empowered by God, Jesus exercises
extraordinary power over people who accept the position of disciple-
companion and over evil, destructive forces in the realm of human life.
This autonomous role, however, also provides the framework for the
limitation of Jesus' power. As a mortal teacher, Jesus cannot escape either
the action of human leaders to bring his adult career to an end or the will
of God that he accept death by means of betrayal, public trial, physical
agony, and estrangement. The cultural role of the itinerant teacher provides a natural setting both for the autonomy and for the limited power of
Jesus in the Gospel of Mark. In this framework, Jesus performs activities
previously associated with Yahweh but he also accepts the limitations
placed upon his activities by the power and authority of other men and
of God.

At this point it is important to recall the care with which Philo of
Alexandria depicts famous Israelites as teachers. Yahweh's role as one who
calls, instructs, and commissions creates the setting for mortals to func-

tion as lawgivers, priests, prophets, kings, and servants. Within this framework, priests and prophets function as the transmitters of tradition. Prior to the first century C.E., significant people in biblical and Jewish tradition tend not to be portrayed as teachers apart from the office of either priest or prophet. The Teacher of Righteousness at Qumran is a priest who interprets the Law and the Prophets for the Sons of Light who constitute a holy temple of people, not made with hands. When Pharisees become famous Jewish teachers, they make decisions with regard to holy rituals and law, and they hand down traditions which they have received from other teachers. But a significant measure of reserve is exercised in the portrayal of Jewish teachers. God's function as the one who summons, teaches, and commissions remains intact. Even the most famous rabbis do not seek people out and encounter them like Yahweh in the biblical tradition, and like Socrates and the sophists in Greek tradition.

Any reserve still extant in first-century Judaism concerning the portrayal of a paradigmatic religious personage as a teacher is bypassed in the portrayal of Jesus of Nazareth in the Gospel of Mark. Throughout the narrative, Jesus approaches people as a teacher who summons them to his point of view and way of life. In cultural terms, Mark's portrayal of summons and response through the protagonist Jesus is an intermingling of Jewish traditions and general cultural traditions. Such intermingling of traditions is characteristic of Hellenistic literature. The heavenly sanction of Jesus' adult activity has strong precedent in Jewish tradition. Abraham, Moses, and the prophets were called and commissioned to their tasks. Yet, a detailed commissioning of Jesus by God is absent from Mark. There are no statements by God telling Jesus to go and do certain things to carry out God's plan. The absence of a detailed commission accords with the imposition of the role of teacher in the tradition. The teacher, in contrast to the prophet, speaks and acts according to the wisdom he has attained. His wisdom is the wisdom of God, but he speaks not simply the words of the Lord but his own words of wisdom. The qualitative progression from the introduction (1:1–13) to the first section of Mark (1:14—3:6) reflects the merger of these traditions. When Jesus comes into Galilee he preaches the gospel of God, but he does not precede his statement with "thus says the Lord." As a teacher of God's gospel, Jesus has received the information through a process different from a scene in which Yahweh tells him what to tell the people. Is the reader supposed to understand that the spirit that descends upon Jesus as a dove after the baptism is a descent of the wisdom of God upon him in a form that allows him to function as an autonomous disciple-gathering teacher? If so, the qualitative progression is certainly distinctive. In prophetic literature, the spirit anoints the specially commissioned prophet for his task. But once he is prepared, the prophet does not adopt the role of a disciple-gathering teacher who chooses disciples whom he himself wants and who perform activities with no instructions from God. As Jesus begins his activity, the gospel of God is present in him like wisdom is present in a philosopher-teacher. Jesus comports himself like a teacher whose message is sanctioned by God. When the assertions are made that Jesus himself possesses authority (1:22) and that the teaching of Jesus is new (1:27), the reader encounters a qualitative progression that has modified categorical expectations arising from biblical tradition. As the scribes accurately point out (Mark 2:6), God is the one who should be credited with these attributes and actions, not Jesus. Jesus should clarify that he is only the mediator of God's word and action. Instead, Jesus adopts the role of an autonomous teacher who possesses the wisdom and authority to command both people and spiritual forces.

In the Socratic tradition, the teacher summons and lures young men into the role of disciple-companion. This characteristic gives Socrates special status among Greco-Roman teachers. In Israelite tradition, such an approach to people is associated with Yahweh. When Hellenistic culture begins to be the setting for the perpetuation of Israelite traditions, the teacher/disciple concept begins to intermingle with the Yahweh traditions. When the role of Yahweh as the only teacher of wisdom and virtue is maintained, human teachers are relegated to an inferior position and famous Israelite leaders are teachers only as a byproduct of their role as philosopher-kings, priests, or prophets. The emphasis upon the teacher and the role of instructional activity in Greco-Roman culture, however, made ever greater inroads into Jewish thought and tradition during the first century. This influence reveals itself in Josephus where Moses and Elijah are portrayed in the role of teachers who select a disciple whom they instruct and designate as a successor. Within a time period virtually contemporaneous with Josephus, the Gospel of Mark represents an avant-garde position within Jewish tradition. Jesus of Nazareth, the Jewish Messiah, is portrayed as an itinerant religio-ethical teacher who summons disciples without specific instructions from God. God is pleased with Jesus (Mark 1:11), God sanctions his activity (Mark 9:7), and God determines the final outcome of his activity. But God does not instruct him at every point like he does Abraham, Moses, and the prophets. Jesus knows what to do as a teacher who says and does the gospel of God. Moreover, Jesus selects the people whom he himself wants as disciple-companions (Mark 3:13), not people whom God tells him to select. In other words, Jesus does not need to be told what to do since he has been designated by God to be a self-possessed teacher. A teacher in Greco-Roman tradition is a more autonomous individual than a prophet in Israelite tradition. A prophet is called and commissioned by Yahweh to say and do certain things. A teacher's activity is sanctioned by God or the gods, but what he says and does is a matter of unifying word and action according to the wisdom that he has attained from God.

The Gospel of Mark revolutionizes Jewish tradition when it portrays Jesus taking over functions of Yahweh with Yahweh's sanction, but without his detailed direction. Jesus' commands, directions, and explanations take the place of Yahweh's commands, directions, and explanations. As a result, Jesus' statements, rather than Yahweh's statements, introduce logical progressions. The attributes of Jesus' character, action, and speech unfold much like the attributes of Yahweh's character, action, and speech in biblical narrative, while the attributes of the disciples unfold much like the attributes of the prophets. In Mark, Jesus' knowledge of the gospel of God allows him to take over Yahweh's role of calling, teaching, and commissioning. Jesus summons, teaches, and commissions with the comportment and authority characteristic of Socrates in Greco-Roman tradition. The distinctiveness of Mark lies in the presence of the God of Israel as one who sanctions the activity of Jesus but does not instruct Jesus in his actions during his adult career. The author of Mark shows very little reserve in the portrayal of Jesus' self-possessed authority to call and commission those whom he wishes to be with him and whom he himself wishes to send out to extend the activity in which he is engaged.

Therefore, a basic dimension of the "messianic" nature of Jesus' activity in Mark arises from the adaptation of the autonomous stature of the teacher in Greco-Roman tradition and the subsequent importation of this emphasis on autonomy into Jewish tradition where God has been the dominant autonomous figure. If interpretation of Mark emphasizes only the last half of the gospel in which Jesus submits to God's will that he die, the influence of the autonomous teacher role in the context of Hellenistic culture is ignored. The tradition of Jesus as a teacher must not be overlooked since it plays a crucial role throughout the second and third centuries as Christianity gradually establishes itself within Greco-Roman culture.[92] The image of Jesus as teacher, as it is portrayed in Mark, establishes a teacher/disciple pattern within Christian tradition that provides a base for the transmission of Jesus tradition and the formation of Christian community in many cultural settings throughout the world.

NOTES

1. A. D. Nock, *Conversion*, 14.

2. Interpreters of the epistles of Paul have recently attended to the overall rhetorical form of the document; see chapter 1, n. 3.

3. For the dominance of the speech in discussions of rhetoric and rhetorical form, see D. L. Clark, *Rhetoric in Greco-Roman Education*, 67–143, 213–61.

4. K. Burke, *Counter-Statement*, 126–27, 204–10.

5. C. H. Weiss, *Die Evangelische Geschichte kritisch und philosophisch bearbeitet*. See also J. M. Robinson, *The Problem of History in Mark: And other Marcan Studies*, 55–56.

6. W. Wrede, *The Messianic Secret*, 132.

7. M. Kähler, *The So-called Historical Jesus and the Historic Biblical Christ*, 80 n. 11.

8. Cf. V. Taylor's outline in *The Gospel According to Mark*, 105–13.

9. T. J. Weeden, *Mark—Traditions in Conflict*, 20–51.

10. See J. D. Kingsbury, "The Gospel of Mark in Current Research."

11. Weeden, *Mark—Traditions in Conflict*, 20–51.

12. Ibid., 52–168.

13. See, e.g., E. Best, "The Role of the Disciples in Mark."

14. Some ancient manuscripts omit the title "Son of God" in the superscription, but the concept and title occur strategically throughout the text of Mark. Cf. W. Marxsen's comments on archē in *Mark the Evangelist*, 132; Robinson, *The Problem of History in Mark*, 69–72; R. A. Guelich, "'The Beginning of the Gospel.'"

15. For a discussion of the pronouns that emerged in the Christian application of these verses to John the Baptist and Jesus, see K. Stendahl, *The School of St. Matthew*, 47–54.

16. The words are actually a combination of words of the Lord in Exod. 23:20; Mal. 3:1; and Isa. 40:3. See Guelich, "'The Beginning of the Gospel,'" 6–8 for Mark 1:2 as a continuation of Mark 1:1.

17. Gen. 12:1–9; Exod. 3:1—4:17; 1 Sam. 3:1–14; Hos. 1:2–11; Jonah 1:1–2.

18. Isaiah 6; Jer. 1:4–19; Ezekiel 1—2.

19. For comparison (*synkrisis*) as a conventional rhetorical procedure, see Clark, *Rhetoric*, 198–99.

20. Cf. Gen. 12:1–3; Exod. 3:7–10; 1 Sam. 3:11–14; Isa. 6:7–13; Jer. 1:5–10; Ezek. 2:3–7. For analysis of prophetic scenes of calling, see N. Habel, "The Form and Significance of the Call Narrative."

21. Weeden, *Mark—Traditions in Conflict*, 20–51.

22. Robinson, *The Problem of History*, 71.

23. For a discussion of complementary roles, see T. R. Sarbin and V. L. Allen, "Role Theory," 498.

24. For an analysis of rhetorical progression in the beginning of the Elijah/Elisha narrative, see R. L. Cohn, "The Literary Logic of 1 Kings 17—19."

25. W. H. Wuellner, *The Meaning of "Fishers of Men*," 68–72.

26. For this tradition, see esp. Plato's *Euthydemus* and *Protagoras*.

27. Book 4 of Xenophon's *Memorabilia* has a coherence of its own that raises the possibility that it was composed independently after the composition of books 1–3; see E. C. Marchant's comments in *Xenophon IV: Memorabilia and Oeconomicus, Symposium and Apology*, xvii–xxiii.

28. See the analysis in Robbins, "Mark I.14–20," 222–25.

29. K. H. Rengstorf has been one of the few to observe this. See "mathētēs," *TDNT* 4 (1967): 426–31.

30. *Môreh* occurs in Isa. 30:20; Prov. 5:13; Hab. 2:18; and 2 Chron. 15:3. *Mēbîn* occurs in 1 Chron. 25:8 and *mĕlamēd*, used as a substantive, occurs in Ps. 119:99.

31. For the manuscript evidence, see R. Hanhard, ed., *Esther*, 175. The articular noun *tōi didaskalōi* occurs in manuscripts B, S, V, O–A', 55, 108, 249', 318, 392, Aeth, Arm. This has been replaced by *tōi diakonōi* in a, b, 542: ex 3 et 5; *pueris* La^x: cf. 3. Both the MT and LXX avoid referring to the one who got the records.

32. For the dating of Esther, see O. Eissfeldt, *The Old Testament*, 510, 591–92.

33. E.g., Josephus, *Antiquities* 13.115; 15.373; 17.325, 334; 20.41, 46.

34. Cf. E. Schweizer, "Anmerkungen zur Theologie des Markus"; A. H. Howe, "The Teaching Jesus Figure in the Gospel of Mark," esp. 5–39.

35. English translations of Greco-Roman literature are based on the LCL edition of the text with occasional modifications to clarify the relation of the passage to other texts being investigated. Quotation of the Greek text is based on the most recent Teubner edition.

36. See G. C. Field, s.v. "Sophists," *OCD*. Cf. G. W. Bowersock, *Greek Sophists in the Roman Empire*.

37. The most comprehensive discussion of these people is found in W. L. Liefeld, "The Wandering Preacher as a Social Figure in the Roman Empire."

38. See D. R. Dudley, *A History of Cynicism;* A. J. Malherbe, s.v. "Cynics," *IDBSup;* idem, *The Cynic Epistles*, 1–5; M. Hengel, *The Charismatic Leader and His Followers*, 27–33.

39. Cf. H. A. Fischel, "Story and History."

40. For a study of the *protrepticus* in the dialogues, see K. Gaiser, *Proptreptick und Paränese bei Platon.*

41. See Liddell, Scott, and Jones, *A Greek-English Lexicon*, 784.

42. P. Friedländer, *Plato*, 1:69–70.

43. Ibid., 2:231–34.

44. Ibid., 236.

45. *Meno, Ion, Menexenus, Phaedrus, Minos.*

46. See, e.g., the *Protagoras* and the *Euthydemus.* Cf. K. J. Dover, *Aristophanes: Clouds*, xlv–lvii.

47. Aristophanes, *Clouds*, 871, 1147, 1467.

48. Aristophanes, *Clouds*, 497–517. For an excellent recent discussion of the portrait of Socrates in Aristophanes, *Clouds*, see J. Beckman, *The Religious Dimension of Socrates' Thought*, 189–201.

49. Cf. Diogenes Laertius, *Lives of the Eminent Philosophers* 7.3; Malherbe, *Cynic Epistles*, 163.

50. See E. Hatch and H. A. Redpath, *A Concordance to the Septuagint*, 892.

51. For Jer. 26:9, see Hatch and Redpath, *Concordance*, 892; for the Daniel references, see J. Ziegler, ed., *Susanna-Daniel-Bel et Draco*, 92–93, 101.

52. In addition to the passage above, see Philo, *Life of Moses*, 2.190.

53. See W. A. Meeks, *The Prophet-King,* 107–31.

54. For the importance of succession in the teacher/disciple tradition, see E. Bickerman, "La chaine de la tradition pharisienne"; Meeks, *Prophet-King,* 142–44, 150, 179–81.

55. See Hengel, *Charismatic Leader,* 16–18.

56. W. D. Davies, *The Setting of the Sermon on the Mount,* 422–25; B. Gerhardsson, *Memory and Manuscript,* 201–2, 324–35.

57. See esp. D. Daube, *The New Testament and Rabbinic Judaism.*

58. Davies, *Sermon on the Mount,* 422–23.

59. Ibid., 423–24.

60. A possible exception exists in Akiba's journeying from Babylon to Jerusalem to find a disciple like Hillel; see ibid., 421.

61. Quoted from J. Neusner, *Development of a Legend,* 242.

62. *Yoma* 35b (Eng. trans. L. Jung), in *The Babylonian Talmud,* 163. See J. Neusner, *The Rabbinic Traditions about the Pharisees Before 70,* Part 1:148, 258–59.

63. This is one of the famous passages in the uncensored versions of the Babylonian Talmud. The name Jesus in the text refers to Jesus of Nazareth; see Neusner, *Rabbinic Traditions,* 83–86.

64. *Sotah* 47a (Eng. trans. A. Cohen), 247–48 = *Sanhedrin* 10b (Eng. trans. H. Freedman), 736 n. 2 in *Babylonian Talmud;* see Neusner, *Rabbinic Traditions,* 83–84.

65. *Shabbath* 30b–31a (Eng. trans. H. Freedman), in *The Babylonian Talmud,* 138–41; see Neusner, *Rabbinic Traditions,* 322–23.

66. In *Megillah* 21a (*Babylonian Talmud*) the tradition is transmitted that the Torah was studied from Moses to Gamaliel (presumably Gamaliel I) standing only, but after his death the Torah was studied sitting. The date of the death of Gamaliel I is not known. In some stories he is featured in conversation with Agrippa I (ruled 37–44 C.E.); see Neusner, *Rabbinic Traditions,* 341–76.

67. See *Babylonian Talmud: Pesahim* 3b; *Shabbath* 17a. See also *Midrash Tanhuma,* Lekh Lekha 10 (Buber, 67–68); Neusner, *Development of a Legend,* 171–72.

68. On *Abot de Rabbi Nathan A,* see chap. 15, in J. Goldin, *The Fathers According to Rabbi Nathan,* 78–82; see Neusner, *Rabbinic Traditions,* 332.

69. *Leviticus Rabba* 34.3; *Sifre Deuteronomy,* 305.

70. G. Kittel, s.v. "akolouthein," *TDNT* 1 (1964): 210.

71. Cf. R. Bultmann, *History of the Synoptic Tradition,* 209–10. He referred to this scene as "paradigmatic" for Jesus' activity in the gospel. See also H. D. Knigge, "The Meaning of Mark," 54–56.

72. Cf. S. Westerholm, *Jesus and Scribal Authority.*

73. Contra W. H. Kelber (*Mark's Story of Jesus,* 22) who takes this scene to be "a first and very subtle indication of a disagreement between Jesus and his disciples."

74. This kind of open-ended reference to the number of people following Jesus is also characteristic of Philostratus's *Life of Apollonius of Tyana;* see, e.g., I.40 (*tous amphi ton Damin*).

75. See R. M. Keesing, "Toward a Model of Role Analysis," 436–40, for the importance of establishing contrast sets to understand a particular social role and competition for fulfilling the role.

76. Cf. Mark 1:15, 17, 25, 38, 41, 44; 2:5, 8–9, 11, 14, 17; 3:3, 4, 5 with 2:19–22, 25–28.

77. See D. E. Aune, "Magic in Early Christianity."

78. On the importance of "polar positions" for establishing a social role, see Keesing, "Role Analysis," 429.

79. For a discussion of rhetorical skill in dividing the issue, see C. Perelman and L. Olbrechts-Tyteca, *The New Rhetoric*, 282.

80. Aune, "Magic," 1529.

81. See R. D. Abrahams, "Introductory Remarks to a Rhetorical Theory of Folklore," 150.

82. Ibid., 149–52. See Abrahams for the difference in rhetorical function between the proverb and the riddle.

83. See Aune, "Magic," 1519–20 for the three major types of religious groups: (1) state cults, (2) mystery cults, and (3) philosophical sects or schools.

84. See J. Z. Smith, "Good News is No News!" 21–38, and the remarks by Aune, "Magic," 1540.

85. Keesing, "Role Analysis," 432–33.

86. On Vespasian, a Roman general who became emperor, see Tacitus, *Histories* 4.81; on Elijah and Elisha, Israelite prophets, see 1 Kings 17:17–24 and 2 Kings 4:18–37; on Apollonius, an itinerant philosopher-teacher, see Philostratus, *Life of Apollonius* 4.20; 4.45; 6.43; and on Iarchus, a sage (sophos) of India, see Philostratus, *Life of Apollonius* 3.38–39.

87. See, e.g. D. Aune, "Septem Sapientium Convivium (*Moralia* 146B–164D)," 54.

88. Hengel, *The Charismatic Leader*, 67.

89. Keesing, "Role Analysis," 424, 427.

90. For the range of activities ascribed to the scribes in Mark, see 2:6, 16; 3:22; 7:1; 8:31; 9:11, 14; 10:33; 11:18, 27; 12:28, 32, 35, 38; 14:1, 43, 53; 15:1, 31.

91. See Robbins, "Mark I.14–20," 220–36.

92. F. Normann, *Christus Didaskalos*.

5

The Intermediate Phase
in the Teacher/Disciple Cycle:
Teaching and Learning
in Mark 3:7—12:44

Learning *how* or improving in ability is not like learning *that* or acquiring
information. . . . We learn *how* by practice . . . often quite unaided by any
lessons in the theory.[1]

In this chapter we will discover the interrelation of Jewish and Greco-
Roman cultural influences in the presentation of the teaching/learning
phase in the Gospel of Mark. After the initial phase in which a relationship is established between a teacher and a disciple-companion, an
intermediate phase ensues in which the teacher and the disciple-companion enter into a teaching/learning process with one another. This period of
interaction is an intermediate phase in the teacher/disciple cycle which
occurs between the initial phase that was necessary to establish the
relation and the final phase in which the disciple-companion becomes
separated from the teacher.

The intermediate phase of the teaching/learning cycle in the Gospel of
Mark occurs in four stages. The first stage, 3:7—5:43, features Jesus
introducing basic details of the system of understanding that underlies his
speech and action. The second stage, 6:1—8:26, shows the disciple-
companions able to perform most of the activities characteristic of Jesus'
ministry but unable to integrate the system of the gospel and the kingdom
of God with the powerful deeds which both Jesus and they are able to
perform. The third stage, 8:27—10:45, portrays full-scale interaction between Jesus and his disciple-companions over central dimensions of the
system of thought and action manifested by Jesus and required for discipleship. The fourth stage, 10:46—12:44, presents Jesus and his disciple-
companions experiencing the ramifications of Jesus' system of thought and
action in the public setting where the dominant ethico-religious group has
religious and political control.

The four stages in the teaching/learning phase as it is manifested in
Mark reveal a merger of both Jewish and Greco-Roman conventions of

teaching and learning in the setting of Mediterranean culture during the Hellenistic period. On the one hand, the teaching/learning phase in a teacher/disciple setting is most highly developed in Greco-Roman culture. Through the activity of Socrates, the Academy, and the later philosophical and rhetorical schools, an entire educational program evolved in which the stages of study were strictly regulated.[2] On the other hand, the basic cycle of teaching and learning is evident in the stages of interaction between Yahweh and the leaders of Israel in biblical tradition. The distinctive dimensions of the Markan portrayal of the teaching/learning phase emerge in a matrix where traditions and conventions from both Jewish and Greco-Roman spheres of influence play a role.

THE TEACHING/LEARNING PHASE IN MARK AND XENOPHON'S *MEMORABILIA*

We may recall, from chapter three above, that the beginning of book 4 of Xenophon's *Memorabilia* (4.1.1–5; 4.2.1–40) contains rhetorical progressions similar to the movement from the introduction to the calling of the disciples in the Gospel of Mark (1:1–13; 1:14—3:6). After both Socrates and Jesus have established teacher/disciple relationships in the beginning of the documents, four sections of material feature the teachers interacting with their disciple-companions and others prior to the scenes that lead to their separation from their disciple-companions. In these four sections, the qualities of the character, action, and speech of the teachers unfold as the teachers take their disciple-companions through a programmatic education in their systems of thought and action.

In *Memorabilia* 4.3.1–18, the first section of the teaching/learning phase, Socrates introduces the themes and issues that lie, in Xenophon's opinion, at the base of the teacher's system of thought and action. Xenophon emphasizes that Socrates tried, "first of all" (*proteron, prōton*), to teach his disciple-companions prudence toward the gods (4.3.1–2). At the end of the section, the narrator asserts that Socrates tried to teach piety and prudence to his companions by both his words and actions (4.3.18). This section has a function in *Memorabilia* 4 similar to the function of Mark 3:7—5:43 in the Gospel of Mark. In Mark 3:7—5:43, Jesus, for the first time, introduces basic details about the kingdom of God. The teaching begins in the setting of conflict with scribes (3:20–34), continues with elaboration about the kingdom in parables (4:1–34), and is enacted in powerful works performed by Jesus in 4:35—5:43. The accusation by the scribes that Jesus casts out demons through allegiance to Beelzebul (3:22) enables Jesus to exhibit the kingdom of God as the fundamental base of his teaching and action. If a kingdom is divided against itself, it cannot stand (3:24). Through possession of the Holy Spirit

(1:12; cf. 3:28–30), Jesus is allied with the kingdom of God that opposes Satan (1:13; 3:23, 26; 4:15) and is able to control spiritual forces allied with Satan (3:27–30; 4:39; 5:2–14). By word and deed, Jesus introduces the base of the system of thought and action that he wishes to transmit to others.

After the section of introductory teaching, the portrayal of the teacher progresses to a stage where the system of thought and action reaches a new level of complexity as a result of its application in the public sphere. *Memorabilia* 4.4.1–25 develops the complexity, first of all, by reference to Socrates' death for the cause of justice (4.4.4) and, secondly, through confrontation with the sophist Hippias in which Socrates presents his understanding of the unwritten laws ordained by the gods concerning justice (4.4.5–25). The narrator ends the section by referring to the words and actions that Socrates used to encourage justice among his companions (4.4.25). This section has a function in *Memorabilia* 4 similar to the function of Mark 6:1—8:26 in the Gospel of Mark. During this stage in the Gospel of Mark, the complexity of Jesus' system of thought and action is developed. First, it is developed through Jesus' rejection in Nazareth (6:1–6) and John the Baptist's death and burial (6:14–29), which set the stage for the mission of the Twelve (6:7–13, 30) and Jesus' feeding of five thousand and then four thousand people (6:31–44; 8:1–10). Secondly, when scribes and Pharisees confront Jesus with the charge that his disciples violate hand-washing laws, Jesus presents a countercharge and displays his understanding of the laws of God that supersede the laws of men (7:1–23). In both documents, the underlying dimensions of the initial teaching are expanded in the setting of public exhibition of the action and direct confrontation with teachers who oppose the system of thought and action.

After the stage in which the teacher's system of thought and action acquires greater complexity through its application in the public sphere, the teacher attempts to teach his disciple-companions the central dimensions of his system of thought and action. In *Memorabilia* 4.5.1–12, Socrates reengages Euthydemus in conversation to teach him the paradox that, although pleasure would appear to be attained through incontinence, which allows a person to avoid everything of displeasure, pleasure actually is attained through self-control which, by causing a person to endure sufferings, allows a person to consider the things that matter most and are most pleasurable (4.5.9). This section has a function in *Memorabilia* 4 similar to the function of 8:27—10:45 in the Gospel of Mark. During this stage in Mark, Jesus teaches his disciple-companions the central, paradoxical dimensions of his system of thought and action. In contrast to the opinions of men that resist the need for suffering, the ways of God require the person who wishes to save his or her life to be willing to deny him- or herself and lose his or her life for the sake of Jesus and the gospel (8:34–37). In practical terms, this means that whoever wishes to be great and first must be a servant and slave of all (10:43–44). In this stage, therefore, the dimensions of the system of thought and action that appear to be contradictory or paradoxical are taught to the disciple-companions.

The fourth stage of the teaching/learning phase features the teacher and his disciple-companions giving public definition to the teacher's system of thought and action. In *Memorabilia* 4.6.1–15, the fourth section of the teaching/learning phase, Socrates briefly analyzes and defines piety, justice, wisdom, goodness, beauty, courage, good government, and good citizenship in a manner that can be understood by people outside the circle of his disciple-companions (4.6.2–14). This section has a function in *Memorabilia* 4 similar to the function of 10:46—12:44 in the Gospel of Mark. During this stage in the Gospel of Mark, the entire range of teachers and leaders in Judaism (Herodians, Pharisees, Sadducees, and scribes) comes to Jesus to hear his public response to issues concerning taxes, resurrection, the commandments, and messiahship (12:13–44). Jesus' responses provide public definitions that do not attempt to communicate the central, paradoxical dimensions of his own system of thought and action. Rather, they address the issues that dominate the thoughts of people in the public domain. The final section in the teaching/learning phase, therefore, presupposes the detailed dimensions of the teacher's system of thought and action and displays the issues that attract attention in the public domain.

Thus, the four sections between the initiation of the teacher/disciple relation and the preparations for the death of the teacher contain scenes of teaching and learning. It is only natural that the sequence in which the author places these scenes should reflect the basic steps of a teaching/learning sequence as they are presupposed in the culture. Both Mark and Xenophon's *Memorabilia* reflect a teaching/learning sequence that proceeds through four stages: (1) basic introduction to the system of thought and action; (2) added complexity of the system when it is applied in the public sphere alongside an alternative system of thought and action; (3) an attempt to teach central, paradoxical dimensions of the system to disciple-companions; and (4) definitions of issues that are of public concern but are not the central dimensions of the teacher's system of thought and action.

TEACHING AND LEARNING IN
THE HEBREW BIBLE

As every interpreter will observe, the four stages of the teaching/learning phase in the Gospel of Mark occur in the midst of a narrative sequence that contrasts with the topical arrangement of Socrates' conversations in Xenophon's *Memorabilia* 4. If the sequence of stages in teaching and learning in Mark's gospel approximates a sequence exhibited in Greek literature, the sequence is thoroughly embedded in a medium of narrative portrayal that is similar to the biblical accounts of Abraham, Moses, Elijah, and Elisha. For this reason, it is necessary to look for stages of teaching and learning in the setting of narrative portrayal in biblical literature.

In the Hebrew Bible, the closest analogies to the teaching/learning phase in Mark occur in Yahweh's interaction with Abraham and Moses. We remember that Yahweh's summons to Abraham in Gen. 12:1–9, 14–18 shows similarities with the summons and response in the initial section of Mark.[3] After the initial summons and response, a process of interaction between Yahweh and Abraham occurs that approximates the teaching/learning process.

After the initial phase of command, promise, and response in Genesis (12:1–9; 13:14–18), the first stage of the teaching/learning phase occurs in Gen. 15:1—17:14. During this stage, Yahweh and Abraham interact for the purpose of understanding the basic tenets of Yahweh's system of thought and action. For the first time in the story the term "covenant" appears (17:12), and Yahweh introduces the basic stipulations of the covenant system (17:10–14). While Abraham never responded verbally to Yahweh during the initial phase of command, promise, and response, the first stage of the teaching/learning phase features Abraham in conversation with Yahweh to discover the fundamental details of the system of thought and action to which he has responded. The first statement of Abraham to Yahweh appears in Gen. 15:2, and the give and take of dialogue provide the setting for Yahweh to teach Abraham.

The first stage of the teaching/learning phase in the Abraham story shares a number of features in common with the Gospel of Mark. First, just as the term "covenant" appears for the first time during this stage, Jesus uses the term "kingdom of God" for the first time with the disciples during this stage (4:11). Second, much as Yahweh instructs Abraham in the basic dimensions of the covenant in Genesis 17, so Jesus instructs his disciple-companions in the basic dimensions of the kingdom of God in Mark 4. In other words, in the same way that a system of covenant ideology establishes the backdrop for the interaction between Yahweh and Abraham, and the introduction of that system of thought to Abraham represents the first stage after the initial summons and response, so the introduction of the ideology of the kingdom of God represents the first stage of interaction between Jesus and his disciple-companions after the initial stage of summons and response.

The second stage of the teaching/learning phase occurs in Gen. 17:15— 18:15 and features amazement and amusement on behalf of Abraham and Sarah. Neither Abraham nor Sarah can understand how Yahweh will give a son to them. Both Abraham (17:17) and Sarah (18:12) laugh in amazement at the suggestion that Sarah will become pregnant and bear a son. In other words, at this point in the interaction between Yahweh and Abraham the system of thought and action has become too complex for Abraham to fathom. Abraham can do the appropriate things like circumcise all the male children according to the instructions of Yahweh (18:22– 27), but he cannot understand the miraculous side of Yahweh's activity.

This second stage in the Yahweh/Abraham story also contains basic features in common with the second stage of the teaching/learning phase in Mark. Much as the disciples are able to carry out the tasks of preaching, casting out demons, healing, and distributing the food to feed the five thousand and four thousand (Mark 6—8), so Abraham dutifully carries out the instructions of Yahweh to circumcise the male children. Nevertheless, neither the disciples nor Abraham is able to correlate the miraculous nature of God's activity with the guidelines for action and expectation that have been introduced to them. For this reason, a significant gap develops between the dynamics of the system that propels the story forward and the understanding of the system by Abraham and Sarah and the disciple-companions of Jesus.

The third stage of the teaching/learning phase occurs in Gen. 18:16— 19:29, and this stage features Abraham and Yahweh in intense discussion over the application of Yahweh's system of thought and action. During this stage, Yahweh decides to reveal to Abraham the complexities of his system of righteousness and justice (18:17–21). In turn, Abraham adopts an aggressive stance with Yahweh to test his application of the principles of righteousness and justice (18:22–33). Abraham is no longer at the stage of receiving basic instructions or of being amazed at the interrelation of miraculous activity with the basic system of thought and action. Rather, on the basis of what he understands he argues with Yahweh about his application of justice on the city of Sodom and does not stop asking questions until he receives the information that allows him to understand in detail how the system works.

This third stage shares much in common with the third stage in the teaching/learning phase in Mark 8:27—10:45. In both contexts, the people being taught engage in intensive interaction with their teacher in order to determine how the system functions in the setting of detailed application. A major difference emerges, however, when the narrative reveals that Abraham understands how Yahweh's system of righteousness works while the disciple-companions of Jesus do not understand how the system of the kingdom and the gospel are to function in the realm of action and expectation.

The fourth stage of the teaching/learning phase occurs in Gen. 19:20—22:24. In contrast to the fourth stage in the Gospel of Mark, this stage features a major test of Abraham. After Yahweh's promise is fulfilled by the birth of Isaac, Yahweh tests Abraham by asking him to offer Isaac as a sacrifice on an altar (22:1–14). When Abraham passes the test in an exemplary manner, Yahweh reiterates the promise he made to Abraham at the beginning of the story (22:17–18; cf. 12:2–3). In other words, in the Abraham story the teaching/learning process ends with a test in the fourth part that exhibits Abraham's comprehension of the system of thought and action.

From the initial summons and response through the first three stages of the teaching/learning process, the Abraham story and Mark's gospel bear similarities. In the Abraham story, however, the dynamics of the covenant system call for a test in the fourth stage of the teaching/learning process, and this test determines the outcome of the story. In contrast, the fourth stage of the teaching/learning phase in Mark calls for the exploration of the ramifications of the system of thought and action in the public setting that will bring about the death of the teacher of that system. At the fourth stage of the teaching/learning process, therefore, the Abraham story and the Gospel of Mark part company. While the system of thought and action based on the covenant calls for a test of obedience to the stipulations of the covenant immediately after they are understood by the student, the system of the gospel and the kingdom calls for the exploration of the public dynamics that bring rejection, suffering, and death upon those who adopt the system of thought and action introduced to them.

Similarities in the sequence of interaction must not lead the interpreter to overlook the differences between a narrative featuring interaction between Yahweh and a mortal and a narrative portraying an extraordinary human teacher interacting with disciple-companions. For this reason, the story of Moses must receive attention, since in the setting of Egypt, the wilderness, and Sinai, Moses performs in a manner closer to the role enacted by Jesus in the Gospel of Mark. In the Hebrew Bible, Moses is an intercessor between Yahweh and the people of Israel, and in this role he summons and teaches the people in a manner similar to Jesus' summoning and teaching of his disciple-companions.

In contrast to the Abraham story, the Moses story manifests three levels of interaction between leaders and followers. On the most well known level, the people of Israel go through a cycle of interaction with Yahweh as they receive the covenant stipulations that establish the conditions for their possession of the land of Canaan. On a second level, Moses and the people of Israel go through a cycle of interaction that involves Moses in the punishment and destruction of those who are unfaithful to the covenant system which he delivered to them. On a third level, Moses goes through a cycle of interaction with Yahweh that finally leads to Yahweh's refusal to allow him to enter into the land of Canaan with the faithful generation that succeeded the people who came out of the land of Egypt.

First of all, the interaction between Yahweh and the people of Israel constitutes the major thematic coherence of the narrative from Genesis through Joshua.[4] Between the promise to the patriarchs (Genesis 12—50) and the fulfillment of the promise in the conquest of Canaan (Joshua 1—24), the narrative contains a four-stage sequence in Exodus through Deuteronomy that establishes the major teaching/learning cycle within Judaism. The stages in the cycle are as follows:

1. Exod. 1—13:16: Exodus from Egypt;
2. Exod. 13:17—18:27: Wilderness Before Sinai;
3. Exod. 19:1—Num. 10:36: Receiving the Covenant at Sinai;
4. Num. 11:1—Deut. 34: Wilderness After Sinai.

The first stage in the cycle portrays the throes of accepting the call out of bondage into a life of identity as the people of Israel. The second stage features the people murmuring about their situation and receiving protection, food, and water from Yahweh when they need it. During the third stage, God teaches the details of his covenant system to the people of Israel through Moses. During the fourth stage, the wilderness after Sinai, the actions of the people are judged on the basis of the stipulations of the covenant. In contrast to the lack of punishment during the wilderness sojourn prior to Sinai, severe discipline and destruction come upon the people of Israel when they murmur and transgress the stipulations of the covenant after Sinai.[5]

The major cycle between Yahweh and the people of Israel in Exodus through Deuteronomy is therefore a cycle of accountability similar to the cycle in the Abraham story. In contrast to the Abraham story, however, the Moses story features the people of Israel being called and taught through an intercessor. In this situation, a stage of unpunished murmuring precedes the stage of detailed teaching. Once the teaching has been given to the people of Israel, their obedience to the stipulations is tested and a blessing or a curse is enacted upon them in accord with their action.

A second level of interaction within the Exodus story features Moses proceeding through stages of interaction with the Israelites, interaction that characterizes the dynamics of human leadership of the people of God. After the section of summons and response to Moses' leadership (Exod. 12:21—15:27), the stages are constituted as follows:

1. Exod. 16—34:28; Num. 11:1—15:41: Interceding for the Murmuring People;
2. Exod. 34:29—Num. 10:36: Teaching the Covenant System;
3. Num. 16—25:18: Confrontation and Punishment;
4. Num. 26—Deut. 30:20: Public Updating of the Teaching.

During the first stage of interaction, the people murmur against Moses (e.g., Exod. 16:2; 17:3; Num. 14:2), but Moses faithfully pleads with Yahweh to meet the needs of the people and refrain from punishing them. During the second stage, Moses presents the detailed requirements of God's system of thought and action to the people. During the third stage, Moses becomes angry with people because of their persistent rejection of him (Num. 16:15), and he participates willingly in the punishment and destruction of the rebellious members of the congregation. During the fourth stage, Moses takes a census of the faithful (Numbers 26) and teaches the additional information necessary before the people enter into the land of Canaan.

Again, this sequence reflects the role of Moses as intercessor. Like the cycle of accountability between Yahweh and Abraham, the teaching of the covenant system is followed by a test of obedience to the stipulations of the covenant. In contrast to the Abraham story, Moses not only sees the unfaithful destroyed (as Abraham sees Sodom destroyed: Gen. 19:27–28), but Moses finally requests the Lord to turn against them when their actions become totally rebellious (Num. 16:15). While Moses participates in the chastisement and destruction of the unfaithful, he accepts the responsibility of organizing the faithful and teaching them in preparation for their entrance into the land of Canaan.

Third, as in the Abraham story, there is in the Exodus story an extensive interaction between Yahweh and the specially commissioned man. While the interaction between Yahweh and the people and the interaction between Moses and the people emphasize the giving of the covenant to the people, the interaction between Moses and Yahweh introduces dynamics between Yahweh and an individual person that are important for understanding the Gospel of Mark. The stages of interaction between Yahweh and Moses, the leader of the people, are as follows:

1. Exod. 3:1—4:17: Summons and Initial Teaching;
2. Exod. 4:18—18:27: Doing and Asking;
3. Exod. 19—Num. 15:41: Argument and Application of the System of Thought and Action;
4. Num. 16—Deut. 4:49: Public Application of the System of Thought and Action.

The first stage is characterized by the summons of Yahweh and the

reluctance of Moses, through humility and apprehensiveness, to accept
the commission to deliver the Israelites from the Egyptians. The second
stage portrays Moses fulfilling all the tasks Yahweh requests and asking
Yahweh for additional instructions when the previous directions have not
covered the situation. The third stage is characterized by Moses' question-
ing of God's decisions for action against his people (Exod. 19:23–24;
32:11–13, 31–34; 33:12–23; Num. 11:11–23; 14:11–35), and in three of
the instances (Exod. 19:23–24; 32:11–13; 33:12–23) Moses convinces
Yahweh to change his mind. The fourth stage portrays Moses united with
Yahweh in the punishment and destruction of those Israelites who have
not fulfilled the requirements of the covenant.

The cycle of interaction between Moses and Yahweh in the story
appears to be something of an expansion of the interaction in the Abraham
story. Like the Abraham story, the Moses story features Moses in a
position of receiving teaching, of fulfilling instructions in a setting of
uncertainty concerning God's overall plan, and of arguing with Yahweh
over the application of the covenant system. Unlike the Abraham story,
Moses has the responsibility of maintaining his faithfulness in a setting
where those following him develop strong resistance to his leadership. In
the end, Moses is punished for "breaking faith" with Yahweh "in the midst
of the people of Israel at the waters of Meribath-kadesh, in the wilderness
of Zin" (Deut. 32:51). His punishment is to die before the people of Israel
enter into the land of Canaan.

The interaction among Yahweh, Moses, and the people of Israel sets the
stage for the way of Torah within Jewish tradition. In essence, the interaction in Exodus through Deuteronomy introduces the dynamics of the
prophet as intercessor between Yahweh and his people.[6] The prophetic
tradition contains interaction at three levels: (1) between Yahweh and the
people; (2) between the prophet and the people; and (3) between Yahweh
and the prophet. Especially in the writings of Philo of Alexandria the
three levels of interaction are incorporated into the Hellenistic system of
paideia.[7] On the first level God teaches lessons to the people of Israel by
his actions both upon them and upon the Egyptians (e.g., *Life of Moses*
1.146). On the second level Moses, as a paradigm of thought and action,
becomes "the hierophant of rites and teacher of divine things" (*On the
Giants* 54)[8] to his disciples (*gnōrimoi*), "the true Jews . . . who are capable
of 'clearly understanding' the symbolic meaning of the Torah."[9] On the
third level Moses, through a period of discipleship to God (*Moses* 1.80;
2.163), becomes the embodiment of the law: a "*nomos empsychos* (living
law), a personal presence of the unwritten universal law, superior to all
statutory law."[10] One of the most interesting discussions in relation to the
levels of interaction occurs in the *Life of Moses* 2.187–292 when Philo

distinguishes between three types of prophecies delivered by Moses. The first type, those spoken by God to Moses (2.189), and the second type, those in which the prophet asks questions of God (2.190; cf. 2.191–245), embody the level of interaction between Moses and God. The third type, in which Moses demonstrates his own power and knowledge of future events (2.190; cf. 2.246–291), emphasizes the interaction between Moses and the people of God.

First and foremost, Moses is portrayed in the Hebrew Bible as an intercessor rather than as a teacher. Accordingly, the rabbis would not call Moses "the law giver," because "only God *gave* the Torah, while it came 'by Moses' hand.' "[11] In the Gospel of Mark it is less clear that Jesus is simply delivering to his disciple-companions information given to him by God. The narrator tells us that Jesus' message is "the gospel of God" (1:14), but this message appears to be as fully "Jesus' message about God" as it is "God's message."[12] In other words, in the Gospel of Mark Jesus is not first and foremost an intercessor. He is a messianic teacher in whom knowledge and power are resident in such a form that he need not continually receive new information from God as the narrative progresses.

The Gospel of Mark portrays Jesus as the messianic teacher by emphasizing his interaction with disciple-companions and other people. Though his heritage lies with the Jewish prophets, interaction between God and Jesus and between God and the people is almost totally absent. In Mark, God and Jesus never interact in dialogue. There are only three instances of communication between God and Jesus, and the discourse is always constituted by a statement from one side only:

1. "Thou art my beloved Son; with thee I am well pleased" (1:11);
2. "Abba, Father, all things are possible to thee; remove this cup from me; yet not what I will, but what thou wilt" (14:36);
3. "My God, my God, why hast thou forsaken me?" (15:34).

Only the first instance represents a statement from God to Jesus; the other two are statements from Jesus to God with no vocal response from God. In addition, God interacts with disciple-companions of Jesus on only one occasion, the transfiguration of Jesus. In this scene, God tells Peter, James, and John: "This is my beloved Son; listen to him" (9:7). Outside of these settings there are no confrontations between God and anyone in the narrative. Even the healings and miracles are narrated in such a manner that Jesus receives as much credit as God for their successful occurrence. The absence of extended interaction between God and Jesus and between God and the disciples (or other people) allows the interaction between the teacher and his disciple-companions to gain center stage.

The Gospel of Mark represents therefore a merger of Jewish and Greco-

Roman traditions that subordinates two levels of interaction in the Jewish prophetic tradition. For this reason, influences from the tradition of Moses and Elijah are embedded within a narrative in which one major cycle of interaction, that between a teacher and his disciple-companions, dominates the narrative structure. The feedings of the five thousand and four thousand people in the wilderness (6:34–44; 8:1–10) reflect influence from the Moses tradition.[13] The role of John the Baptist (1:4–6; 9:13), expectations concerning Jesus (6:15; 8:28), Jesus' raising of Jairus's daughter (5:21–24A, 35–43), and Jesus' cry from the cross (15:36–37) call forth traditions related to Elijah and Elisha.[14] In the transfiguration story (9:2–8), Moses and Elijah share the spotlight with Jesus, and Elijah attracts the attention in the discussion as Jesus and his disciples descend the mountain (9:9–13). Yet neither the Moses nor the Elijah tradition fully explains the cycle of interaction between Jesus and his disciple-companions in Mark. While one might expect the biblical account of Elijah's relationship with Elisha to reflect the cycle, in fact it does not.[15] After Elijah's call of Elisha (1 Kings 19:19–21), there is no interaction between Elijah and Elisha until the setting in which Elijah is taken up into heaven (2 Kings 2). To explain the cycle of interaction between Jesus and his disciple-companions it is necessary to examine Greco-Roman documents that exhibit the cultural conventions operative within the teacher/disciple relationship from the fifth century B.C.E. onward.

TEACHING AND LEARNING
IN PLATO'S DIALOGUES
AND THE GOSPEL OF MARK

The most complete exhibition of the dynamics of interaction between a teacher and his disciple-companions in Greco-Roman literature is to be found in Plato's dialogues and Philostratus's *Life of Apollonius of Tyana*.

Plato's *Theaetetus* and *Meno* and Philostratus's *Apollonius* will be analyzed here for the purpose of exploring the dynamics of the teaching/learning process in Hellenic and Hellenistic culture. Both Plato's dialogues and Philostratus's *Apollonius* share a number of features with the gospels, and are dramatic narratives designed to transmit religio-philosophical wisdom in Greco-Roman culture.[16]

In both Plato's dialogues and Mark's gospel, interaction between the teacher and the disciple-companions creates tension in the plot as the teacher works through the ambiguities that attend his system of thought. Both Plato's *Theaetetus* and *Meno* display the sequence of interaction vividly and efficiently. The *Theaetetus* begins with a section in which Socrates summons Theaetetus to become his disciple-companion in learning (143D–151D) while the *Meno* begins immediately with a question by

Meno. After the section of summons, the *Theaetetus* progresses through three stages of the teaching/learning phase comparable to Mark 3:7—5:43; 6:1—8:26; 8:27—10:45. In the *Theaetetus*, the stages emerge as follows:

1. *Theaetetus* 151E–160E: Initial Teaching;
2. *Theaetetus* 160E–186E: Refutation of the Dominant Traditional System in Front of the Learner;
3. *Theaetetus* 187A–210D: Interchange Between Teacher and Learner Over Central Dimensions of the System.

The three stages of the teaching/learning phase emerge in the *Theaetetus* through interchange between Socrates, a student, and an established teacher in Athens. During the first stage, *Theaetetus* 151E–160E, Socrates engages a student, Theaetetus, in a conversation in which they attempt to define knowledge. Socrates begins with Theaetetus's state of understanding and introduces a basic view of knowledge as Theaetetus can understand it. Since Theaetetus thinks knowledge is perception, Socrates examines the meaning of perception at length. In the process, Socrates introduces those aspects of the doctrines of Protagoras and Heracleitus that he himself accepts.[17] At the end of the section, Theaetetus agrees with Socrates that all is motion and flux, man is the measure of all things, and therefore perception is knowledge.

This initial exploration of the meaning of knowledge in a philosophical domain bears similarities with Jesus' exploration of the meaning of the kingdom of God in a religious domain. The kingdom of God is a message that bears fruit among some but not all people (Mark 4:14–20). Dimensions of the kingdom of God that are now hidden will become clear (4:21–22), and the degree to which one gives to the kingdom determines the degree to which one will receive in the future (4:24–25). The kingdom of God functions on its own terms like grain that grows by itself (4:26–29), and the smallest instance of it can become an overwhelming amount, like a tiny seed that becomes the greatest of all shrubs (4:30–32). This is an initial definition of the kingdom of God that hardly gives the information necessary to fully comprehend its meaning. This explanation provides a beginning point for exploring the implications of the kingdom and the gospel through a sequence of interaction with the teacher.

In both the *Theaetetus* and the Gospel of Mark the initial explanation of the teacher occurs in an interrogative setting in which the true understanding of the concept is the goal to be reached by the student and by the reader. In both the *Theaetetus* and Mark the theme of "secret" understanding among disciples arises. As Socrates begins the discussion of knowledge as perception, he introduces an ironic statement that Protagoras, who held this view, must have been a very ingenious person "who spoke these things in a dark saying (*ēinixato*) to the common herd like ourselves, but told the truth in secret (*en aporrhētōi*) to his own disciples (*tois mathētais*)" (152C). In the parallel setting in the Gospel of Mark, Jesus speaks ironically to those around him with the Twelve:

> "To you has been given the secret of the kingdom of God, but for those outside everything is in parables; so that they may indeed see but not perceive, and may indeed hear but not understand; lest they should turn again, and be forgiven." And he said to them, "Do you not understand this parable? How then will you understand all the parables?" (4:11–13).

Just as the reader detects that Socrates is being ironical, so the reader's suspicion that Jesus is being ironical is confirmed in Mark 8:17–18 when Jesus applies the same verse concerning seeing but not perceiving and hearing but not understanding to his own disciples. The irony of this is driven home by the narrator when he tells the reader in Mark 4 that Jesus spoke with many parables to the people "as they were able to hear it . . . but privately to his own disciples he explained everything" (4:33–34). In Mark's gospel the reader is treated much like Socrates treats Theaetetus. The narrator's statement in Mark is especially exasperating since Jesus told those around him with the Twelve that they have "been given the secret of the kingdom of God" (4:11). Is the reader supposed to know what the secret of the kingdom of God is? Is the secret that the time is fulfilled (1:14)? Is the secret that repentance and belief will allow a person to participate in the benefits of the kingdom of God (1:14)? If so, repentance and belief in what precisely? That God is acting? That Jesus manifests the kingdom of God in his thought and action? Or is the secret that the kingdom of God is a call that a person must follow (1:16–20)? Is the kingdom of God a system of thought and action that a follower must adopt? Is this the essence of the parable of the sower of the seed and its explanation (4:1–20)? The unfulfilled answers create a cognitive setting similar to Plato's *Theaetetus*. What is knowledge? What is the kingdom of God? The questions and the initial explanations establish an interrogative setting for the student and the reader that forces cognitive activity. The interplay between the teacher's rhetoric with the student and the narrator's rhetoric with the reader creates a dramatic setting for learning that can be satisfied only by following the teacher and the student into the next stage of interaction.

Theaetetus 151E–160E therefore represents a parallel to Mark 3:7—5:43 from the point of view of the stages of interaction between a teacher and a disciple. During this stage, the teacher introduces the newly won disciple to the system of thought underlying the words and actions of the teacher. In both the *Theaetetus* and Mark the section raises the issue of special understanding among the disciples who have been taught in private and enigmatic understanding that exists among others outside the circle of discipleship (*Theaetetus* 152E; Mark 4:11, 34). In the *Theaetetus* the issue is: What is knowledge?; in Mark the issue is: What is the kingdom of God? While the subject matter is vastly different, the logic of the developing relationship between teacher and disciple reflects a cultural sphere in which public teachers and students have an established social identity. The relationship is understood to be a customary means by which religious and philosophical teaching is transmitted in the culture.

The second section of the teaching/learning phase in the *Theaetetus* (160E–169D) features Socrates "running round . . . in a circle" (160E) with the idea that was given birth in the first section (151E–160E). The introductory teaching is tested, examined, and exposed to see if it holds up in the face of challenge and alternative points of view. In the previous section Theaetetus and Socrates concluded that perception is knowledge. In this section Theaetetus participates but is unable to answer because Socrates begins modifying the point of view he represented in the preceding section. Theaetetus confesses that he is lost in wonder now. He was quite satisfied, "but now it has suddenly changed to the opposite" (162C–D). In this setting Socrates insists on arguing against the position of Protagoras with Theodorus, an adult geometrician, lest he be accused of winning a victory over Protagoras by discussing his views with a child. Theodorus considers himself "being forced to give an account of himself" (169A) by Socrates. The discussion with Theodorus occupies the major part of the section (168C–184B) and features intense disagreement between Socrates' view and a dominant tradition in the culture. Theaetetus observes the dialogue, gaining confidence to assert his own views forthrightly with Socrates. After the discussion, Theatetus comes back into the conversation with renewed confidence.

The second section of the *Theaetetus* therefore shares a number of similarities with the second section in the teaching/learning phase in the Gospel of Mark (6:1—8:26). Much as Theaetetus moves beyond his initial hesitation to participate fully in the teacher/disciple interchange, so the disciples preach repentance, cast out demons, anoint sick people with oil, heal, engage Jesus in dialogue, and distribute food to five thousand and four thousand people (6:7–13, 30, 35–44; 7:17–23; 8:1–10, 14–21). Also, much as Socrates' teaching suggests that knowledge is *not* perception, so Jesus' feeding of five thousand and four thousand people and his refusal to give a sign extend the meaning of the kingdom of God beyond the performance of exorcisms and the teaching in parables in 1:21—5:43. In this setting the disciples become confused about the system of thought and action that Jesus manifests in the narrative. Their confusion leads to a concern that they have forgotten to take bread with them in the boat (8:16), even though they have just participated with Jesus in feeding huge crowds of people with a few loaves. The ensuing discussion (8:17–21) indicates that the system of thought and action which Jesus teaches and manifests has become too complex for them to understand. They have become like those outside who having eyes do not see, and having ears do not hear (8:18).

In the midst of the second stage of the teaching/learning phase Jesus attacks a dominant alternative system of thought and action in the cultural setting. When Pharisees together with scribes from Jerusalem see Jesus' disciples eat with unwashed hands, they do not simply ask Jesus to explain the basis for this action (as in Mark 2—3) but they attack Jesus' entire approach whereby his disciples do "not live according to the tradition of the elders" (7:5). In turn Jesus upbraids the Pharisees and scribes because they "leave the commandment of God and hold fast the tradition of men." This illustrates Jesus' change with the provision for Corban (7:8–9, 12–13). Through this encounter the disciples see the moves that Jesus makes to present an alternative system of thought and action in the cultural setting. They ask Jesus to explain the parabolic teaching he uses to instruct the people (7:14–17), and they discuss bread (8:16) when they have just finished feeding four thousand people with seven loaves (8:1–10). In other words, in this section the disciples participate actively in Jesus' ministry, and they see Jesus' basic principle for presenting the alternative system of thought and action, yet they are unable to comprehend the overall system their teacher is systematically attempting to unveil to them.

The second stage of the teaching/learning phase in the *Theaetetus* and the Gospel of Mark, therefore, features disciples unable to comprehend the complexity of the teacher's understanding. During this stage, the teacher's system of thought is clarified for the reader through confrontation with one or more representatives of a point of view to which the teacher presents an alternative system of understanding.

The third stage of the *Theaetetus* (187A–210D) features an extensive discussion between Socrates and Theaetetus as they explore the meaning of knowledge from a new angle, knowledge as "thinking" or "making judgements." The section opens with Socrates' probing of Theaetetus to discover what knowledge is, rather than what it is not. When Theaetetus suggests that knowledge is true opinion or belief, Socrates responds with:

"That is the right way, Theaetetus. It is better to speak up boldly than to hesitate about answering, as you did at first. For if we act in this way, one of two things will happen: either we shall find what we are after, or we shall be less inclined to think we know what we do not know at all; and surely even that would be a recompense not to be despised" (187C–D).

As the discussion continues, Theaetetus shows an aggressiveness he did not previously possess. He persistently challenges Socrates to explain himself more clearly so that Socrates finally observes that Theaetetus's fear has disappeared, and that he is beginning to despise him (189C). Nevertheless, Theaetetus does not possess the ability to lead the discussion to its appropriate conclusion. Theaetetus admits that he understands Socrates less than ever now (192D), yet he answers confidently. Accordingly, Socrates approves of Theaetetus's ready responses and does not hesitate to disagree forthrightly with the statements Theaetetus brings forth (204B).

The third stage of the teaching/learning phase in the *Theaetetus* bears features similar to the third stage in the Gospel of Mark (8:27—10:45). During this stage, Jesus begins an entirely new tack with the disciples, teaching that the Son of man must be rejected, must be killed, and must rise again. The section begins with a question by Jesus to the disciples concerning who he is, and their answer provides the starting point for the section (8:27–30). When Peter disagrees with Jesus, he engages Jesus in vigorous dialogue (8:32–33). As the section progresses, Peter and the other disciples unhesitatingly assert what they think (9:5; 10:28, 39), do what they want to do (9:38; 10:13), respond as they wish to respond (10:24, 26, 41), and ask whatever they wish (9:11; 10:10, 35–37). Correspondingly, Jesus freely criticizes their actions and points of view (9:19, 39–41; 10:14–16, 38–40). Despite the confidence of the disciples, they do not understand the system of thought and action well enough to avoid mistakes. Like Theaetetus, they have learned to participate in their teacher's system of thought and action, but they have no mastery of the overall system and thus no ability to take a major step beyond what they have been taught without making an error.

Plato's *Theaetetus* ends after the third stage in the teaching/learning phase. The progressive form of the dialogue emerges as the teacher introduces a concept that is difficult to understand, gives the learner the confidence to participate in the exploration of the concept, exhibits an alternative point of view held by others, challenges this point of view with his own system of understanding, and interacts boldly and aggressively with the student over detailed application of the system. As Socrates indicates to Theaetetus that their solution is still problematic although they have clarified a few things for themselves (210B–C), so Jesus' responses to the disciples indicate that the disciples are still having difficulty with Jesus' system of thought and action in Mark 8:27—10:45. In the *Theaetetus,* the dialogue ends as Socrates asserts that his goal is simply to help other people bring their own thoughts to birth. After this, he excuses himself to go to meet with Meletus who is issuing an indictment against him. In Mark, the third stage of the teaching/learning phase ends as Jesus tells the disciples that he came not to be served but to serve and to give his life as a ransom for many (10:45). Immediately after this, he goes through Jericho, Bethphage, and Bethany to the Mount of Olives where he prepares his entry into Jerusalem.

While the *Theaetetus* presents the first three stages of the teaching/ learning phase, the *Meno* presents the last three stages. Omitting the phase of summons and response and the stage of initial teaching, Plato's *Meno* begins with the second stage of the teaching/learning phase in which disciple-companions are already participating freely in the actions characteristic of the teacher. The *Meno* therefore presents stages comparable to Mark 6:1—8:26; 8:27—10:45; 10:46—12:44—the second, third, and fourth stages of the teaching/learning phase.[18] The structure of the *Meno*, using the numbers of the stages in the teaching/learning phase, is:

2. *Meno* 70A–79E: Refutation of the Dominant Traditional System in Front of the Learner;
3. *Meno* 79E–89C: Interchange Between Teacher and Learner Over Central Dimensions of the System;
4. *Meno* 89D–100C: Exploration of the System with a Public Official Who Initiates the Trial of the Teacher.

Plato's *Meno* begins with Meno asking Socrates if virtue can be taught or learned by practice, or if virtue is transmitted by nature (70A). Socrates immediately distinguishes his own system of thought and action from the dominant cultural approach instituted by Gorgias whereby such a question is asked without the prior question of definition. Socrates insists that the question be changed to "What is virtue?" and asks Meno to define virtue for him (70B–D). The response by Socrates indicates that Meno, as a student of the sophists, is beyond the initial stage of the teaching/ learning phase where he needs to be gently introduced to a procedure for pursuing the meaning of a question. Meno is ready for the second stage of the teaching/learning process. He knows how to participate, but his ability to participate outruns his ability to understand. In order to work with Meno at this stage, Socrates exhibits a basic refutation of the sophistic position before Meno with the aid of Meno's participation. In response to Socrates' request that Meno define virtue, Meno describes, in the tradition of the sophists, a major virtue of a man and a major virtue of a woman and indicates that there are numberless virtues (71E–72A). Socrates immediately attacks this procedure of listing virtues, indicating that the goal is to arrive at a definition that describes what is common to all virtues (72A–D). In this setting, Socrates asks Meno if he understands, and Meno says: "My impression is that I do; but still I do not yet grasp the meaning of the question as I could wish" (72D). When Meno tries again, he admits that he really does not know what to say, but in the tradition of the sophists he defines virtue by suggesting *a* virtue, justice (73C–D). After a short time longer, Meno finds himself unable to answer (75C), so Socrates leads Meno through a definition of "figure" (75C–76A). When Meno then asks Socrates to give a definition of color (76A), Socrates asks Meno if he would like him to answer "in the manner of Gorgias" (76C) so that he can follow him. After Socrates continues with Meno in this vein, he finally upbraids Meno for having forgotten what he has already discussed with him (79A). Socrates then reviews their discussion (79B–C) and asks Meno if he remembers how the procedure worked in the definition of "figure" (79C). When Meno responds that he does remember, Socrates is ready to begin the next stage of the discussion with him (79E).

This stage of the *Meno* (70A–79E), like *Theaetetus* 160E–169D, bears many similarities to the second stage in the teaching/learning phase in Mark 6:1—8:26. In addition to an exhibition of a dominant point of view held by others (as in Mark 7:1–23), Socrates turns the initiative back to Meno much as Jesus turns the initiative back upon the disciples in the feeding of the five thousand. When the disciples ask Jesus to "send them away, to go into the country and villages round about and buy themselves something to eat" (6:36), Jesus tells them, "You give them something to eat" (6:37). This is similar to the procedure whereby Socrates tells Meno that he himself should define virtue. Likewise, as the disciples show themselves to be inept when they try to figure out how to proceed (6:37), so Meno is unable to devise an appropriate answer (71E–72A). Moreover, when Jesus is in the setting where the disciples do not understand, he reviews the feedings with them and asks them to remember what happened (Mark 8:19–21). Although both Meno and the disciples remember what previously occurred, they are still without the understanding necessary to proceed in the thought process to an accurate conclusion. In the second stage of the interrogative enterprise, therefore, there is an ironic interplay between understanding and not understanding, remembering and not remembering. On the one hand, a person may know the conclusion because that person may have been told or may even have said it himself. Yet, on the other hand, complete understanding of a concept escapes each and every person. As a religious teacher, Jesus appears to possess the complete answer to the questions he probes for the disciples and for the reader. In contrast, Socrates asserts that he himself does not possess this knowledge but simply brings it forth like a midwife. Yet

Socrates clearly knows where he is going, and the impression lies near at hand that he actually does know the answer to the question he has asked. Yet neither Socrates nor Jesus ever completely answers the question. One attains a better understanding of the constituents of the answer, but the question escapes an absolutely clear answer. In this manner, the Gospel of Mark shares a dimension with Plato's *Theaetetus* and *Meno* that is not present in the story of Abraham or Moses. Both Socrates and Jesus are engaged in a cycle of interaction in which the answer to the questions lies somewhere in the future. In contrast, the Abraham and Moses stories introduce a system of thought and action for the purpose of testing the obedience of the student to the stipulations in the system.

Similar to *Theaetetus* 187A–210D, *Meno* 79E–89C features Socrates approaching the issue from another point of view. For the first time in the dialogue, Socrates and Meno have an exceptionally aggressive exchange. Meno verbally attacks Socrates, accusing him of casting a spell on him, comparing him to the flat torpedo fish who numbs all who touch him, and telling him that if he traveled outside Athens he would be cast into prison as a magician (80A–B). In response, Socrates calls Meno a rogue but says that he has no objection to join with him in the inquiry (80B–D). Meno then taunts Socrates, asking him how he will investigate something he knows nothing about, how he will find a starting point in the region of the unknown, and how he will know if he lands upon the thing which he has never known (80D). When Socrates begins, Meno interrupts him and abruptly asks him to tell what certain men and women skilled in divine things have said about learning (81A). After Socrates tells Meno the myth about recollection, Meno asks Socrates if he can teach him about recollection. Socrates again calls him a rogue and criticizes him for imagining that he could expose him in a contradiction when he has said that virtue could only be recalled and not taught (81E–82A). This exchange is characteristic of the third stage of the teaching/learning phase. The disciple-companion is past the stage of initial teaching and observation of the refutation of the dominant cultural point of view, and he is ready for a battle of wits over detailed application of the system of thought. In this setting, Socrates asks a servant boy of Meno a series of questions about mathematical numbers and figures that demonstrate the view of recollection that Socrates has described (82C–85B). After this, when Socrates asks Meno if he would like to return to a discussion of the nature of virtue and Meno says that he would rather return to the original question that he asked about acquiring virtue, Socrates objects that Meno never thinks about self-control but only of controlling him (86C–D). After further discussion, the section ends when Meno asks Socrates why he is so difficult, so slow to believe that virtue is knowledge (89D).

Meno 79E–89C is similar to the aggressive interaction between Jesus and his disciple-companions in Mark 8:27—10:45. Peter's strong objection to Jesus' teaching and Jesus' strong response to it (8:32–33) are similar in tone to *Meno* 80A–82A. In fact, Meno's comment about Socrates' attempt to cast a spell on him like a magician is an exceptionally interesting parallel to the exorcism language concerning rebuking and Satan in Mark 8:32–33. Additionally in the same way that Meno attempts to gain control over Socrates, so James and John attempt to commandeer Jesus into giving them a place at his right and left hand in his kingdom (10:36–37). Thus, *Meno* 79E–89C represents the third stage of the teaching/learning phase, parallel to Mark 8:27—10:45, which features the battle of wits between teacher and disciple over central dimensions of the system of thought and action that the teacher is systematically introducing to his disciple-companions.

With *Meno* 89D–100C, the dialogue enters a stage comparable to Jesus' teaching in the Temple area in Mark's gospel. When Meno cannot understand why Socrates is so slow to believe that virtue is knowledge so that it can be taught and learned, Socrates engages Anytus in conversation (90A–95A). Anytus is a well-educated Athenian—chosen for political office by the Athenians—who is one of Socrates' accusers at the trial. As part of the Athenian political establishment, Socrates asks him to advise him concerning the transmission of virtue. Socrates' dialogue with Anytus is very aggressive. He asks Anytus what is wrong with the sophists and whether they corrupt consciously or unconsciously (92A). Finally Anytus tells Socrates he is "too apt to speak ill of people" and tells him to be careful since "in most cities it is probably easier to do people harm than good" (94E). Socrates suggests to Meno that Anytus is in a rage especially because he thinks he is one of them whom Socrates accuses of being unable to teach virtue (95A). After further discussion with Meno, the dialogue ends with a reference by Socrates to Anytus. If Meno is able to persuade Anytus and to conciliate him, he "will do a good turn to the people of Athens also" (100C).

Meno 89D–100C is similar in a number of ways to Mark 10:46—12:44. Much as Socrates engages Anytus with questions and insists that he try to answer, so Jesus returns questions to the chief priests, scribes, and elders and insists that they answer. The reluctance of both Anytus and the Temple hierarchy to answer reveals the hostility that leads them to have the teacher tried and condemned to death. The major encounter in Mark occurs in 11:27—12:12. When the chief priests, scribes, and elders ask Jesus by what authority he does these things, he says to them:

"I will ask you a question; answer me, and I will tell you by what authority I do these things. Was the baptism of John from heaven or from men? Answer me" (11:29–30).

The aggressiveness of Jesus' statements to the Temple hierarchy is similar to the aggressiveness of Socrates' statements to Anytus in *Meno* 91A–95A. The interaction becomes most intense when Socrates insists upon an answer to his questions:

> "I only ask you to tell us, and do Meno a service as a friend of your family by letting him know, to whom in all this great city he should apply in order to become eminent in the virtue which I described just now" (*Meno* 92D).

When Anytus responds, "Why not tell him yourself?" Socrates tells him that he has answered but now wishes to know Anytus's suggestions:

> "Now you take your turn, and tell him to whom of the Athenians he is to go. Give us a name—any one you please" (*Meno* 92D–E).

As Anytus will not answer Socrates, so the Temple representatives will not answer Jesus. As the conversation breaks off between Socrates and Anytus, Socrates says:

> "Meno, I think Anytus is angry, and I am not at all surprised: for he conceives, in the first place, that I am speaking ill of these gentlemen; and in the second place, he considers he is one of them himself" (*Meno* 95A).

Similarly, when Jesus tells the Temple hierarchy the parable of the vineyard: "they tried to arrest him, . . . for they perceived that he had told the parable against them" (Mark 12:12).

The similarities between the Gospel of Mark and Plato's *Theaetetus* and *Meno* arise as the teacher aids the student in developing the ability to pursue the meaning of a concept in the arena of thought and action. Instead of a sequence in which Jewish thought dominates so that the role of the teacher is to introduce a series of requirements that test their obedience, Jesus teaches basic dimensions of thought and action that accompany the kingdom and gospel of God. Instead of direct commandments, therefore, Jesus teaches concepts in Mark:

> "There is nothing outside a man which by going into him can defile him; but the things which come out of a man are what defile him" (7:16).

> "Whoever would save his life will lose it; and whoever loses his life for my sake and the gospel's will save it" (8:35).

> "If any one would be first, he must be last of all and servant of all" (9:35).

As a result, Jesus' words and deeds create difficulty in understanding that is similar to the difficulty which the student has following Socrates. Both Jesus and Socrates say and do things that people cannot understand. While Socrates works hard to bring understanding to birth in the student and the reader, so Jesus and the narrator of Mark raise an expectation that the disciples and the reader will reach understanding sometime in the future: "there is nothing hid, except to be made manifest; nor is anything secret, except to come to light" (4:22). In Plato's dialogues and the Gospel of Mark there is a rhetorical play upon the reader so that the teacher appears to have the information toward which he leads the student, but the information is never entirely clear either to the student or to the reader.

Both Plato's *Theaetetus* and *Meno* exhibit the dynamics of teaching and learning in a setting that eventually leads to the arrest, trial, and death of the teacher. The teacher introduces a system of thought and action that is an alternative to a system maintained by established members in the culture. The teacher's system highlights the integrity of the teacher rather than the obedience or disobedience of the student which is characteristic of the cycle in biblical tradition. The fourth stage of the teaching/learning phase in Mark and Plato's dialogues exhibits the public hostility that brings about the teacher's indictment and death rather than a test of the student's obedience to the teaching. The intellectual climate of Mark's gospel extends beyond the religious environment of obedience into the Hellenistic cultural environment where the search to understand life and death creates admiration for the sage who challenges dominant points of view. The sage challenges viewpoints in order to introduce a system of thought and action that calls for an integrity that transcends obedience to the established customs of society.

TEACHING AND LEARNING IN PHILOSTRATUS'S *LIFE OF APOLLONIUS OF TYANA*

Philostratus's *Apollonius* presents an extended narrative sequence that contains the entire cycle of the teacher/disciple relationship in contrast to individual dialogues that contain segments of the cycle. Since Damis accompanies Apollonius throughout Apollonius's adult career as a philosopher-teacher, the full cycle of relationships between a teacher and a disciple-companion is manifested most vividly between these two in Philostratus's *Apollonius*. As we recall, the initial stage of their relationship contains no summons by Apollonius. Instead, this stage is characterized by resolve on behalf of Damis, a resolve that meets with approval by Apollonius (1.19).

The teaching/learning phase in Philostratus's *Apollonius* unfolds in the setting of a novelistic biography. The narrative explores the domain of knowledge by means of travel through foreign lands. As Apollonius and Damis travel to different countries and peoples, they move through the cycle of teacher/disciple relationships as they encounter the manifold forms of thought and action that constitute the wisdom of the world. The stages of interaction that emerge between Apollonius and Damis are as follows:

1. *Apollonius* 1.21–40: Initial Teaching;
2. *Apollonius* 2: Major Demonstration of the Superiority of the Teacher's System of Thought and Action Through Encounter with King Phraotes;
3. *Apollonius* 3: Exploration of the Depths of the Teacher's System Through Mutual Learning from the Sages of India;
4. *Apollonius* 4–6: Foreshadowing of Arrest and Trial Through Encounter and Exploration of the System with a Range of Public Groups.

The first stage of the teaching/learning phase (1.21–40) features Apollonius teaching Damis his basic Pythagorean system of thought and action. During this stage Apollonius does not expect Damis to have accurate knowledge, so he does not ask him questions that call for substantive answers. Damis, however, never takes a passive role in the relationship. On his own initiative he offers answers and gives advice from the very beginning. During the initial stage of the teaching/learning phase, Damis's suggestions are usually off the mark.

The initial stage in the teaching/learning phase bears similarities with Mark 3:7—5:43.[19] In two instances, a circumstance similar to the parable of the sower and its explanation (4:1–20) arises. First, Apollonius and Damis come across a slain lioness from which the hunters cut eight whelps (1.22). When Apollonius interprets this as a sign that they will stay with the king of Babylon for a year and eight months, Damis wonders, alternatively, if it might mean that their stay abroad will extend to nine years. In response, Apollonius explains to Damis that his own interpretation is based on an understanding of the whelps as incomplete animals who signify months rather than years. Second, when Apollonius tells Damis the dream he had the night before, Damis fears that it is a bad omen for their trip and attempts to persuade Apollonius to turn back (1.23). Apollonius then explains to Damis the real meaning of the dream, and they continue on their way. As Apollonius and Damis travel to Babylon and reside there, Apollonius never begins a discussion by asking Damis a question. Their relation is characterized by Apollonius's direct teaching which ends with a command or an explanation. Finally, while Apollonius and Damis are in Babylon, the king's offer of ten gifts to

Apollonius raises the issue of greed between the teacher and his disciple-companion. After Apollonius teaches Damis about the evils that attend greed, laziness, anger, passion, and love of drink, Damis blushes at his own stupidity and asks Apollonius to pardon him for misunderstanding so badly. In turn, Apollonius says:

> "Never mind, for it was not by way of rebuking and humbling you that I spoke of this, but in order to give you some idea of my own point of view" (1.34).

In other words, during the first stage of the teaching/learning phase, Apollonius, like Jesus in Mark 3:7—5:43, does not expect his disciple-companion to have correct answers to questions. For this reason, Apollonius does not ask Damis questions nor rebuke Damis when he makes an incorrect statement or gives wrong advice. Rather, Apollonius reveals his abilities and teaches his point of view to Damis, correcting Damis whenever necessary but not reprimanding him for erroneous thinking. Throughout the first stage Damis, like the disciple-companions of Jesus in Mark 3:7—5:43, remains at a notable distance from Apollonius in understanding. This distance leads Apollonius to forbid Damis to visit the Magi with him (1.26; cf. Mark 5:37 where Jesus does not let all twelve disciples accompany him). Also, the natural lack of understanding that characterizes the disciple-companion during the first stage of the teaching/learning phase motivates Apollonius to teach Damis directly and to deal with his wrong ideas gently.

The initial stage of the teaching/learning phase in Philostratus's *Apollonius* represents the portrayal of a teacher and his disciple-companion in a mode that lies somewhere between the portrayal in Socrates' dialogues and the Gospel of Mark. On the one hand, Damis's active role in dialogue is more like the conversations between Socrates and a student during the initial stage of the teaching/learning phase. On the other hand, the authority with which Apollonius comports himself is more like Jesus in the Gospel of Mark so that the following parallels occur: the question arises, "By the gods, who are you?" (1.21; cf. Mark 5:41), the title "divine Apollonius" is used (1.21; cf. Mark 5:11), Apollonius's disciple-companion becomes afraid (1.23; cf. Mark 4:38), and people are astonished at Apollonius's actions (1.27, 35; cf. Mark 5:20, 42). Common to Plato's dialogues, the Gospel of Mark, and Philostratus's *Apollonius* is an initial stage in which the teacher devotes his efforts to teaching and exhibiting basic dimensions of the system of the thought and action which he manifests throughout the narrative.

The second stage of the teaching/learning phase (book 2) emphasizes Apollonius's demonstration of the superiority of his system of thought and action over royal wisdom in India. Apollonius initiates long conversations with Damis by means of direct questions to him, and much of Damis's lack of understanding is overcome through Apollonius's conversations both with him and with King Phraotes. The stage represents a shift from direct teaching to teaching by means of dialogue with the student and with an established adult in the cultural setting.

The second stage of the teaching/learning phase opens in 2.5 where the new tactic of Apollonius appears. As they are walking along on foot, Apollonius asks Damis: "Tell me where we were yesterday." When Damis replies that they were on the plain, Apollonius asks him: "And to-day, O Damis, where are we?" In this way, Apollonius leads Damis to make the observation that today they are much higher up toward the heavens than they were the day before. When Apollonius asks Damis: "Can you tell me then, O Damis, what understanding of divine mystery you get by walking so near the heavens?" Damis replies: "None whatever." First Apollonius tells Damis he ought to have greater understanding today, then finally he tells Damis, "So then you are, O Damis, still below, and have won nothing from being high up, and you are as far from heaven as you were yesterday. And my question which I asked you to begin with was a fair one, although you thought that I asked it in order to make fun of you." This scene, which opens the second stage of the teaching/learning phase, depicts Damis at a stage similar to the stage depicted in Mark 8:14–21. When the disciples are asked how many loaves they distributed and picked up during the feedings, they remember. Still they are not able to make any progression in their understanding on the basis of this information. Likewise, when Damis is asked if he can remember what they did the day before, Damis can remember; but he is unable to venture an answer to the significance of the new circumstance in which they find themselves. As in Mark 8:17–18, Apollonius does not drop the matter, but needles Damis about being "as far from heaven as you were yesterday" (2.5).

The second stage of the teaching/learning process continues with a series of discussions between Apollonius and Damis, each opening with a question by Apollonius to Damis. In 2.7 when Damis thinks Apollonius will drink some Indian wine that has been poured out as a libation to Zeus, Apollonius asks Damis if it is not necessary to abstain from both money and wine on the basis of his previous statements. After Damis admits that they should abstain from money, Apollonius gives a long speech that contains a series of questions in the first half which he answers in the last half. Finally, Apollonius finishes with: "The abstinence from these things has, I perceive, profited you nothing, though it has profited me in the philosophic profession which I have made from boyhood." In other words, Damis, as Jesus' disciples in Mark 8, is unable to draw appropriate conclusions on the basis of participation in events that should have been a learning experience for him.

In 2.11 the mood begins to change, because Damis is able to provide good answers to a series of questions that Apollonius asks him about good horsemanship. Through this series of questions, Apollonius leads Damis to recognize that his understanding was deficient, yet Damis's participation shows an ability and an interest in pursuing philosophical subjects in a thoughtful and detailed manner. At the end of the conversation Apollonius does not make a comment about Damis's lack of understanding but simply states the conclusion in direct relation to the discussion. In 2.14–16 the discussion deepens as Apollonius asks Damis a long, involved question about affection in animals, and Damis asks Apollonius perceptive questions that provide the setting for Apollonius to explain further details. This time when the discussion ends the narrator comments: "Many such learned discussions were suggested to them as one occasion after another worth speaking of arose" (2.16). In other words, dialogue between Apollonius and Damis becomes easier as Damis begins to understand and to accept the revision of his understanding by Apollonius. This continues in 2.22 when Apollonius asks Damis what painting is. Soon after the beginning of the discussion, Damis is embarrassed at the foolishness of his first answer, but the narrator comments that Apollonius had no desire to humiliate him and continued the conversation so that Damis engaged willingly in the rest of the discussion. During this stage, therefore, Damis becomes a capable partner in dialogue, gradually overcoming his embarrassment at slightly wrong suggestions since he has shown himself to be committed to a philosophical quest of understanding.

After these events, Apollonius and Damis arrive at King Phraotes' palace in Taxila, and Apollonius's interaction and dialogue with King Phraotes (2.23–39) change the relationship between Damis and Apollonius. While King Phraotes exhibits exceptional wisdom and capability both in discussion and action, Apollonius shows himself time after time to possess a system of thought and action superior to the king. In the midst of these events, Damis gains further confidence in himself. He aids Apollonius by encouraging him to continue his debate with King Phraotes (2.36) and makes arrangements with the king for provisions to continue their journey (2.40). At the end of the first stage in the teaching/learning phase, Apollonius had made his own arrangements for the journey to Taxila (1.40). At the end of the second stage, Apollonius allows Damis to negotiate for the provisions (2.40). The second stage has been a period of learning so that Damis is able to participate fully in the enterprise in which Apollonius is engaged.

The second stage in the teaching/learning phase in Philostratus's *Apol-*

lonius possesses dimensions in common with the second stage in the Gospel of Mark and Plato's dialogues. The disciple-companion partici-pates without hesitation in the teacher's activity but is unable to com-prehend the ramifications of previous experiences. During this stage the teacher's encounter with a well-educated and established adult in the presence of the disciple-companion provides a setting for the growth of confidence within the disciple-companion. During this stage, however, a major difference emerges between Philostratus's *Apollonius* and the other documents. In neither the Gospel of Mark nor the dialogues of Plato does the disciple-companion attain the ability to take the correct initiative at the end of the second stage. The nature of the system of thought and action introduced by Jesus and Socrates appears to disallow such natural growth in the process of understanding. In contrast, Damis is able, by the end of the second stage of the teaching/learning phase, to give Apollonius good advice concerning their provisions as they continue their travels. One of the characteristics of a novelistic narrative may therefore be a more positive portrayal of the disciple-companion's ability to grow in under-standing.

The third stage in the teaching/learning phase (book 3) features Apol-lonius and Damis learning together from the sages of India. Rather than featuring a battle of wits between Damis and Apollonius, the third stage portrays teacher and disciple-companion clarifying the details of the teacher's system of thought and action in a setting where the teacher learns from sages of India for whom he has the deepest respect. During this stage, Apollonius accepts Damis as a wise and trusted companion. In turn, Damis does not attempt to correct Apollonius's answers or give him advice that will keep him from taking advantage of the things people offer him. In other words, the positive portrayal of Damis eliminates a stage featuring an intensive battle of wits between the teacher and the learner. The battle of wits has taken place during the first two stages of the teaching/learning phase through Damis's vigorous interaction with Apol-lonius from the first encounter. During the third stage, therefore, Apol-lonius and Damis explore the depths of Apollonius's system of thought and action by having the teacher himself submit to the role of student among people whom he considers to have wisdom greater than his own.

During the third stage Damis is allowed to sit with the sages while Apollonius converses extensively with them, and Damis observes their healing of various people (3.34–39). Only Apollonius, however, is allowed to converse with Iarchus about the innermost mysteries of astronomy, divination, foreknowledge, sacrifices, and invocations to appease the gods (3.41). Damis is less concerned to guess what Apollonius will do next, and Apollonius no longer considers it necessary to tutor Damis. Apollonius allows Damis to learn with him, though of course Apollonius is able to go deeper into the mysteries of understanding than Damis himself.

The third stage of the teaching/learning phase in Philostratus's *Apollonius* shares in common with Plato's dialogues and the Gospel of Mark a detailed exploration of the teacher's system of thought and action. The means by which the detail is explored, however, are different. The battle of wits that characterizes *Theaetetus* 187A–210D, *Meno* 79E–89C, and Mark 8:27—10:45 is replaced by extensive discussion with a person who possesses greater wisdom than either the teacher or his disciple-companion.

The fourth stage in the teaching/learning phase takes place in books 4–6 and portrays Damis in the background as Apollonius encounters a variety of people and discusses a variety of public issues that set the stage for his imprisonment and death. Damis willingly does whatever Apollonius asks him and participates freely in discussion with Apollonius and others around him. This stage manifests the final stage in the teaching/learning phase which features the student-disciples accompanying the teacher as he addresses the major public issues and performs the major public activities that set the stage for the final phase of the teacher/disciple relation.

During the fourth stage Damis travels to Greece and Rome, and these travels introduce the topic of Nero and the danger of imprisonment and death for anyone who teaches philosophy. The theme of danger arises in 4.11 when:

> Having purged the Ephesians of the plague, and having had enough of the people of Ionia, he [Apollonius] started for Hellas. Having made his way then to Pergamum . . . he came to the land of Ilium . . . he went to visit the tombs of the Achaeans, . . . then he bade his companions go on board ship, for he himself, he said, must spend a night on the mound with Achilles. Now his companions tried to deter him . . . alleging that Achilles was still dreadful as a phantom . . . (4.11).

From this point on, Apollonius begins to rebuke people who run temples and to correct the rites that are being observed there (4.21, 22, 23, 24, 26, 27–28, 30). Then, in 4.35 the subject of Nero and his opposition to philosophy is introduced, and this concern hovers over almost every remaining episode in book 4 as Apollonius travels into Rome. The unwillingness of twenty-six of his thirty-four companions to accompany him to Rome (4.37), the surveillance and interrogation of Apollonius by Tigellinus (Nero's informant) while in Rome (4.42–44), Apollonius's correspondence with Musonius in prison (4.46), and Nero's prohibition of the teaching of philosophy in public (4.47) foreshadow the arrest, trial, and death of Apollonius in the final section of the story.

Much as the disciples in Mark's gospel assist and accompany Jesus into Jerusalem in 10:46—12:44, so Damis and seven other companions accompany and assist Apollonius. This is not a stage for disagreement between the teacher and his disciple-companions. Rather, the teacher rebukes, corrects, and encounters people with a combination of aggressiveness, wit, and charm that creates animosity among the establishment which in turn leads to his death. Meanwhile Damis, like the disciples in Mark, obediently fulfills duties he is asked to perform (e.g., 4.46; 5.13; 5.43) and listens perceptively to the comments of his teacher (e.g., 4.37; 5.31).

In book 6, Apollonius himself occupies center stage as the narrator introduces the public activity that immediately precedes the trial and death which end the story. Apollonius goes to the academy of naked sages in Egypt and in face of strong criticism argues his point of view with courage and wisdom (6.6–11). At the end of the initial encounter, Thespesion, the spokesperson for the naked sages, visibly blushes "in spite of the blackness of his complexion, . . . while the rest of them seemed in some way stunned by the vigorous and fluent discourse which they listened to" (6.12). However, the youngest of the naked sages, named Nilus, admires Apollonius and seeks to become his disciple (6.12). As the conversations continue, Apollonius describes the Egyptian sages as inferior to the wise men of India who receive the gift of foreknowledge as the crown of their wisdom (6.13). In response, both Nilus and Thespesion encourage Apollonius to converse with them about the gods (6.19), government and justice (6.20–21), immortality of the soul, and nature (6.22). At the end of this series of episodes, Apollonius and his companions visit the source of the Nile (6.23–28). Then, accounts are given of Apollonius's exchanges with Titus after his destruction of Jerusalem (6.29–33); his interactions with the inhabitants of Tarsus (6.34); and his successful efforts to convince a youth to go to school (6.36), to influence the thinking of the inhabitants of Sardis and Antioch (6.37–38), to help a man establish a dowry for his four daughters without depleting his own resources (6.39), to purge a man and some temples from improper worship (6.40–41), to force Domitian to change his decree about vineyards, and to heal the madness in both a man and a dog (6.43). These public activities represent the final stage of the teaching/learning phase before Apollonius faces imprisonment and death under Domitian's directions. This stage portrays the public activity that creates the setting for his unjust trial and death. The section ends with the comment:

> Such were the exploits of our sage in behalf of both temples and cities; such were the discourses he delivered to the public or in behalf of different communities, and in behalf of those who were dead or who were sick; and

such were the harangues he delivered to wise and unwise alike, and to the sovereigns who consulted him about moral virtue (6.43).

The fourth stage of the teaching/learning phase in Philostratus's *Apollonius* again bears similarities with the fourth stage in Plato's dialogues and in the Gospel of Mark. The role of Anytus in Plato's *Meno* (90A–95A) is similar to the role of Tigellinus in Philostratus's *Apollonius* (4.42–44). Almost every dimension of Mark 10:46—12:44 is paralleled in *Apollonius* 4–6. Jesus enters into the city in which he is eventually tried and killed (11:1–11), he reforms practices in the Temple (11:15–19), he argues with political people who finally succeed in killing him (11:27—12:17), and he discusses basic issues of belief and practice with a range of people in the cultural setting (12:18–40). Common to these documents is a final stage in the teaching/learning phase where the disciple-companions accompany the teacher as he engages in a range of activities that creates the setting for his trial and death.

Philostratus's *Apollonius* 1.21–6.43 therefore illustrates the intermediate phase in the teacher/disciple relationship as it may manifest itself in a biographical romance or novel. This phase contains a sequence of four stages characterized by: (1) initial teaching; (2) dialogue with Damis and an established adult to exhibit the alternative principles at work in the system of the teacher; (3) exploration by the teacher and his disciple-companion of the depths of the system by means of mutual learning from the sages of India; (4) presence of the disciple-companion with the teacher as he performs the major public activities that create the setting for his imprisonment, trial, and death. This sequence replaces a section in which the teacher and his disciple-companion explore the details of his system of thought and action through a battle of wits with a section that explores those details through mutual learning from sages for whom the teacher has deep respect.

THE DISTINCTIVE CHARACTERISTICS OF
THE TEACHING/LEARNING PHASE

The purpose of comparative analysis is to gain a more detailed understanding of the major document that the interpreter analyzes. Toward this end, a closer look at the teaching/learning phase in the Gospel of Mark is now in order. During the first stage of the teaching/learning phase in Mark 3:7—5:43, Jesus issues commands and asks only rhetorical questions that do not call for an answer from the person being addressed. All the commands of Jesus occur in the setting of a powerful work of Jesus (4:39; 5:8, 19, 34, 36, 41), except one (4:35). In other words, Jesus continues to perform acts of power during the first stage of the teaching/

learning phase. In fact, the acts of power reach new heights in this section (4:35—5:43). Within this authoritative mode, Jesus' rhetorical questions provide a setting for him to teach people:

1. "How can Satan cast out Satan?" (3:23);
2. "Who are my mother and my brothers?" (3:33);
3. "Do you not understand this parable? How then will you understand all the parables?" (4:13);
4. "Is a lamp brought in to be put under a bushel, or under a bed, and not on a stand?" (4:21);
5. "With what can we compare the kingdom of God, or what parable shall we use for it?" (4:30);
6. "Why do you make a tumult and weep?" (5:39).[37]

Only one of these questions is addressed to scribes (3:23); another is addressed to a crowd in the setting of a mighty work (5:39). The rest are addressed to those who have gathered around Jesus. In contrast to Mark 1:14—3:6 where rhetorical questions lead to proverbial wisdom that defends the actions of Jesus and the disciples, the rhetorical questions in 3:7—5:43 lead to statements that inform the hearers about the basic system of thought and action that Jesus manifests in the narrative.

A dramatically new feature in 6:1—8:26 arises as the disciples participate in miraculous events performed by Jesus and replicate certain miraculous events previously performed only by Jesus. This shift in the role of the disciples begins in 6:1–13, the progression that introduces the section. This stage of the teaching/learning cycle, coming after the stage in which Jesus introduces basic details of his system of thought and action, shows the disciples able to perform basic activities characteristic of Jesus' action but unable to perceive the meaning of the teaching and the significance of the actions.[20]

Within this section Jesus issues commands both to his disciples and to various people amidst both healing and teaching:

1. "Come away by yourselves to a lonely place, and rest a while" (6:31);
2. "Take heart, it is I; have no fear" (6:50);
3. "Hear me, all of you, and understand" (7:14);
4. "Let the children first be fed, for it is not right to take the children's bread and throw it to the dogs" (7:27);
5. "For this saying you may go your way; the demon has left your daughter" (7:29);
6. "Ephphatha" ("Be opened") (7:34);
7. "Take heed, beware of the leaven of the Pharisees and the leaven of Herod" (8:15);
8. "Do not even enter the village" (8:26).

A new dimension emerges in the teaching/learning cycle, however, when Jesus commands the Twelve in Mark 6:8–11. In the setting where Jesus sends the Twelve out two by two:

1. He charged them to take *nothing* for their journey *except* a staff; *no* bread, *no* bag, *no* money in their belts; *but* to wear sandals and *not* put on two tunics;
2. And he said to them, "Where you enter a house, stay there until you leave the place. And *if* any place will *not* receive you and they refuse to hear you, when you leave, shake off the dust that is on your feet for a testimony against them."

Within the setting of the negative, adversative, and conditional features characteristic of Jesus' speech in the Gospel of Mark, the disciples are commanded to go out into the kind of activity in which Jesus has been engaged. In the setting of these commands, Jesus gives the disciples authority over the unclean spirits (6:7), and they: go out; preach that men should repent; cast out many demons; anoint with oil many that are sick; and heal (6:12–13).

A different set of responses emerges between Jesus and his disciples after the disciples attain the ability to perform activities similar to Jesus. First, the disciples presuppose that they have the right to give advice to Jesus. Coming to Jesus, they instruct him saying:

"This is a lonely place, and the hour is now late; send them [the five thousand] away, to go into the country and villages round about and buy themselves something to eat" (6:35–36).

Second, Jesus turns the responsibility for action back upon the disciples. In the feeding of the five thousand, he tells them, "You give them something to eat" (6:37). Third, the questions that Jesus asks the disciples are no longer simply rhetorical but require the disciples to produce accurate but simple information and to remember the information. These questions emerge during and after the feedings:

1. "How many loaves have you? Go and see" (6:38);
2. "How many loaves have you?" (8:5);
3. "When I broke the five loaves for the five thousand, how many baskets full of broken pieces did you take up?" (8:19);
4. "And the seven for the four thousand, how many baskets full of broken pieces did you take up?" (8:20).

Fourth, in the midst of this new participation and responsibility the disciples begin to show confusion and lack of understanding. For this reason, the narrator describes the disciples as "arguing among themselves" (*dialogizesthai pros allēlous:* 8:16), much as the scribes did during the first phase of the narrative (cf. 2:6, 8). The confusion and lack of understanding call forth rhetorical questions from Jesus that contain the same biting characteristics as those previously launched against the scribes and Pharisees:

1. "Then are you also *without* understanding? Do you not see that whatever goes into a man from outside *cannot* defile him, since it enters, *not* his heart *but* his stomach, and so passes on?" (7:18–19);
2. "Why do you discuss the fact that you have *no* bread? Do you *not* yet perceive or understand? Are your hearts hardened? Having eyes do you *not* see, and having ears do you *not* hear? And do you *not* remember?" (8:17–18);
3. "Do you *not* yet understand?" (8:21).

The negative and adversative features now characterize the disciples as confused and lacking understanding. They know how to perform many activities similar to the one who has called them into the role of disciple-companion. Yet during the second stage of the teaching/learning phase, confusion emerges as the disciple-companions attempt to extend their basic knowledge of the system into new circumstances.

Disciple-companions are expected to learn specific duties and accept specific responsibilities from their teacher. Modern theory holds that people learn how to do things before they understand the implications of what they do.[21] Moreover, when they are adults in the process of learning a new role, they are expected to know the art of integrating knowledge about things with knowledge of how to do things. The second stage of the teaching/learning phase in Mark reflects this dimension of learning. The disciples are able to perform duties that they are instructed to perform, but they are unable to understand the relation of Jesus' activities to the system of thought and action he introduced to them in the prior section. In other words, the disciples are unable to find a means to satisfactorily interrelate their response to the call of the kingdom of God with their ability to perform activities in a manner similar to the way in which Jesus performs them. Although five thousand and four thousand people were successfully fed with five and seven loaves, the disciples remain concerned that they brought only one loaf with them in the boat (8:14). At this stage the disciples are being introduced to complexities of the system of thought and action that they are not able to comprehend. As a result, they become confused and lack understanding.

The third stage of the teaching/learning phase in Mark (8:27—10:45) contains a series of differences in the interaction between Jesus and the disciples. First, except for two instances, Jesus introduces his statements with questions requiring direct answers rather than rhetorical questions that he himself answers. In the setting of the healing of the epileptic boy, Jesus says about the crowd and the disciples who were not able to heal the boy: "O faithless generation, how long am I to be with you? How long am I to bear with you?" (9:19). Then in response to the rich man who addresses him as "Good Teacher," he says: "Why do you call me good?" (10:17). Otherwise, throughout the section Jesus responds even to the Pharisees with questions requiring answers. Accordingly, questions by Jesus, the disciples, and others are questions which call for, and usually receive, direct answers:

1. "Who do men say that I am?" (8:27);
2. "But who do you say that I am?" (8:29);
3. "Why do the scribes say that first Elijah must come?" (9:11);
4. "What are you discussing with them?" (9:16);
5. "How long has he had this?" (9:21);
6. "Why could we not cast it out?" (9:28);
7. "What were you discussing on the way?" (9:33);
8. "What did Moses command you?" (10:3);
9. "What do you want me to do for you?" (10:36);
10. "Are you able to drink the cup that I drink, or to be baptized with the baptism with which I am baptized?" (10:38).

These questions call for people to produce information that has not otherwise come to light in the narrative. Moreover, five of the questions between Jesus and the disciples (8:27, 29; 9:11, 28; 10:38) require the person who is questioned to give an interpretative answer or an answer based on inference. In other words, this section now features a stage of reciprocal questions and answers between Jesus and his disciples. Jesus no longer simply presents basic details of his system of understanding. Also, the disciples are not simply caught in confusion and failure to understand. Rather, this stage features a full-fledged interchange between Jesus and his disciples over the central dimensions of his system of thought and action.

Second, the new relation between Jesus and the disciples calls forth a large number of statements that contain neither negative nor adversative features in them. Many of these are characterized by conditional constructions, imperatives, the positive "whoever" or "anyone" rather than "no one" (*hos* [*e*]*an* or *tis* rather than *oudeis*), and the explanatory conjunction "for" (*gar*):

1. "*If any man* would come after me, *let him deny* himself and *take up* his cross and *follow* me" (8:34);

2. *"For whoever* would save his life will lose it; and *whoever* loses his life for my sake and the gospel's will save it" (8:35);

3. *"For whoever* is ashamed of me and of my words in this adulterous and sinful generation, of him will the Son of man also be ashamed, when he comes in the glory of his Father with the holy angels" (8:38);

4. *"If any one* would be first, *he must be* last of all and servant of all" (9:35);

5. *"Whoever* receives one such child in my name receives me" (9:37);

6. *"Have* salt in yourselves, and *be at peace* with one another" (9:50);

7. *"Whoever* divorces his wife and marries another, commits adultery against her; and *if* she divorces her husband and marries another, she commits adultery" (10:11–12);

8. "How hard it will be for those who have riches to enter the kingdom of God" (10:23);

9. "Children, how hard it is to enter the kingdom of God! It is easier for a camel to go through the eye of a needle than for a rich man to enter the kingdom of God" (10:24–25).

In contrast to other sections of Mark, this section contains extensive positive teaching about the system of thought and action that Jesus manifests in the narrative.

Still, in this section Jesus' teaching remains aggressive. In three instances, a unit of one or more positive statements is followed by a rhetorical question:

1. "For what does it profit a man, to gain the whole world and forfeit his life? For what can a man give in return for his life?" (8:36–37);

2. "And how is it written of the Son of man, that he should suffer many things and be treated with contempt?" (9:12);

3. "Salt is good; but if the salt has lost its saltness, how will you season it?" (9:50).

Moreover, when Jesus makes a series of statements, the positive statements lead to statements characterized by negative and adversative features. On four occasions these sayings are introduced with the formula, "Truly, I say to you" (*amēn legō humīn*). The first three contain an emphatic negative construction (*ou mē* with aorist subjunctive):

1. "Truly, I say to you, there are some standing here who *will not* taste death before they see that the kingdom of God has come with power" (9:1);

2. "For truly, I say to you, whoever gives you a cup of water to drink because you bear the name of Christ, *will by no means* lose his reward" (9:41);

3. "Truly, I say to you, whoever does *not* receive the kingdom of God like a child *shall not* enter it" (10:15);

4. "Truly, I say to you, there is *no one* who has left house or brothers or sisters or mother or father or children or lands, for my sake and the

gospel, who will *not* receive a hundredfold now in this time, houses and brothers and sisters and mothers and children and lands, with persecutions, and in the age to come eternal life. *But* many that are first will be last, and the last first" (10:29–31).[22]

Other statements use "not . . . but," "no one . . . but," or "but . . . not" to provide contrast or antithetical parallelism:

5. "And whoever receives me, receives *not* me *but* him who sent me" (9:37);
6. "*No one* is good *but* God alone" (10:18);
7. "With men it is impossible, *but not* with God; for all things are possible with God" (10:27);
8. "You know that those who are supposed to rule over the Gentiles lord it over them, and their great men exercise authority over them. *But* it shall *not* be so among you; *but* whoever would be great among you must be your servant, and whoever would be first among you must be slave of all. For the Son of man also came *not* to be served *but* to serve, and to give his life as a ransom for many" (10:42–45).

In addition, three statements contain direct prohibitive pronouncements:

9. "*Do not* forbid him, for *no one* who does a mighty work in my name will be able soon after to speak evil of me. For he that is *not* against us is for us" (9:39–40);
10. "For your hardness of heart he wrote you this commandment. *But* from the beginning of creation, 'God made them male and female.' 'For this reason a man shall leave his father and mother and be joined to his wife, and the two shall become one flesh.' So they are *no longer* two *but* one flesh. What therefore God has joined together, *let not* man put asunder' " (10:5–9);
11. "Let the children come to me, *do not* hinder them; for to such belongs the kingdom of God" (10:14).

Four statements attain their forcefulness through comparison:

12. "Whoever causes one of these little ones who believe in me to sin, it would be *better* for him if a great millstone were hung round his neck and he were thrown into the sea" (9:42);
13. "And if your hand causes you to sin, cut it off; it is *better* for you to enter life maimed *than* with two hands to go to hell, to the *un*quenchable fire" (9:43);
14. "And if your foot causes you to sin, cut it off; it is *better* for you to enter life lame *than* with two feet to be thrown into hell" (9:45);
15. "And if your eye causes you to sin, pluck it out; it is *better* for you to enter the kingdom of God with one eye *than* with two eyes to be thrown into hell, where their worm does *not* die, and the fire is *not* quenched. For every one will be salted with fire" (9:47–49).

In other words, direct conversation between Jesus and his disciples establishes the program for this section of the Markan narrative. These conversations contain direct positive teaching, direct negative teaching, antithetical parallelism, and comparison. First and foremost, the activities in the section are correlated with Jesus' teaching about the suffering, rejection, death, and resurrection of the Son of man. After the transfiguration, Jesus discusses the suffering, rejection, and resurrection of the Son of man (9:9–13) with Peter, James, and John. Then as Jesus travels with his disciples through Galilee and Judea he reiterates the teaching that the Son of man must be rejected, killed, and raised up (9:31; 10:33–34). In each instance this teaching produces the occasion for dialogue between Jesus and his disciples. The direct speech is persistently concerned with a system of understanding that the disciples must correlate with their activities. They must understand the significance of what they do in order to be able to respond appropriately in widely different situations and to prepare for the public reaction that will result from their activities.

For the disciples, Jesus' approach in 8:27—10:45 represents a transition, for the disciples not only learn how to do many of the things Jesus does but they also learn the meaning of those activities.[23] Up to 8:26 the Twelve learn how to preach, cast out demons, anoint with oil, and heal (6:12–13). Moreover, they participate in the feeding of multitudes of people with meager supplies (6:34–44; 8:1–10). Beginning with 8:27, Jesus begins to require that they understand that the activities in which both he and they have been involved have a particular significance within the realm of both human and divine thought and action. The time has come for the disciples to learn that the mode of thought and action in which Jesus and they have been involved brings suffering, rejection, and death. Prior to this section the disciples have learned how to perform tasks for which they received specific directions, and they have adopted certain practices as a result of their association with Jesus. Learning an adult role, however, requires the person to acquire the conceptual framework that enables him or her to respond appropriately to a range of situations which arise in the midst of the performance of the role and to understand the overall significance of the role. This aspect of learning is a matter of integrating cognition with performance.[24] Such integration occurs only through a long process of action and interchange, attempt and evaluation.

To achieve the goal of understanding, Jesus begins specific evaluation of the disciples' activities in their conversations together. Prior to this section, Jesus does not evaluate the activities in which the disciples engage with others. At the outset of their association, Jesus defends their activities concerning fasting and plucking grain on the Sabbath (2:18–28). Later on, the narrator is noncommittal concerning Jesus' response to the Twelve when they return from their initial mission (6:30). Jesus assaults the disciples for not understanding the significance of the feedings of the four thousand and the five thousand in which they have participated (8:14–21). But only in 8:27—10:45 does Jesus evaluate their independent decisions and correct their points of view. He challenges their understanding of who is the greatest (9:33–37), reprimands them for hindering an exorcist who does not follow them (9:38–41), corrects their attempt to prevent little children from coming to him (10:13–16), and criticizes their desire to have positions of power at his right and left hands (10:35–45). Jesus thus inaugurates a new phase in his relationship to his disciple-companions. He engages in a direct attempt to take them beyond simple imitation of him to a system of understanding that guides thought and action toward the saving of oneself through the willingness to lose oneself.

Throughout this section people refer to Jesus regularly as "teacher." The father of the epileptic boy (9:17), the disciple John (9:38), an unnamed person (10:17, 20), and James and John the sons of Zebedee (10:35) address Jesus as teacher, as they direct their requests to him. Moreover, the author uses the verb *didaskō* (to teach) in the narrational framework to indicate the nature of Jesus' action.[25] In other words, even though the section features Jesus' attempt to establish his identity as the suffering, dying, and rising Son of man, he is persistently identified by his sociocultural role as teacher, and he performs the basic functions of that teaching role in an exemplary manner.

A remarkable aspect of Mark 8:27—10:45 is the manner in which Jesus maintains his public teaching even as he concentrates on a special program of instruction for his disciple-companions. At the beginning of the section, Jesus begins a program of instruction with his disciple-companions concerning his identity (8:27–33). In the next scene, Jesus summons the crowd along with his disciples to transfer the implications of his identity to any who wish to achieve the status of a follower (8:34—9:1). Throughout the section, teaching and interaction with potential followers are interspersed between scenes in which Jesus converses with his disciples (9:14–29, 10:1–12, 17–22). Even the special teaching about Jesus' identity as the rejected, dying, and rising Son of man is communicated to potential followers, as well as to his specially selected followers.

The fourth stage of the teaching/learning process occurs in 10:46—12:44. During this stage the disciples are obedient and respectful, and they accompany Jesus into the city of Jerusalem where they do not wish him to go. The tension exhibited in the relationship during the prior stage disappears while Jesus goes into a public setting to discuss general issues of concern—taxation, divorce, resurrection, the authority of John the Baptist and himself, and the relationship of the Messiah to the Son of

David. During this stage the disciples appear to have a better understanding of Jesus' system of thought and action than they did before.

One of the most noticeable characteristics of this section is the questions of chief priests, scribes, elders, Pharisees, Herodians, and Sadducees. Four times Jesus is confronted with questions which require an interpretative answer:

1. "By what authority are you doing these things, or who gave you this authority to do them?" (11:28);
2. "Is it lawful to pay taxes to Caesar, or not? Should we pay them, or should we not?" (12:14–15);
3. "In the resurrection whose wife will she be? For the seven had her as wife" (12:23);
4. "Which commandment is the first of all?" (12:28).

In turn, Jesus' questions are accompanied either by a scriptural quotation or command:

1. "Is it not written, 'My house shall be called a house of prayer for all nations'? But you have made it a den of robbers" (11:17);
2. "Was the baptism of John from heaven or from men? Answer me" (11:30);
3. "What will the owner of the vineyard do? He will come and destroy the tenants, and give the vineyard to others. Have you not read this scripture:
   'The very stone which the builders rejected
   has become the head of the corner;
   this was the Lord's doing,
   and it is marvelous in our eyes'?" (12:9–11);
4. "Why put me to the test? Bring me a coin, and let me look at it" (12:15);
5. "Whose likeness and inscription is this?" . . . "Render to Caesar the things that are Caesar's, and to God the things that are God's" (12:16–17);
6. "Is not this why you are wrong, that you know neither the scriptures nor the power of God? . . . And as for the dead being raised, have you not read in the book of Moses, in the passage about the bush, how God said to him, 'I am the God of Abraham, and the God of Isaac, and the God of Jacob'? He is not the God of the dead, but of the living; you are quite wrong" (12:24–27);
7. "How can the scribes say that the Christ is the Son of David? David himself, inspired by the Holy Spirit, declared,
   'The Lord said to my Lord,
   Sit at my right hand,
   till I put thy enemies under thy feet.'
   David himself calls him Lord; so how is he his son?" (12:35–37).

The authoritative approach characterized by Jesus' commands and references to Scripture persists to the end of the section where Jesus commands the people to beware of the scribes and then issues a summons to his disciples:

> And in his teaching he said, "Beware of the scribes, who like to go about in long robes, and to have salutations in the market places and the best seats in the synagogues and the places of honor at feasts, who devour widows' houses and for a pretense make long prayers. They will receive the greater condemnation" (12:38–40);

> And he called his disciples to him, and said to them, "Truly, I say to you, this poor widow has put in more than all those who are contributing to the treasury. For they all contributed out of their abundance; but she out of her poverty has put in everything she had, her whole living" (12:43–44).

While 8:27—10:45 portrays Jesus teaching the disciples that they must anticipate his suffering, rejection, and death in Jerusalem, in 10:46—12:44 Jesus takes his disciples into the public arena where the system of understanding that he has taught is explicitly enacted. For the disciples, this is a shift from anticipatory learning to actual performance of activities in the setting they have been taught to anticipate. Since the actual performance of activities in an unfamiliar or unwanted context is the most effective means of changing one's attitudes,[26] the disciples are now involved in the stage of learning that can most successfully nurture their independent manifestation of a value system that they have been reluctant to accept. Having learned how to perform duties that Jesus gives them, they procure the colt for Jesus' entrance into Jerusalem with no errors or complaints (11:1–7). Beyond this, they are taught that having faith in God is the means by which mighty works are performed (11:20–25). But a significant change has taken place. Both Jesus and the disciples are in Jerusalem, and the disciples have been told that rejection and death will emerge out of this activity. Having been introduced conceptually to rejection and death in Jerusalem, the disciples are now participating in the events. The disciples accompany Jesus as he curses the fig tree and disrupts the market in the Temple (11:12–25), and they hear the chief priests, scribes, and elders question Jesus' authority (11:27–33). They observe Jesus' response to the Temple hierarchy with the parable of the vineyard and the scriptural quotation, and they see his response to the Pharisees and Herodians (12:13–17), the Sadducees (12:18–27), and a scribe (12:28–34). Finally, they hear Jesus' challenge to the scribes' understanding of messiahship (12:35–37) and the scribes' pompous public activities (12:38–40). In the Temple itself, Jesus teaches the disciples that giving of one's whole livelihood is the greatest offering to God (12:41–44). The disciples participate in the events that they have been reluctant to accept and have found difficult to understand. This participation provides the best hope for their final acceptance of the task of perpetuating Jesus' thought and action after he is absent from them.

Again in 10:46—12:44 Jesus is regularly perceived as a teacher and addressed in the manner appropriate for this social identity. All kinds of people gather in the Temple area to ask Jesus about basic religio-ethical issues. Chief priests, scribes, elders, Pharisees, Herodians, and Sadducees come to Jesus with questions to test his point of view and to trap him in illegal or inaccurate teaching. These people constitute the entire set of established people who oppose Jesus' system of thought and action. Jesus responds to their questions with counter questions, commands, and scriptural quotations. Pharisees and Herodians (12:13), Sadducees, (12:19), and a scribe (12:32) refer to him as teacher, and the narrator again emphasizes Jesus' teaching role in his comments (12:35, 38).

The final stage of the teaching/learning process leaves the impression that Jesus' disciple-companions have benefited from the interaction by which they were introduced to the teacher's system of thought and action. After the basic introduction to the system, the stage of confusion, and the stage of intense conversation, the disciple-companions and the teacher enter into a stage where they are relaxed with one another. However, Jesus is still intensely engaged with representative groups in the cultural setting.

THE MERGER OF JEWISH AND GRECO-ROMAN PATTERNS AND FORMS IN THE TEACHING/LEARNING PHASE IN MARK

The Gospel of Mark has been influenced both by stages of interaction characteristic of Israelite/Jewish tradition and by stages of interaction characteristic of the teaching/learning process in Greco-Roman culture. One of the major characteristics of the Greco-Roman teaching/learning process is the lack of a dramatic test of the student at the end of the teaching/learning sequence. Rather, the sequence ends with the suggestion that the encounter has been informative and beneficial, but not complete. In contrast, Jewish tradition introduces an expectation of obedience that carries a warning of punishment if there is disobedience. Mark intermingles Jewish thought patterns with Greco-Roman thought patterns in a manner that does not exhibit the decisive tests and punishments portrayed in biblical literature. To be sure, this gospel contains warnings against a failure to heed the words of Jesus (e.g., 8:38; 13:33–37; cf. 3:29), and in one setting the conventional punishments associated with Gehenna are invoked (9:43–48). But descriptions of judgment and punishment for disobedience are minimal in the Gospel of Mark. Test and punishment are projected until the end, but the system of thought and action contains ambiguities, complexities, and paradoxes that require that the test be applied by assessing a person's fulfillment of a role *throughout* his or her adult life. In the domain of obedience and disobedience, testing and punishing, therefore, the system of thought and action in the Gospel of Mark is more like the religio-ethical system of Xenophon's *Memorabilia* than the covenant system that informs the stories of Abraham, Moses, Elijah, and Elisha. For this reason, the issue, first and foremost, is not obedience or disobedience, but whether a person is able to comprehend a system of thought and action that deviates from established systems, a system that grounds its appeal in the portrayal of an authoritative person- age who appears to have the rhetorical advantage in every interchange, yet is killed by established authorities for his thought and action.

The Gospel of Mark represents a biographical account produced in a cultural setting that took Jewish prophetic traditions into an intellectual environment engaged in the dynamics of Greco-Roman paideia. For this reason, the Gospel of Mark virtually eliminates interaction between God and Jesus and between God and the followers of Jesus in order to focus on the interaction between Jesus and his disciple-companions. Sole con- centration on Jesus' interaction with his disciple-companions and other people produces an unusual dimension within Jewish literature. Usually such interaction is between God and a prophet, an angel and a prophet, or a prophet and a king or a nation of people. The influence from Greco- Roman traditions about wandering preacher-teachers who gathered disci- ple-companions created an intellectual milieu that gave birth to a Chris- tian document written in Greek. The document was dominated by the cycle of relationships that emerges around a teacher who gathers disciple- companions; communicates and manifests his system of thought and action in their presence; and accepts arrest, trial, and death because he presents an alternative system of thought and action in a cultural setting dominated by an established legal system with political power.

Unfortunately, both sides of the debate about the success or failure of the disciples in Mark have operated, either consciously or unconsciously, with a presupposition that Jewish intellectual heritage establishes the guidelines for understanding the role of the disciples in Mark.[27] The well- known interpretation that the disciples in Mark are depicted in a failure to understand because they represent the opponents of the author of the gospel presupposes that the accountability sequence based on covenant ideology dominates the Markan narrative. The Jewish sequence of inter- action would require punishment and exclusion of the disciple-compan- ions of Jesus for trangressing the stipulations of the accountability system that Jesus has introduced to them. Instead, this gospel is influenced by Greco-Roman cultural dynamics between teacher and disciple where the disciple is never completely able to fathom the system of thought and action taught and manifested by the teacher. This mode of thought and interaction had been nurtured for four centuries within the cultural sphere of Greek and then Greco-Roman heritage in settings where philosophical and religio-philosophical groups, movements, and individuals perpetuated dynamics related to the tradition of Socrates. By the first century of the Common Era, these dynamics had infiltrated virtually every sector of popular Hellenistic culture. The Gospel of Mark reveals the manner in which certain Christian groups participated in those dynamics without perpetuating specific tenets of Socratic or Platonic philosophy.

NOTES

1. G. Ryle, *The Concept of Mind*, 59, 41.
2. H. I. Marrou, *A History of Education in Antiquity*, 102–216.
3. V. K. Robbins, "Mark I.14–20," 225–26.
4. G. von Rad, "The Form-Critical Problem of the Hexateuch."
5. J. A. Wilcoxen, "The Making of Israel."
6. W. A. Meeks, *The Prophet-King*, 125–29.
7. For a discussion of paideia in the writings of Philo, see B. L. Mack, "IMITATIO MOSIS"; W. H. Wagner, "Philo and Paideia."
8. See Meeks, *Prophet-King*, 121, for this translation based on Colson (LCL) vol. II, 473.
9. Ibid., 103.
10. Ibid., 110.
11. Ibid., 132.
12. The issue, of course, is whether *tou theou* is subjective or objective genitive. Even though W. Marxsen (*Mark the Evangelist*, 133) and K.-G. Reploh (*Markus—Lehrer der Gemeinde*, 21–22) disagree with nuances of each other's meaning, they appear to presuppose that it is subjective genitive, i.e., that Jesus is preaching God's gospel about himself rather than his gospel about God.
13. F. Hahn, *The Titles of Jesus in Christology*, 379; R. H. Fuller, *The Foundations of New Testament Christology*, 171.
14. See Fuller, *Foundations*, 125–29; Hahn, *Titles of Jesus*, 365–72.
15. Despite the many parallels between the Elijah/Elisha material and the Gospel of Mark (as discussed, e.g., in R. E. Brown, "Jesus and Elisha"), the stages of teaching and learning which constitute such an important part of this gospel do not appear in the Elijah/Elisha material.
16. Initial comparative work between the gospels and Plato's dialogues is to be found in D. L. Barr, "Toward a Definition of the Gospel Genre." For important work on Philostratus's *Life of Apollonius of Tyana* see G. Petzke, *Die Traditionen über Apollonius von Tyana und das Neue Testament*; D. Esser, "Formgeschichtliche Studien zur hellenistischen und zur frühchristlichen Literatur

unter besonderer Berucksichtigung der Vita Apollonii des Philostrat und der Evangelien."

17. See the comments in F. M. Cornford, *Plato's Theaetetus*, 58–59. See also P. Friedländer, *Plato*, 3:145–89.

18. For an interpretation of the dramatic features of the *Meno* that produce the stages, see J. Eckstein, *The Platonic Method*. For additional commentary on the *Meno*, see Friedländer, *Plato*, 2:273–90.

19. There are three questions in the section that do not provide a setting for teaching: Mark 4:40; 5:9, 30.

20. T. J. Weeden (*Mark—Traditions in Conflict*, 26–51) distinguishes between lack of perception prior to Mark 8:27–33 and misunderstanding after it.

21. Ryle (*Concept of Mind*, 25–61) distinguishes these two types of learning as learning *how* and learning *that*. See T. R. Sarbin and V. L. Allen, "Role Theory," 546–47.

22. On this passage, see R. C. Tannehill, *The Sword of His Mouth*, 147–52.

23. See Sarbin and Allen, "Role Theory," 546–47.

24. Ibid.

25. Mark 8:31; 9:31; 10:1.

26. Sarbin and Allen, "Role Theory," 554–55; " . . . changes in attitudes are contingent upon changes in role enactment . . . the change in role enactment is antecedent to the change in attitude."

27. See a major exception by J. Z. Smith, "Good News is No News."

6

The Final Phase of the Teacher/Disciple Relation: Farewell and Death in Mark 13:1—16:8

Few of us live beyond our three score and ten years and yet in that brief time most of us create and live a unique biography and weave ourselves into the fabric of human history.[1]

The final phase of the teacher/disciple cycle in the Gospel of Mark contains two stages. The first stage, 13:1–37, portrays Jesus giving a lengthy discourse about the future to the four disciples whom he called at the beginning of the teacher/disciple cycle (1:16–20: Peter, Andrew, James, and John). The second stage, 14:1—15:47, features Jesus accepting arrest, trial, and death.

In both stages of the final phase, biblical and Jewish patterns again intermingle with Greco-Roman patterns of understanding. In the first stage, 13:1–37, material in the tradition of farewell discourses and apocalyptic visions in Israelite and Jewish literature is placed in the framework of the Greco-Roman tradition of the Temple dialogue. The result is a pastiche of conventional forms in which the prophet-teacher prepares his disciple-companions for independent perpetuation of the system of thought and action which he has introduced to them during their relationship as teacher and disciple-companion.

During the second stage, 14:1—15:47, the title "king" suddenly emerges as a designation for Jesus (15:2, 9, 12, 18, 26, 32). With the emergence of the title, the tradition of the suffering king intermingles with the portrayal of the rejected prophet-teacher who gathers disciple-companions. This feature in the portrayal of Jesus gains special prominence, since it occurs in the final phase where both logical and qualitative progressions reach their goals in the narrative. The previous assertions that "The Son of man . . . [will] come in the glory of his Father with the holy angels" (8:38; cf. 13:24–27) culminate in Jesus' statement during the trial before the Sanhedrin that they "will see the Son of man seated at the right hand of Power, and coming with the clouds of heaven" (14:62). Also,

Jesus' assertions that "The Son of man must suffer many things, and be rejected by the elders, and the chief priests and the scribes, and be killed, and after three days rise again" (8:31; 9:9, 12, 31; 10:32–34) are fulfilled in the final stage of the narrative and the conclusion (14:1—16:8). The emergence of the title "king" in this setting represents a new step in the portrayal of Jesus, the messianic prophet-teacher. Our analysis of the final stage of the teacher/disciple cycle will seek to understand this progression on the basis of antecedent and contemporary influences in Mediterranean culture.

THE FINAL PHASE IN MARK AND
XENOPHON'S *MEMORABILIA*

After the four stages of the teaching/learning phase both in the Gospel of Mark and in Xenophon's *Memorabilia* 4, the final phase of the teacher/ disciple cycle begins. In both documents, the phase contains two stages: (a) preparation for separation from the teacher, and (b) the teacher's acceptance of death.

The first stage of the final phase in Xenophon's *Memorabilia* 4 and the Gospel of Mark features the teacher preparing his disciple-companions for his absence from them. *Memorabilia* 4.7.1–10 recounts the admonitions and directions Socrates offers to his disciple-companions to encourage them in the wise pursuit of independent skills. In the midst of the section, Socrates warns his disciple-companions to watch themselves lest they lose sight of the system of thought and action which he has transmitted to them. Naturally, the warnings emphasize prudence and self-control:

> Everyone should watch himself throughout his life, and notice what sort of meat and drink and what form of exercise suit his constitution, and how he should regulate them in order to enjoy good health. For by such attention to yourselves you can discover better than any doctor what suits your constitution (*Memorabilia* 4.7.9).

This section has a function in *Memorabilia* 4 similar to the function of Mark 13:1–37 in the gospel. In Mark, Jesus' warnings have an eschatological focus:

> "Take heed, watch; for you do not know when the time will come. . . . And what I say to you I say to all: Watch" (13:33, 37).

Preparation for independence from the teacher brings exhortation to remember the mandates laid upon them by the system of thought and action transmitted to them during their time with the teacher. Before the teacher goes to his death, he talks with them about the situation they will face when he is no longer with them.

After the preparation of the disciple-companions for their absence from the teacher, both *Memorabilia* 4 and the Gospel of Mark portray the teacher accepting a sentence of death, a death he thinks the deity requires, through a legal process involving the established court system. In *Memorabilia* 4.8.1–11, Xenophon discusses Socrates and his death, then recounts discussions that Socrates had with his companions during his imprisonment. This section leads to the conclusion of the document where the author summarizes the importance of Socrates' life and death. His unjust death will be remembered, and the recitation of the account of his death will assure that people in the future know the beneficial influence he had upon the people around him (4.8.9–10). The function of the final section in *Memorabilia* 4 is similar to the function of Mark 14:1— 15:47 in the gospel. During this stage, Jesus accepts death according to the will of God (14:36). His disciple-companions are present with him during the final evening of his life, and they try, without success, to remain with him until his death (14:12–72). In the end, women who see him die are told that he has risen and will go before his disciples to Galilee (16:6–7). This conclusion verifies Jesus' promises to the disciples on earlier occasions in the document (8:31; 9:31; 10:32–34; 14:28). As the account of Jesus' adult life ends, Jesus' actions and the events that happen to him are shown to be consistent in every way with the things Jesus taught. Just as Socrates' words and deeds were thoroughly unified, so Jesus' words and deeds as recounted in Mark stand as a testimony to the integrity of the disciple-gathering teacher who will return as Son of man.

As was noted in the preceding chapters, while the rhetorical progression from one phase to another in the teacher's relation to his disciple-companions is similar in *Memorabilia* 4 and the Gospel of Mark, the medium of the portrayal is significantly different. The differences result from the imbalance of influence in the biblical and Greek traditions of Mark's gospel. The gospel exhibits an intermingling of the Greek pattern of the disciple-gathering teacher and the biblical pattern of the prophet. The patterns are intermingled, however, in a literary medium that bears marks of direct literary influence from biblical and Jewish literature. It is necessary once again, therefore, to probe both Jewish and Greco-Roman literature to describe the intermingling of conventional patterns and forms in the Gospel of Mark.

MARK 13 AND CONVENTIONAL PREPARATION FOR FUTURE ACTION IN BIBLICAL AND JEWISH LITERATURE

While comparative research on the activities of Jesus—other than miracles—has been unsystematic, comparative research on the accounts of

Jesus' death is at a fairly advanced stage. As a result, this section of our investigation can depend heavily upon recent analyses that shed light on the intermingling of Jewish and Greco-Roman traditions in the final phase of the account of Jesus' adult life in the Gospel of Mark. Mark 13:1–37, the well-researched chapter that presents Jesus' speech about the future to the four disciples he called in Mark 1:16–20, intermingles dimensions of farewell speeches, apocalypses, and Temple dialogues. The manner in which Mark 13 intermingles the three forms of tradition provides a clue for understanding the role of both Jewish and Greco-Roman influences upon its formulation.

One of the most well developed traditions in the Hebrew Bible and Jewish literature is the *Abschiedsrede,* the "farewell," or "departure," speech. In biblical literature, a farewell speech is present for Jacob (Gen. 47:29—49:33), Moses (Deut. 31:1—34:38), Joshua (Josh. 23:1—24:30), Samuel (1 Sam. 12:1–25), and David (1 Kings 2:1–9; 1 Chron. 28–29).[2] In the Apocrypha, farewell speeches are found for Tobit (Tobit 14:3–11) and Mattathias (1 Macc. 2:49–70).[3] Outside the Hebrew Bible and the Apocrypha, departure speeches are present in Jubilees, the Testament of the Twelve Patriarchs, the Testaments of Isaac and Abraham, the Life of Adam and Eve, the Biblical Antiquities of Pseudo-Philo, the Assumption of Moses, 4 Ezra, 2 Baruch, and slavonic Enoch.[4]

Research on the farewell, or departure, speeches reveals that in these speeches of biblical and Jewish literature there are thirteen potential components:

1. reference to being old and near death either within the narration or the direct speech of the leader;
2. summoning of one individual, a select group, or all the people of Israel;
3. admonitions, in the setting of the rehearsal of the past actions of Yahweh, to accept the covenant promises as their own inheritance and to keep the laws which have been given to them as requirements for receiving benefits of the covenant;
4. a prophetic account of the near future and/or the end of time;
5. self-exoneration of the dying person;
6. appointment of a successor;
7. blessing;
8. prayer;
9. specific mandates;
10. directions for burial;
11. promise and oath;
12. final departure activities (i.e., kissing, embracing, weeping, eating, etc.);

13. the end of the person's life on earth.[5]

A reference to the advancing age of the speaker (1), the summoning of one or more people to hear the speech (2), admonitions to accept the covenant promises and keep the laws (3), and reference to the end of the speaker's life (13) are constant features in farewell discourses. A prophetic account of the near future and the end of time (4), self-exoneration of the dying person (5), a blessing (7), directions for burial (10), and final farewell activities (12) are highly frequent. The appointment of a successor (6), prayer (8), and specific mandates (9) are less frequent. In only a few speeches is there recitation of a specific promise and oath (11).[6]

Mark 13:1–37 is dominated by a prophetic account of the near future and the end of time (4). Within this setting, there are admonitions and warnings (3) based on the system of thought and action that constitutes the gospel. The major promise is presented in an assertion that "he who endures to the end will be saved," that is, "gathered together" by the Son of man (13:13, 27). The major responsibility is to avoid being led astray by false messiahs and false prophets (13:5–6, 21–22). In the midst of the speech, a specific mandate (9) is placed upon these four men to inaugurate the activity by which the gospel will be preached to all nations (13:10). Summoning (2) of the four disciples to hear the speech has been replaced by inquiry from the disciples about the near future and the end of time. All items concerning the speaker himself (1, 5, 10, 13) are absent from Mark 13, and final departure activities, for example, eating together (12), are reserved for Mark 14—16. Appointment of the four disciple-companions as successors (6) is implicit in Mark 13:9–13. In contrast to biblical and Jewish farewell speeches, Mark 13 contains no reference to past events. All of the events referred to and implied (i.e., Jesus' arrest, trial, beating, and death: 13:9–11) are events in the future of the speech.

In the traditional farewell speech in biblical and Jewish traditions the leader has already completed the tasks necessary before his death. The farewell speech is therefore a death speech. In contrast, in Mark 13 Jesus does not rehearse his past activities. He tells the disciples that they will encounter the same kind of thing that he will encounter in the final section of the narrative. The speech prepares the disciple-companions for a mission that includes arrest, court trials, beatings, and widespread hatred prior to the acceptance of these ignominies by the teacher himself.

Mark 8:27—10:45 confronted the disciples with assertions about Jesus' death in Jerusalem. In that setting, the teaching concerning the disciple-companions' future was couched in terms of "whoever wants to follow" or "whoever wants to be first." In 13:5–37, the statements about the future are formulated directly to the first four disciples whom Jesus called.

Statements containing second-person plural verbs or pronouns addressing the four disciple-companions establish the basic dynamics of the speech. The four disciple-companions are warned about self-proclaimed leaders who will attempt to lead people astray during the time of the Jewish-Roman wars. They are told that they themselves will be brought to trial and beaten. But they have been told all things beforehand and are to watch carefully for the signs of the end. Most of all, they are not to be led astray by people who misconstrue the time of wars as the end of time.

Within the setting of direct address to the four disciple-companions, a series of statements is made about people outside the circle of primary discipleship:

1. "Many will come in my name, saying, "I am he!" and they will lead many astray" (13:6);
2. And brother will deliver up brother to death, and the father his child, and children will rise against parents and have them put to death (13:12);
3. False Christs and false prophets will arise and show signs and wonders, to lead astray, if possible, the elect (13:22);
4. And then they will see the Son of man coming in clouds with great power and glory. And then he will send out the angels, and gather his elect from the four winds, from the ends of the earth to the ends of heaven (13:26).

While Jesus warns the four disciple-companions to beware of false leaders, he does not predict that any of those to whom he speaks will be led astray. Jesus does predict, however, that many other people will be led astray (13:6). In the midst of the speech, a dictum is introduced in the form of earlier discipleship statements: "He who endures to the end will be saved" (13:13). Only one "woe-statement" is introduced: "Alas for those who are with child and for those who give suck in those days" (13:17). In the midst of the speech stands one necessity statement. "And the gospel must first be preached to all nations" (13:10). Beyond the circle of the four disciple-companions, Jesus speaks directly about "the elect" who will escape the catastrophe of the end time. The elect are those who live according to the system of thought and action introduced in Mark's gospel.

The dominance of future events including the passing away of heaven and earth (13:31) in Mark 13 calls for comparison not only with farewell speeches but with apocalypses. Since Mark 13 often is called the "Little Apocalypse" or the "Markan apocalypse," it may be startling to suggest that this chapter is only marginally related to the apocalypse form. Yet recent analysis has revealed that Mark 13 lacks essential features of the apocalypse genre. On the basis of extensive analysis of Jewish, Christian, Gnostic, Greco-Roman, Rabbinic, and Persian apocalypses, the common core of constant elements leads to this definition of the genre:

"Apocalypse" is a genre of revelatory literature with a narrative framework, in which a revelation is mediated by an otherworldly being to a human recipient, disclosing a transcendent reality which is both temporal, insofar as it envisages eschatological salvation, and spatial insofar as it involves another, supernatural world.[7]

This definition points to six constant components in apocalypses:
1. a narrative framework describing the manner of revelation;
2. an otherworldly mediator and a human recipient;
3. both an eschatological salvation which is temporally future, and present otherworldly realities;
4. some form of personal afterlife;
5. activity of otherworldly, angelic, or demonic beings;
6. the existence of another world beyond.[8]

Mark 13 contains an introductory narrative framework introducing brief dialogue followed by a discourse (1), human recipients (2), an eschatological salvation that is temporally future (3), some form of personal afterlife (4), activity of otherworldly beings (5), and the existence of another world beyond (6). Mark 13 is a marginal apocalypse, however, since the narrative framework does not introduce an otherworldly mediator (2) and the speech does not include an experience of present otherworldly realities (3). When Jesus enters into dialogue as he exits from the Temple (13:1–2) and delivers a discourse as he sits on the Mount of Olives opposite the Temple (13:3–37), he functions as a prophetic teacher or oracle-giver rather than as an otherworldly being.[9]

The apocalyptic contents that occur in Mark 13 are the contents common to the eschatological farewell speech. The near future (13:5–13), events leading up to the end (13:14–23), and the final events (13:24–27) are told to successors in a framework of admonition (13:5, 9, 23, 28–37). Contents compatible with the apocalypse and the eschatological farewell speech are placed in a specific setting. In this setting an itinerant teacher delivers a farewell address to his inner circle of disciple-companions in order to prepare them for the independent continuation of the itinerant activity in which he himself has been engaged. In this setting the incredible difficulty of leading a life committed to the system of thought and action receives central attention. The Jewish covenant system containing blessings and curses is replaced by a system of paideia that focuses upon the benefits that come from remaining steadfast to the system taught and manifested by the teacher. In other words, Mark 13 combines a marginal farewell speech with a marginal apocalypse, since the beginning of the chapter (13:1–4) contains neither a reference to the approaching death of

Jesus nor the introduction of an otherworldly mediator to articulate the speech.

THE TEMPLE DIALOGUE
IN GRECO-ROMAN LITERATURE

The opening verses of Mark 13 (vv. 1–4) intermingle the tradition of the *Tempeldialog*, or *Kirchendialog*, in Greco-Roman tradition[10] with features of the conventional farewell speech and the apocalypse. The customary summons of Jesus to his disciples takes place inside the Temple (12:43) prior to the *peripatos* (stroll with the teacher) in which a disciple raises a question about the Temple.[11] The question leads into a speech by Jesus that is designed to instruct the listeners in appropriate understanding in regard to the sanctuary, which provides the setting for the dialogue. The dialogue begins with questions by the disciple-companions and leads to a speech by Jesus that relates the destruction of the Temple to the future activity of the disciples. There is little interest in exploring the destruction or judgment of people who do not follow the insights of the system of thought and action introduced by Jesus. Rather, the speech teaches the listeners about the nature of their future action vis-à-vis this sanctuary which has been the center of Jewish piety and expectation for many years.

The earliest known example of a temple speech or dialogue in Greco-Roman tradition is the *De re rustica* (On Farming) of Varro (first century B.C.E.).[12] As a means of instructing his wife, Fundania, so that she will be able to farm the estate she bought "not only during his life but after his death as well" (1.1.2), Varro employs the literary device of a recollected temple conversation. Entering the temple of Tellus at the time of the Festival of the Sementivae (Festival of Sowing), he meets people who engage with him in conversation (1.2.1). After an introductory question and response, they sit down together and a question by Agrasius initiates the dialogue (1.3.1).

During the first and second centuries C.E., the temple dialogue became a widespread literary form. One was written by Cebes of Thebes (first century C.E.),[13] two were written by Plutarch (late first or early second century),[14] one was written by Florus (ca. 122 C.E.),[15] and one was written by Numenius (late second century C.E.).[16] The literary framework of Mark 13 (vv. 1–4) places the chapter in the domain of this literary phenomenon in Greco-Roman culture. When Jesus sits down opposite the Temple on the Mount of Olives (13:3), the author presents the counterpart to his sitting down opposite the treasury while he was in the Temple (12:41). In the earlier setting Jesus asserted that the poor widow had cast into the treasury her whole living (*holon ton bion autēs*). In the speech while he is sitting opposite the Temple itself, Jesus describes the arrests, trials, beatings, and hatred that accompany a commitment to the task of preaching the gospel to all nations (13:9–13). Immediately after the Temple speech, the author has enframed the story of the woman who anointed Jesus before burial (14:3–9) with references to the betrayal, arrest, and death of Jesus which was brought about by the convergent actions of Judas Iscariot, the chief priests, and the scribes (14:1–2, 10–11).

The literary device of the temple dialogue links the giving of one's livelihood to the temple with the giving of one's life for the gospel. Giving to the temple treasury is replaced by preaching the gospel to all nations. The willingness of Jesus to accept arrest, trial, and death through the conspiracy of one of his disciples, the chief priests, and the scribes is the means by which the replacement is made. During the Temple speech itself Jesus talks about the future time in which he will be absent from his disciple-companions. During this time they have the responsibility of continuing with the work he began in Mark 1:14–20.

In summary, conventions from Jewish and Greco-Roman farewell speeches, apocalypses, and Temple dialogues intermingle in Mark 13, creating an excellent transition from the teaching/learning phase to the account of Jesus' arrest, trial, and death. As a farewell speech, or testament, the opening imperative statement in 13:5 is thoroughly at home: "Take heed that no one leads you astray." As a speech designed to prepare disciple-companions for perpetuation of the prophet-teacher's system of thought and action, conventional curses and blessings are replaced with a charge to "preach the gospel to all nations" (13:10) and an explanation of the hardships that will arise as they undertake the charge (13:9–13). As a result of the function of the speech, only one "woe-statement" occurs (13:17), and this refers to a woman who happens to be pregnant or suckling a child, not to someone who has transgressed any of the stipulations of the system of thought and action that constitutes the gospel.

In Mark 13, knowledge of a transcendent realm containing heavenly beings (characteristic of the apocalypse) and *paraenesis* (characteristic of the farewell speech) are placed in the setting of the Temple dialogue. In other words, features from these three literary forms intermingle in an overall narrative setting appropriate for introducing the final stage of the teacher/disciple cycle. In this context, suffering and rejection carry no connotation of sinfulness. Suffering is changed from a negative association with sinfulness to a positive achievement in preaching the gospel to all nations. The merging of Jewish concepts with Greco-Roman concepts and traditions provides an opportunity to advance from the system of blessings and curses in the covenant system toward a system of thought and action that accepts suffering and rejection as a natural part of fulfilling the "new" system, which is called gospel.

THE ARREST, TRIAL, AND DEATH
THAT SEPARATES THE TEACHER
FROM HIS DISCIPLE/COMPANIONS

The second stage of the final phase, 14:1—15:47, moves dramatically through the events of Jesus' arrest, trial, crucifixion, and burial. In this section, the portrayal of the disciples reaches a conclusion as the disciples are implicated in betrayal (14:10–11, 17–21, 41–45), unable to remain alert (14:32–41), caught in denial (14:27–31, 54, 66–72), and set into flight (14:50–52). Also in this section, the portrayal of Jesus reaches a conclusion as Jesus resolutely accepts arrest, trial, and death. From the perspective of the teacher/disciple cycle, the events represent the stage in which the disciple-companions are separated from their teacher after the drama of the initial summons, the teaching and learning, and the speech preparing them for the time when they are expected to "preach the gospel to all nations" without the aid of the teacher.

In the section in which Jesus and his disciple-companions become separated from one another, an extended logical progression in the narrative reaches its conclusion. Logical progressions, as we recall, occur as the result of specific clues given to the reader concerning events that will happen in the future. In the Gospel of Mark, God (through biblical quotations), the narrator, and Jesus make assertions and give explanations that point to future events. The kind of logic in Mark's logical progressions derives from the conventional logic of assertion and fulfillment in biblical and Jewish literature. As in the introduction to Mark, so in the section that portrays the arrest, trial, and death of Jesus, assertions in the initial span of narrative direct the reader toward future events that are logical fulfillments of the previous assertions. There are two assertions by Jesus near the beginning of the final section that set the stage for assertion and fulfillment in the final section. First, Jesus tells those with him in the house of Simon the leper at Bethany, "For you always have the poor with you, and whenever you will, you can do good to them; but you will not always have me" (14:7). This statement is a reiteration of a statement already made by Jesus in chapter 2: "The days will come, when the bridegroom is taken away from them" (2:20). A general expectation for a time of Jesus' absence was established early in the narrative, and an assertion that renews the expectation occurs on the lips of Jesus at the beginning of the final section. Second, the reliability of Jesus' assertions is reconfirmed when Jesus tells two of his disciples that a man carrying a jar of water will meet them when they go into Jerusalem to prepare the Passover meal, and they find it "as he told them" (14:13–16).

The two statements by Jesus function in a setting that is given more specific direction by the narrator in Mark 14:1, 10–11. The narrator tells the reader that the chief priests and scribes were seeking a means to kill Jesus, and Judas entered into an agreement and began to seek an opportunity to hand Jesus over to them. The narrator has carefully prepared the reader for this event from the second verse of the document through a chain of statements made by himself, Jesus, and characters other than Jesus. The arrest, trial, death, and burial of Jesus is a logical fulfillment of the Baptist's arrest, death, and burial as God's preparation of the way for the mightier One, Jesus. The narrator builds this progression out of specific assertions that are fulfilled by specific events later in the narrative. The specificity of assertion and fulfillment in the narrative creates a logic that makes the narrative function for the reader like a rhetorical syllogism. The syllogism works as follows: (a) God sent the Baptist to prepare the way for Jesus (1:2); (b) the Baptist was arrested, killed, and buried (1:14; 6:17, 27, 29); (c) therefore, Jesus will be arrested, killed, and buried. The essential steps in the logical progression are presented in the following sequence:

1. Introduction

As is written in Isaiah the prophet [i.e., God said to the Messiah through Isaiah],
"Behold, I send my messenger before thy face,
who shall prepare thy way" (Mark 1:2).

John the baptizer appeared . . . saying, "After me comes he who is mightier than I" (1:4, 7).

2. Summons and Response

John was arrested, Jesus came into Galilee (1:14).

The Pharisees went out, and immediately held counsel with the Herodians against him [Jesus], how to destroy him (3:6).

3. Teaching and Learning

And he appointed twelve . . . and [including] Judas Iscariot, who betrayed him (3:14, 19).

For Herod had sent and seized John, and bound him in prison (6:17, 27).

When the disciples [of John the Baptist] heard of it [his death], they came and took his body, and laid it in a tomb (6:29).

And he began to teach them that the Son of man must suffer many things, and be rejected by the elders and the chief priests and the scribes, and be killed, and after three days rise again (8:31; developed in Mark 9:9, 12–13, 31).

[Jesus said,] "Behold, we are going up to Jerusalem; and the Son of man will be delivered to the chief priests and the scribes, and they will condemn him to death, and deliver him to the Gentiles; and they will mock him, and spit upon him, and scourge him, and kill him; and after three days he will rise: (10:33–34; developed in 10:45).

[The chief priests and scribes and elders] tried to arrest him, but feared the multitude; . . . so they left him and went away. And they sent to him some of the Pharisees and some of the Herodians, to entrap him in his talk (12:12–13).

Within the section of the narrative that presents the farewell speech and the separation of Jesus from his disciples, the sequence continues and culminates in specific events that are logical fulfillments of the chain of previous assertions:

4. Farewell and Death

The chief priests and the scribes were seeking how to arrest him by stealth, and kill him (14:1).

Jesus said, . . . "You will not always have me . . . she has anointed my body beforehand for the burying" (14:7–8).

Judas Iscariot, who was one of the twelve, went to the chief priests in order to betray him to them. . . . they . . . promised to give him money. And he sought an opportunity to betray him (14:10–11).

Jesus said, "Truly, I say to you, one of you will betray me, one who is eating with me. . . . It is one of the twelve, one who is dipping bread into the dish with me" (14:18, 20).

[Jesus said,] "It is enough; the hour has come; the Son of man is betrayed into the hands of sinners." . . . Judas came, one of the twelve, and with him a crowd with swords and clubs, from the chief priests and the scribes and the elders. . . . And they laid hands on him and seized him (14:41, 43, 46).

They led Jesus to the high priest; and all the chief priests and the elders and the scribes were assembled (14:53).

[The chief priests, scribes, and elders] condemned him as deserving death. And some began to spit on him, and to cover his face, and to strike him, saying to him, "Prophesy!" And the guards received him with blows (14:64–65).

As soon as it was morning the chief priests, with the elders and scribes, and the whole council held a consultation; and they bound Jesus and led him away and delivered him to Pilate (15:1).

The soldiers led him away . . . and they clothed him in a purple cloak, and plaiting a crown of thorns they put it on him. And they began to salute him, . . . struck his head with a reed, and spat upon him, and they knelt down in homage to him. And when they had mocked him, they stripped him of the purple cloak, and put his own clothes on him. And they led him out to crucify him (15:16–20).

They crucified him . . . And those who passed by derided him. . . . So also the chief priests mocked him to one another with the scribes. . . . Those who were crucified with him also reviled him" (15:24, 29, 31–32).

And Jesus uttered a loud cry, and breathed his last (15:37).

[Joseph of Arimathea] laid him in a tomb . . . and he rolled a stone against the door of the tomb (15:46).

5. Conclusion

[The young man at the tomb said,] "He has risen, he is not here" (16:6).

The care with which this extended logical progression is executed in the Gospel of Mark dispels previous theories that this gospel is not a unified literary document.[17] The sequence provides a logical unfolding of events from the beginning to the end of the document.

In the setting of the logical progression that unifies the gospel, attributes of Jesus and his disciples unfold in qualitative progressions which the reader is less prepared to anticipate but is prepared to accept when they occur. During the final stage, the portrayal of the disciples reaches a dramatic conclusion that represents a qualitative progression from the initial stage of the teacher/disciple cycle. During the earlier stages of the cycle, the disciples responded to Jesus' commands and adopted features of his activity as Jesus initiated new action in each section. With the third stage in the teaching/learning phase (Mark 8:27—10:45), the disciples began to initiate activity on their own and Jesus forthrightly evaluated the action and speech they initiated (8:32–33; 9:38–41; 10:13–16, 35–40). In the final stage of the teacher/disciple cycle, Judas, one of the twelve disciples, takes the initiative to assist the chief priests and scribes in their plot to kill Jesus (14:10–11). His initiative is no surprise to the reader, since Judas was identified early in the narrative as the person who would deliver Jesus over (3:19). When Judas takes the initiative, Jesus evaluates his action severely:

"Woe to that man by whom the Son of man is betrayed! It would have been better for that man if he had not been born" (14:31).

Judas's action results from his own initiative, and he is the object of a woe-statement from Jesus as a result.[18] In contrast to Judas's initiative on his own accord, the remaining disciples fall away in accord with an assertion by God in Scripture:

Jesus said to them, "You will all fall away; for it is written 'I will strike the shepherd, and the sheep will be scattered' " (14:27).

Concerning Peter specifically, Jesus says:

"Truly, I say to you, this very night, before the cock crows twice, you will deny me three times" (14:30).

When the remaining disciples, including Peter, fall away, they portray a quality of character for which the reader is prepared by their previous obtuseness and resistance, but which the reader could have hoped would not emerge. The disciples, however, are controlled by an assertion of God which Jesus recites to them. Once Jesus makes the statement, the action of falling away occurs as he asserts it: (a) they all forsook him and fled (14:50); (b) Peter denied him three times (14:68–72).

While the activity of the disciples other than Judas is influenced during the final stage by God's assertions through Scripture, the assertions, predictions, promises, instructions, and explanations of Jesus to the disciples during the teacher/disciple cycle will guide their activity from the time of their separation from Jesus until they see the Son of man in the glory of the Father. In fact, it would appear that even God's assertions are known to the disciples only through Jesus.[19] The system of thought and action taught to them by Jesus places them under a charge to save their lives by losing them for Jesus and the gospel. When the disciples fall away, they must call this system of thought and action to remembrance. Peter begins this process when, finding himself in a situation where he denies any association with Jesus, he himself remembers Jesus' prediction of his denial, judges his own action as unacceptable and weeps (14:71–72). From the perspective of the teacher/disciple cycle, Peter has reached a point of consciousness of his own activity whereby he brings the words and deeds of Jesus to remembrance, judges his activity according to the system of thought and action taught to him, and responds with the appropriate emotions. No longer is it necessary, or possible, to report action and speech to Jesus for evaluation (as the disciples did in 6:30; 9:38–41). Rather it is necessary for the disciples to remember the words and deeds of Jesus that will guide and evaluate their action and speech until the Son of man comes.

During the final stage, the qualitative progression in the portrayal of Jesus also reaches its goal. As we recall, the progression began with the assertion in the first verse of the narrative that Jesus is the Messiah, Son of God. During the final stage of the teacher/disciple cycle, Jesus himself affirms that he is the Messiah, Son of the Blessed, and that people will see the Son of man seated at the right hand of Power and coming on the clouds of heaven (14:62). Then, after Jesus breathes his last, a centurion declares that Jesus was truly the (or a) Son of God (15:39). For this progression, the reader has been fully prepared by the use of the titles Messiah, Son of God, and Son of man through the narrative.[20] Also, twice in the section Jesus' role as teacher, well known from the previous narrative, is reiterated (14:14, 49). A significantly new dimension arises in the portrayal of Jesus, however, when Jesus accepts Pilate's designation of him as King of the Jews (15:2), Pilate presents Jesus to the crowd as King of the Jews (15:9, 12), the soldiers use the title King of the Jews when they mock Jesus (15:18), the inscription on the cross contains the title King of the Jews (15:26), and the chief priests and scribes refer to Jesus as Messiah, King of Israel as he hangs on the cross (15:32).[21]

The title "King of the Jews" emerges with notable contrast to the titles Messiah, Son of God, and Son of man, since the term *basileus* (king) has been applied only to King Herod, who was responsible for the death of John the Baptist (Mark 6:14, 22, 25, 26, 27), and to leaders before whom the disciples will stand in the future (13:9). It is even more notable that the term emerges from the lips of non-Jews, namely, Pilate and the soldiers under his charge. When chief priests and scribes join in the comments as Jesus is hanging on the cross, they adapt the title to Messiah, King of Israel (15:32). In the qualitative progression of the narrative, therefore, the last stage of the teacher/disciple cycle features a declaration that Jesus dies as King.

BIBLICAL AND JEWISH TRADITION
OF THE SUFFERING RIGHTEOUS ONE,
THE TEACHER, AND THE KING

The presence of the title "King" on the lips of non-Jews involved in the death of Jesus raises the issue of the intermingling of Jewish and Greco-Roman traditions in the final section of Mark. According to a recent study by George W. E. Nickelsburg, the tradition of the suffering righteous one became a common genre in biblical and Jewish literature in the Joseph narratives in Genesis 37—50; the story of Ahikar; the book of Esther; Daniel 3 and 6; Susanna; Wisdom of Solomon 2—5; 3 Maccabees; and 2 Maccabees 7. All the stories contain a common theme: "the rescue and vindication of a persecuted innocent person or persons." Wisdom of Solomon 2—5 and 2 Maccabees 7 have been particularly influenced by the last servant song in Second Isaiah (Isa. 52:13—53:12).[22] According to Nickelsburg, this genre is constituted by twenty-one components of which fifteen are clearly manifested in the Gospel of Mark: introduction (chaps. 1—10); provocation (11:15–17; 14:3–9); conspiracy (11:18; 12:12–13; 14:1–2, 10–11); trial and accusation (14:53–64; 15:1–15); rescue and exaltation (14:62); reactions (14:63; 15:5); assistance (15:9–14); condemnation (14:64; 15:15); investiture (15:16–20); ordeal (15:29–32, 36); prayer (15:34); vindication (15:38); and acclamation (15:18, 26, 39). Two more components—decision and obedience—may be manifested in Mark 14:62. Only four components of the genre—trust, protest, reactions to the vindication, and punishment of the prosecutors—are not manifested in Mark.[23]

The components of this genre, as Nickelsburg suggests, have been integrated into the overall structure of the narrative so that the messiahship of Jesus is construed "in terms of willing death at the hands of those whose existence and authority was bound up with the temple, and he cast the shape of discipleship in a similar mold."[24] The major question for our study is: through what influences was the author of the Gospel of Mark able to integrate Jesus' role as a teacher who gathered disciple-companions with his role as a suffering, dying king?

The strongest traditions within Judaism for the teacher who accepts rejection, and if necessary death, lie in the domain of the rejected prophet.[25] One of the most extensive efforts to demonstrate that the coherence of the mighty works, the powerful teaching, and the acceptance of rejection and death in the Gospel of Mark arose directly from prophetic-apocalyptic circles within Judaism is to be found in the work of Howard C. Kee.[26] Observing that "Mark's favorite designation for Jesus is teacher," he argues that "Jesus is a charismatic prophet whose words and works are self-authenticating."[27] While Jesus' mighty works recall the prophetic figures of Moses and Elijah (Mark 6:31; 8:28; 9:4, 11), the Teacher of Righteousness at Qumran represents the closest parallel. In Kee's words:

> While the content of the teaching of Jesus as Mark presents it is radically different from that of the Qumran prophet, the intent is the same: to interpret past and present trials in preparation for the future of the community of the elect to whom these mysteries have been vouchsafed (Mark 4:11).[28]

There should be no denial that prophetic-apocalyptic circles within Judaism provided central content, concepts, and dynamics for the creation of the Gospel of Mark. Jesus' preparation of the community for future vindication and his authentication of himself through mighty works reveal direct influence from prophetic-apocalyptic traditions nurtured within first-century Judaism.[29] The role of the teacher to prepare the community for future vindication, the mighty works to validate Jesus' authority, and the title "Son of man" to link the authoritative earthly ministry of Jesus with the authoritative action within the heavenly realm reveal direct influence from prophetic-apocalyptic traditions nurtured within first-century Judaism.

Strong traditions concerning kingship also emerge from biblical and Jewish traditions. A recent study by Frank J. Matera suggests that the concept of kingship in the Gospel of Mark provides a unified presentation of Jesus as a royal Messiah.[30] Special reflection on Psalm 118 in the Markan community, as well as influence from Psalm 2, provides a royal background for God's statements at the baptism (1:11) and the transfiguration (9:7). It also provides background for Jesus' discussion with the disciples after the transfiguration (9:11–13); his recital of the parable of the vineyard to the chief priests, the scribes, and the elders (12:1–12); and his teaching about the Messiah as Son of David in the Temple (12:35–37).[31] Therefore, there should also be no denial that concepts of kingship in biblical and Jewish traditions played an important role in the portrayal of Jesus' authority and power as Messiah. To a marked degree the attribution of the Psalms to David during the first century created a royal framework of understanding that nurtured a kingly understanding of Jesus' messiahship within early Christianity.[32]

Yet the author of Mark wrote in a Hellenized environment where it was necessary to explain Aramaic words[33] and the eating rituals of the Pharisees.[34] His readers are outside the ambiance of central Jewish heritage. In this setting the author perpetuates biblical and Jewish traditions through structures, modes, and cycles that are deeply embedded within popular Greco-Roman culture.[35] The cultural milieu in which the author lives places a high value on poignant, proverbial teaching that exposes the evils and pretenses of established teachers in the culture. Moreover, the intellectual environment in this setting presupposes a coherent unity among the wise teacher, the suffering king, and the Son of God. The interpreter must seek the intellectual environment in eastern Mediterranean culture that converged with Jewish prophetic-apocalyptic traditions as the author of Mark integrated Jesus' activity as an itinerant, prophetic, disciple-gathering teacher with his activity as a suffering, dying king.

GRECO-ROMAN TRADITION
OF THE SUFFERING TEACHER-KING

In Sam K. Williams's recent search for the background and origin of the concept of death as a saving event, he found that the well-established Greek and Hellenistic tradition of death as a benefit to others provided a crucial cultural influence for the portrayal of death in 4 Maccabees and in early Christianity.[36] In turn, Sherman Johnson has shown that the conceptual unity of the Gospel of Mark derives from "a coalescence of Jewish and pagan elements" similar to the status of traditions in 4 Maccabees.[37] Our survey of biblical, Jewish, and Greco-Roman literature suggests that not enough attention has been given to the shift from the term "Messiah" to the term "king" in the Markan passion narrative. The term "king" and the concept of kingship have a well-developed tradition in Greco-Roman literature and culture as well as biblical and Jewish traditions. In Greco-Roman circles, the term and concept go back to Homer and Plato, and extensive discussion of kingship occurred especially after the exploits of Alexander the Great. As in other sections in Mark, patterns and concepts known to Greek and Roman authors outside of Jewish and Christian circles intermingle with explicit influences from biblical and Jewish literature and traditions.

In the Markan passion narrative, after Jesus admits, under interrogation among Jews, to be the Messiah Son of God, people outside Jewish circles of thought refer to Jesus as the King of the Jews. The portrayal of the crucifixion as resulting from the conviction that Jesus was a messianic pretender is likely to stand at the beginning of Christian tradition.[38] The early tradition in 1 Cor. 15:3–5 about Jesus' crucifixion, death, and resurrection features the title "Messiah" and presupposes that messiahship was integrally linked with Jesus' death on the cross. Undoubtedly, the concept of a crucified Messiah was a highly offensive thought, and much has been made of this in modern interpretation.[39] From the perspective of a socio-rhetorical interpretation, it is important to discover streams of tradition in the Mediterranean world that made it plausible for early Christians to persist with an emphasis on the crucifixion of their Messiah. Analysis of Greco-Roman literature suggests that streams of tradition in Mediterranean culture outside of Jewish and Christian circles provided an excellent milieu for integrating the portrayal of Jesus as a wise disciple-gathering teacher with his portrayal as a suffering, dying king.

The association of the title "King of the Jews" with the crucifixion of Jesus during the last half of the first century appears to have been supported by the tradition of the suffering, dying king in Greek and Roman tradition. In Greco-Roman tradition, the concept of dying as a benefit for one's people was a well-established tradition by the first century B.C.E., as exhibited by the well-known verse of Horace (65–68 B.C.E.), *"dulce et decorum est pro patria mori"* ("sweet and fitting it is to die for one's fatherland").[40] Moreover, the tradition of a king's voluntary sacrifice exists in the "example of Codrus, the legendary last king of Athens, who on the basis of an oracle went out to meet the enemy alone in slave's clothing; unrecognized, he was killed by them and in so doing saved Athens."[41] Direct evidence for the interest of Christians in the tradition of kings dying for their subjects is known from Clement of Rome:

"Many kings and rulers, when a time of pestilence has set in, have followed the counsel of oracles, and given themselves up to death, that they might rescue their subjects through their own blood" (*1 Clement* 55:1–5).[42]

Dio Chrysostom (ca. 40–after 112 C.E.) wrote four discourses on kingship which should be explored more fully in relation to gospel traditions.[43] Dio emphasizes the willingness of the true king to endure hardship (3.2) and to serve others (4.66). Moreover, the true king, who is a shepherd of peoples (*Dio* 3.41; 4.43; cf. Mark 6:34; 14:27), considers himself to be doing his duty only when he helps people: "having been appointed to this work by the greatest god, whom it is not right for him to disobey in aught nor yet to feel aggrieved, believing, as he does, that these tasks are his duty" (*Dio* 3.55). The king depends upon the loyalty (*pistis*) of his friends, whom he needs as co-workers (*Dio* 3.86), and his greatest sufferings arise when he is wronged by friends whom he did not know to be his enemies (*Dio* 3.114).

As Dio discusses the nature of true kingship, he relates activities of the Persians at the Sacian feast that parallel closely the soldiers' mocking of Jesus in Mark 15:16–20. According to Dio, the Persians:

take one of their prisoners . . . who has been condemned to death, set him upon the king's throne, give him the royal apparel, and permit him to give orders, to drink and to carouse, and to dally with the royal concubines during these days, and no one prevents his doing anything he pleases. But after that they strip (*apodusantes*) and scourge (*mastigōsantes*) him and then hang him (*ekremasan*) (*Dio* 4.67).

If the prisoner understands the meaning of the action, he is likely "to break out into wailing and refuses to go along without protesting" (*Dio* 4.69) in order to show that the true meaning of kingship involves suffering and service.[44] The lesson to be learned, therefore, is: "Do not attempt to be king before attending to wisdom" (*Dio* 4.70).

The integration of Jesus' teaching with his death as a suffering, obedient king is highly understandable in first-century Mediterranean culture influenced by these traditions. The relationship of the model king to the man of wisdom is explored with great interest in Mediterranean culture through a portrayal of an encounter between Alexander the Great with Diogenes the Cynic. The necessity of wisdom for true kingship is explored in *Dio Chrysostom* 4, where Alexander, who possesses power and might (*exousia kai dunamis: Dio* 4.2) consults with Diogenes who possesses great wisdom (*phronēsis*). Alexander learns that if a king is a son of Zeus (*Dios pais/huios*: 4.21), he knows the attributes of true kingship. The king will know the foolishness of attempting to gain (*kerdainein*) money and possessions (*Dio* 4.6; cf. Mark 8:36) and to clamor after wealth (*ploutos: Dio* 4.10; cf. Mark 4:19; 10:25; 12:41). The model king possesses truth and frankness (*alētheia kai parrēsia: Dio* 4.15; cf. Mark 8:32). The instruction in kingship is of two kinds: the divine (*hē theia/daimonios*) and the human (*hē anthrōpinē: Dio* 4.29; cf. Mark 8:33). These two ways are distinguished by the possession of virtues or vices. Virtues and vices are not something outside (*exōthen*) the person but the actions that result from each man's intelligence (*ho idios nous*), which is his guiding spirit (*Dio* 4.79; cf. Mark 7:20–23). The king who has received divine instruction as a son of Zeus at once recognizes and knows the road (*hē hodos: Dio* 4.33; cf. Mark 1:2–3; 8:27; 9:33–34; 10:17, 32, 52; 12:14). The divine instruction leads a person on a road that is great (*megalē: Dio* 4.29) and strong (*ischuros:* cf. Mark 1:7; 3:27), while the human instruction leads to seduction (*apatē: Dio* 4.29) by wealth and other desires, weakness (*asthenes*), and cowardice (*deilos*).

An awareness of the presence of these traditions in first-century Mediterranean culture allows the interpreter to understand the patterns of unity presupposed by the author of the Gospel of Mark. For him, the role of a suffering, wise teacher was an essential part of the role of an authentic Messiah-King. Especially, his integration of traditions in Mark 15 shows the intermingling of Jewish and Christian traditions with Greco-Roman patterns of understanding. The high priest's understanding of Jesus as Messiah, Son of the Blessed (14:61–62), is directly juxtaposed with Pilate and the soldiers' understanding of Jesus as King of the Jews (15:2, 9, 12, 18). As the title "king" emerges from the lips of non-Jewish people, the concept of kingship from Greco-Roman circles intermingles with the concept of kingship from Jewish circles. Kingship as manifested in the mockery, abuse, crying out, and death of Jesus is well understood by the general member of Mediterranean society as authentic kingship that does not lord it over others, but serves people, suffering and dying for them as the true shepherd of the people over whom he has domain.

Mark appears to have structured the scenes from Jesus' hearing before Pilate until his death according to the tradition among the Persians as recounted by Dio Chrysostom.

1. "They take one of their prisoners . . . who has been condemned to death" (*Dio* 4.67).

Jesus, who has been condemned to death by the Sanhedrin, is taken by Pilate and his soldiers (Mark 15:15–16).

2. "[They] set him upon the king's throne . . . [and] give him the royal apparel" (*Dio* 4.67).

Jesus is clothed in a purple cloak; a crown of thorns is placed on his head; he is hailed as "King of the Jews"; and they kneel down in homage to him (Mark 15:17–19).

  3. "They strip and scourge him and then hang him" (*Dio* 4.67).

Jesus is stripped (Mark 15:20), and since he has already been scourged (15:15), he is led out to be hung on a cross (15:20).

  4. "[If the prisoner understands the meaning of the action, he] breaks out in wailing and refuses to go along without protesting" (*Dio* 4.69).

Jesus cries out, "My God, my God, why hast thou forsaken me?" (Mark 15:34). This cry, which is an astonishing cry of abandonment on the lips of the Messiah, is an indication to the general member of Mediterranean society that Jesus understands the process as a necessary route to true kingship.

When Jesus cries out with a great cry just prior to his death, the centurion knows that Jesus has manifested the true nature of kingship as a Son of Zeus manifests it. Naturally, however, his language is adapted to the language of the Christian community. Just as the chief priests and scribes adapt the title of Messiah to kingship by calling Jesus "Messiah, King of Israel" (Mark 15:32) instead of "King of the Jews," so the centurion adapts the title "Son of Zeus" to "Son of God."[45]

Again the interpreter discovers patterns in Hellenistic literature outside of Jewish and Christian circles that intermingle with biblical and Jewish traditions in the Gospel of Mark. Explicit influences from biblical and Jewish literature and traditions are obvious from biblical quotations and Jewish titles of honor. Yet patterns of understanding and action at home in first-century Mediterranean literature outside of Jewish and Christian circles intermingle with the patterns, traditions, and titles from biblical and Jewish literature. As a result, the actions of Jesus as a disciple-gathering teacher are integrated with his actions as a suffering, dying king in a manner that provides the possibility for living with the offense of the crucifixion of the Messiah. Jesus, the Messiah, possessed the wisdom and power to live the life of a true king. Through his system of thought and action as a true king, the kingdom of God is near at hand.[46]

THE CONCLUSION OF MARK

After the burial of Jesus, three women who saw where the body was laid went to the tomb on the first day of the week with the purpose of anointing his body (Mark 15:47—16:2). The scene is brief, and the young man at the tomb conveys two major pieces of information to the reader: (a)

Jesus is no longer in the tomb, but has arisen (16:6); (b) The disciples and Peter are to be told that Jesus goes before them to Galilee, because they will see him there, as he told them (16:7). The first item is a fulfillment of Jesus' repetitive assertions during the third stage of the teaching/learning phase that he would rise up after three days (8:31; 9:9, 31; 10:34). The second item is a reiteration of the statement in Mark 14:28 where Jesus expanded the assertion about his resurrection to include his going before the disciples into Galilee.

Extensive debate continues concerning whether these verses refer to a resurrection appearance of Jesus or his appearance when he returns as Son of man, and we cannot pursue the debate here.[47] Indeed, the ambiguity of the statement may derive from an intermingling of Jewish and Greco-Roman patterns of thought. On the one hand, Jesus' resurrection has been preceded by a transfiguration scene in which Jesus talks with Elijah and Moses (9:4). Likewise, Jesus has explained the nature of resurrected persons by referring to the nature of angels in heaven (12:25), citing Scripture from the book of Moses (12:26), and calling attention to the power of God (12:24, 27). These features support a Jewish understanding of Jesus as one who, after death, has been transformed into a heavenly being called the Son of man who will "come in clouds with great power and glory and then will send out the angels and gather his elect from the four winds, from the ends of the earth to the ends of heaven" (13:26–27). On the other hand, the empty tomb story emphasizes well-known phenomena from Greek tradition contemporary with the gospels: the disappearance of the one who has died so that his remains are nowhere to be found,[48] an interpretation by someone that the one who has disappeared has been transformed from a mortal to an immortal being,[49] and an announcement to people that they will see him again.[50] If the Gospel of Mark ended with 16:8, and recent analysis has given renewed support to this possibility,[51] then the ending of Mark leaves the reader on common ground between Jewish and Greco-Roman traditions, with an opportunity to understand the ending in quite Jewish or quite Greco-Roman terms, or a mixture of both.[52]

The participation of the women in the scene brings the narrative to a dramatic close. As a recent study by Thomas E. Boomershine has shown, the women are the first followers of Jesus since the flight of the disciples and Peter's denial.[53] For this reason, the reader watches with interest to see the women's faithful activity in contrast to the disciples' flight and denial. Instead, the women also flee (Mark 16:8), and thus they directly disobey the command of the young man to go and tell the disciples and Peter (16:7) by telling nothing to anyone (16:8). What, then, is the reader to think? As Boomershine has demonstrated so well, while the narrator judges the flight and silence as wrong, he creates strong sympathy on the part of the reader for the women, by explaining that they fled and remained silent because they were afraid to respond to the command to announce the resurrection of Jesus.[54] The women, as the reader knows, have every reason to be afraid of responding to the command. As Jesus clearly told Peter, Andrew, James, and John, those who accept this responsibility will be delivered up to councils, beaten in synagogues, will stand before governors and kings for the sake of Jesus and will be hated by all for the sake of the name of Jesus (13:9–11). Yet "the gospel must first be preached to all nations" (13:10). Someone must accept the responsibility. The portrayal of the women's flight and silence, in trembling, astonishment, and fear, leaves the task to the reader. The disciples are at a disadvantage because they have not been told that Jesus' resurrection has taken place, and the women who know are too afraid to tell them or anyone else. The reader knows that the task will bring hardship, but the reader also knows that "whoever loses his life for my [Jesus'] sake and the gospel's will save it" (8:35). Thus, the narrator provokes the reader to undertake the words and deeds that are the necessary response to this final scene when the disciples have fled without experiencing the real outcome of the story and the women have not told the end of the story because they are afraid.

SUMMARY

In sum, the final phase of the teacher/disciple cycle and the conclusion of Mark portray an end and a beginning. They elaborate the end of the time in which Jesus transmitted his system of thought and action to his disciples and the beginning of the period of absence and anticipation in which the charge of preaching the gospel to all nations must be accepted with the insight that this means saving one's life by losing it. Both stages of the final phase—the farewell and the occurrence of Jesus' death—unfold special attributes of Jesus and the disciples in the midst of an extended logical progression that began with the announcement that a messenger was being sent to prepare the way for the Messiah.

As the narrative unfolds the final attributes in the portrayal of Jesus and his disciple-companions, conventions that accompany farewell discourses, apocalypses, and temple dialogues intermingle in a scene in which Jesus prepares Peter, Andrew, James, and John for his absence from them. Then, the tradition of the suffering king intermingles with the portrayal of Jesus as a rejected prophet-teacher in the final stage of the narrative where Jesus and his disciples become separated from one another. The final phase completes both logical and qualitative progressions as it sets the stage for the period of time in which people face the commands in the narrative through remembrance rather than through the actual presence of Jesus with them.

NOTES

1. E. Kübler-Ross, *On Death and Dying*, 276.
2. H.-J. Michel, *Die Abschiedsrede des Paulus an die Kirche Apg 20, 17–38*, 36–39.
3. Ibid., 39.
4. Ibid., 40–47.
5. Ibid., 48–53.
6. Ibid., 54.
7. J. J. Collins, "Introduction: Towards the Morphology of a Genre," 9.
8. Ibid.
9. A. Y. Collins, "The Early Christian Apocalypses," 97.
10. I am indebted to D. E. Aune for observing the importance of the Greco-Roman *Tempeldialog* for interpreting Mark 13. See his *Prophecy in Early Christianity*, 184–87.
11. Aune, *Prophecy*, 399–400n.93: "By the second century A.D., when Plutarch and Lucian had revived the dialogue as a literary form suitable for ethical, religious and philosophical discussion, the *peripatos* had become, to judge by Plutarch's fourteen surviving dialogues, an essential feature (Plutarch *Amatorius* 771d; *De facie* 937c; *Non posse suav.* 1086d, etc.). In Plutarch's dialogues one frequently finds a seated conversation following a *peripatos* (R. Hirzel, *Der Dialog* [Leipzig: S. Hirzel, 1895] II, 187); thus a *peripatos* can provide the setting for part or all of a Plutarchian dialogue, or it may be regarded as having already occurred prior to the beginning of the seated dialogue. Thus *De def. orac., De E apud Delphos, De Pythia orac.* and *Sept. sap. conv.* all begin with a *peripatos* and conclude with a seated dialogue. *De sera num.* contains a dialogue which occurs during a *peripatos* which lasts throughout the entire composition."
12. See Aune, *Prophecy*, 400n.93; R. Hirzel, *Der Dialog*, 1:558. Hirzel observes (558n. 3) that Plato, *Alcibiades* 2 was "auf dem Wege eine Tempeldialog zu werden."
13. Ibid., 2:254–59.
14. Ibid., 2:197–98: *De def. orac.* and *De E apud Delphos*.
15. Ibid., 2:66.
16. Ibid., 2:358–59.
17. Cf. N. Petersen, *Literary Criticism for New Testament Critics*, 49–80.
18. V. K. Robbins, "Last Meal: Preparation, Betrayal, and Absence (Mark 14:12–25)," 31–34.
19. Contrast Matt. 13:52, where the disciples are depicted as scribes who will, through their own work in the Scriptures, bring out "what is new and what is old."
20. Extensive analyses of these titles in Mark have been undertaken: 1:1, 11; 2:10, 28; 3:11; 5:7; 8:29, 31; 9:9, 12, 31; 10:33, 45; 12:35; 13:26; 14:21, 41. See N. Perrin, "Towards an Interpretation of the Gospel of Mark," 14–50; J. R. Donahue,

Are You the Christ? 139–87; W. H. Kelber, ed., *The Passion in Mark*; D. Juel, *Messiah and Temple*, 77–116.

21. See the analysis of Mark 15 by F. J. Matera in *The Kingship of Jesus*.

22. G. W. E. Nickelsburg, "The Genre and Function of the Markan Passion Narrative," 156.

23. Ibid., 157–67.

24. Ibid., 182.

25. Cf. O. H. Steck, *Israel und das Gewaltsame Geschick der Propheten*.

26. H. C. Kee, *Community of the New Age*.

27. Ibid., 117.

28. Ibid., 118.

29. W. Roth (in "The Biblical Matrix of Literary Structure and Narrative Execution of the Synoptic Gospel") argues that the synoptic gospels derive from a basic biblical genre established by the Elijah/Elisha narrative.

30. Matera, *Kingship of Jesus*, 147–51.

31. Ibid., 67–119.

32. Ibid., 81–82.

33. Mark 3:17; 5:41; 7:11, 34; 15:34. In contrast, the narrator presupposes that the reader will understand the meaning of the Greek cognate of the Latin *legio* in Mark 5:9.

34. Mark 7:3–4; cf. 7:19.

35. See V. K. Robbins's review of H. C. Kee's *Community of the New Age* in *JBL* 98 (1979): 147–49.

36. S. K. Williams, *Jesus' Death as Saving Event*, 137–254.

37. S. Johnson, "Greek and Jewish Heroes," 165.

38. N. A. Dahl, *The Crucified Messiah and Other Essays*, 10–36.

39. Reemphasized recently by M. Hengel in *Crucifixion*; idem., *The Atonement*, 31–32, 44–75.

40. Horace, *Odes* 3.2.13; see Hengel, *Atonement*, 13, 82n. 47. I am grateful to David Seeley, Claremont Graduate School, for discussing this material with me.

41. Hengel, *Atonement*, 14, 82n. 48.

42. Ibid., 14.

43. These discourses were analyzed in relation to Cynic tradition by R. Höistad in *Cynic Hero and Cynic King*.

44. Cf. *Dio Chrysostom* 4.43–44. For a similar tradition of importance, see Philo, *Flacc.* 36–40; cf. J. Gnilka, *Das Evangelium nach Markus (Mk 8, 27–16, 20)*, 308–9.

45. See *Dio Chrysostom* 4.39–45; contra M. Hengel (*The Son of God*, 30n. 57) who argues that "Son of Zeus" is fundamentally distinct from "Son of God."

46. W. H. Kelber, "The Hour of the Son of Man and the Temptation of the Disciples (Mk 14:32–42)," 45–46.

47. R. H. Stein, "A Short Note on Mark xiv. 28 and xvi. 7."

48. Cf. Aristeas of Proconnesus in Herodotus, *Persian Wars* 4.14.3 and Plutarch, *Romulus* 28.4; Cleomedes of Astypaleia in Pausanias, *Descriptions of Greece* 6.9.6–8 and Plutarch, *Romulus* 28.5; and Alcmene in Plutarch, *Romulus*

28.6. See J. E. Alsup, *The Post-Resurrection Appearance Stories of the Gospel Tradition*, 226–28, 235–36.

49. Cf. esp. Pausanias, *Descriptions of Greece* 6.9.8. See C. H. Talbert, "The Concept of Immortals in Mediterranean Antiquity"; idem, *What Is A Gospel?* 25–52.

50. Cf. esp. Philostratus, *Life of Apollonius of Tyana* 7.41; 8.12. See Alsup, *Post-Resurrection Appearance Stories*, 221–24.

51. T. E. Boomershine and G. L. Bartholomew, "The Narrative Technique of Mark 16:8."

52. See Talbert, *What Is a Gospel?* 42: "A Hellenistic reader confronted with this structure would have understood the Gospel [of Mark] in much the same terms as he would have used in interpreting Laertius's *Life of Empedocles*. Here is a *theios anēr* about whom the claim is made that he became an immortal at the end of his career."

53. T. E. Boomershine, "Mark 16:8 and the Apostolic Commission," 231.

54. Ibid., 227–30.

7

Messianic Expectation and Cultural Fulfillment: An Explanation of the Preservation of Mark

I have attempted to move beyond an interpretation of the Gospel of Mark based on its minor forms toward an interpretation based on its overall rhetorical form. During the last sixty years, form has referred to discrete units in the gospels. In this study, the form of the entire Gospel of Mark has been held in view as the minor forms in the document have been investigated. When the interpreter keeps the form of the whole document in view, he or she is challenged to look beyond the confines of biblical and Christian literature for the patterns, conventions, and traditions in first-century Mediterranean culture that explain the interpenetration of form and content in the narrative sweep of the document.

From this perspective, most exegesis of Mark's gospel never really allows the overarching repetitive and progressive forms to control the interpretation. With an eye on minor forms in Mark, most interpreters have allowed the passion narrative to control the interpretation, or they have pitted miracle stories against the passion narrative. Such a procedure has also encouraged interpreters to pit biblical and Jewish conventional forms against Greek and Greco-Roman conventional forms. As a result, one interpreter argues that only biblical and Jewish literature contain precedents for the gospel form, while another argues that *theios anēr* traditions provide the essential structure of the document. These approaches should be revised to reflect our awareness that Christianity resulted from multiple influences during the first century C.E. Thus, the literature produced by its adherents reflects an extensive and often subtle intermingling of traditions and conventions from people who had previously claimed to have distinct political, social, and cultural identities.

My agenda, therefore, moves beyond previous interpretations that imply an essential conflict between minor forms in this gospel. This analysis leads directly to a discussion of the interrelation and conflict of forms—different from previous analyses. I will now explore the interrelation and conflict of repetitive, progressive, and conventional forms in the overall narrative of Mark.

THE RHETORIC OF
REPETITIVE FORMS IN MARK

Through repetition, things in our world become familiar to us. Those familiar things provide a base for us to accept new ideas. The Gospel of Mark acquires repetitive form at the beginning of the narrative as it presents Jesus going to locations where he preaches, teaches, summons, casts out demons, and heals. The basic pattern is established in the introduction when John the Baptist goes into the wilderness preaching, and people, including Jesus, come to him (1:4–5, 9). The activity of Jesus expands the pattern. Jesus comes into Galilee and preaches (1:14–15), then goes to the sea of Galilee and summons four disciples (1:16–20). Then Jesus goes to Capernaum where he teaches and casts an unclean spirit out of a man (1:21–28). Then Jesus goes to a house where he heals Simon's mother-in-law of a fever (1:29–31), and in the evening people bring sick and demonized people to him to be healed (1:32–34). With these episodes, the basic repetitive patterns of the narrative are established. Throughout the rest of the narrative, Jesus continually goes to new places, preaches, teaches, summons, casts out unclean spirits, and heals. In turn, people come to him to engage him in conversation about his teaching, to request healing, and to follow him to new locations.

This repetitive form sustains a familiar pattern of expectation and fulfillment throughout the narrative. This pattern establishes a bond between the narrator and the reader and provides a basic social role for Jesus out of which the narrator may portray the distinctive characteristics of Jesus' activity. The preaching of Jesus (1:34, 38, 39, [45]; 5:20) establishes a basic pattern of activity among himself, John the Baptist (1:4, 7), and his followers (3:14; 6:12; 7:36; 13:10; 14:9). Yet, through repetition, the distinctive quality of Jesus' activity is teaching (1:21–22; 2:12; 4:1–2; 6:2, 6, 34; 8:31; 9:31; 10:1; 11:17; 12:14, 35; 14:49). His activity brings forth the title "Teacher" on the lips of people who either address Jesus (4:38; 9:17, 38; 10:17, 20, 35; 12:14, 19, 32; 13:1) or speak about him (5:35). Once Jesus even refers to himself with the title "Teacher" (14:14). Through repetitive form, Jesus' distinctive role in the narrative is teaching. This role establishes competition with the teaching of the scribes and Pharisees (1:21; 7:7) and provides a distinctive quality for the activity of those whom he sends out as apostles (6:30). The special authority of Jesus' teaching manifests itself in exorcisms (1:21–28, etc.), healings (2:1–12, etc.), and in the repetition of the phrase "Truly, I say to you" at the beginning of many sayings (Mark 3:28; 8:12; 9:1, 41; 10:15, 29; 11:23; 12:43; 13:30; 14:9, 18,

25, 30). The special goal of Jesus' teaching manifests itself in Jesus' gathering of disciple-companions, calling them to follow him (1:20; 2:17), and subsequently summoning the disciples and other people to adopt his system of thought and action (3:13, 23; 6:7; 7:14; 8:1, 34; 9:35; 10:42; 12:43). The presence of these disciple-companions with Jesus, together with their role in relation to Jesus' activity, causes the term "disciple" (*mathētēs*) to occur forty-four times in the narrative. Thus repetitive form establishes the role of the itinerant, wonderworking, disciple-gathering teacher as the base of familiarity between the narrator and the reader.

In the setting of these basic repetitive forms, two special titles acquire rhetorical importance through repetition: Son of man and Son of God. The title "Son of man" appears in relation to Jesus' authoritative teaching (2:10, 28), his suffering, rejection, death, and resurrection (8:31; 9:9, 12, 31; 10:33, 45; 14:21, 41), and his return in the future in the glory of the Father with the holy angels (8:38; 13:26; 14:62). Likewise, the title "Son of God" appears before Jesus' ministry begins (1:1, 7), at strategic places during his ministry (3:11; 5:7; 9:7; [12:6; 13:32]; 14:61) and immediately after his death on the cross (15:39). These minor repetitive forms in the midst of the basic repetitive forms that exhibit Jesus' role as a disciple-gathering teacher give special identity to Jesus as Son of God who will return as Son of man in the future.

THE RHETORIC OF
CONVENTIONAL FORMS IN MARK

While repetitive forms create the familiar, conventional forms presuppose the familiar. As we recall from chapter one, conventional forms exist prior to the reading of the document. Their rhetorical significance arises as expectations from the social, cultural, and literary milieu are either fulfilled or modified. As we recall, when the gospel begins with a quotation attributed to Isaiah (1:2–3) and portrays John the Baptist attired and eating food in a wilderness setting reminiscent of Elijah (1:4, 6), it raises expectations that emerge from conventional forms accompanying biblical prophets. We also recall that as soon as Jesus calls disciple-companions to follow him and begins to teach them his system of thought and action, expectations that emerge from conventional forms accompanying disciple-gathering teachers arise from the reader. The intermingling of these two spheres of conventional forms provides a distinctive social, cultural, and literary quality for the portrayal of Jesus in the Gospel of Mark.

Conventional forms from the biblical sphere of the prophet of the Lord and from the Greco-Roman sphere of the disciple-gathering teacher intermingle so that the autonomy and authority of Yahweh characteristic of biblical literature is transferred to Jesus via the autonomy and authority of the disciple-gathering teacher characteristic of Greco-Roman literature. Instead of Yahweh calling, teaching, summoning, and testing his prophet and his people, Jesus calls, teaches, summons, and sends out his disciple-companions with no specific commands, directions, or instructions from Yahweh. A major characteristic of God's beloved Son is his possession of authority, wisdom, and power in the form in which an autonomous teacher possesses such attributes. As a result, Yahweh functions in the narrative in a manner similar to the function of the god in Xenophon's *Memorabilia*. The wisdom of both Socrates and Jesus and the necessity of accepting death as a result of a verdict by the established representatives of the people have their ultimate source in the will of the deity. Yet no scenes depict the deity giving specific instructions, and no repetitive phrases continually defer the wisdom of Socrates and Jesus to the deity. Rather, in contrast to the biblical prophets, both Socrates and Jesus manifest an autonomy of their own that exhibits itself in the unity between speech and action in their lives.

Another result of the intermingling of the two spheres of conventional forms is the lack of an emphasis on punishment in the cycle of interaction between Jesus and his disciple-companions. In the Jewish cycle of calling, teaching, and learning, the system of thought and action that is taught is the covenant system. Since a system of blessings and curses accompanies the covenant system, the cycle of interaction between Yahweh and his prophet or people ends with a test that results either in a reward for obedience or a punishment for disobedience. In contrast, the Greco-Roman cycle of teaching and learning presupposes that the system is so complex that only one's complete life can produce the evidence to determine the commitment or lack of commitment to the system of thought and action. The system of thought and action transmitted in Mark contains the kind of complexity that requires a stance similar to the one exhibited in Greco-Roman literature featuring disciple-gathering teachers. For this reason, Mark's gospel emphasizes the Son of man's gathering of his elect rather than his punishing of the disobedient as in the Gospel of Matthew (24:51; 25:26–46).[1] Jesus' teaching lacks the repetitive statements about judgment, punishment, and destruction characteristic of the Gospel of Matthew.[2] Only Judas, those who directly cause people to sin, and those who blaspheme against the Holy Spirit are the objects of statements of curse from Jesus (Mark 14:21; 9:42–48; 3:29). Even then, no direct punishment of Judas is narrated, nor are examples of punishment presented in parables or in scenes of interaction between Jesus and other people. Likewise, punishment of Peter and the rest of the disciples who flee is held in suspension until such time as it becomes clear that they manifest a life of commitment or lack of commitment to the system of thought and action that Jesus manifested during his life.

THE RHETORIC OF PROGRESSIVE FORMS IN MARK

While repetitive forms establish the familiar, and conventional forms presuppose the familiar, progressive forms build upon repetitive and conventional forms to produce rhetorical argumentation. In a discursive essay, progressive forms result from direct statements by the narrator that assert one or more theses, demonstrate the theses, and draw conclusions from the theses—using brief stories, if the narrator wishes, to support or elaborate the theses, demonstrations, or conclusions. Since the literary form of Mark's gospel is a narrative rather than a discursive essay, the major theses, demonstrations, and conclusions emerge from the progressive forms that portray Jesus and the disciples. Assertions by the narrator, by God, and by characters in the story introduce theses, demonstrate those theses—either partially or fully—and call for specific conclusions from the reader.

The overall thesis of Mark's gospel is that the gospel of Jesus Christ is the story portrayed in the narrative. This thesis is introduced in the opening verse of the document which claims to be the beginning of the gospel of Jesus Christ (1:1). Within this thesis, two specific theses are presented—one concerning the Messiah and another concerning discipleship. The basic argument concerning the Messiah unfolds in both logical and qualitative progressive forms in Mark. Logical progressive form emerges from God's assertion (through Isaiah) that he is sending a messenger to prepare the way of the Messiah (1:2). When the Baptist arrives and is arrested, killed, and buried (1:14; 6:17, 27–29), the arrest, death, and burial of Jesus (14:1—15:47) emerge as a logical result of the initial assertion. This progression is logical, because it advances through assertions that produce a chain of argumentation that extends the terms in the original assertion. The extension of the terms occurs according to the logic of rhetorical syllogisms in which the action of a personage is a demonstration of something in the initial assertion. The first syllogism proceeds as follows:

1. Assertion: Isaiah says that God is sending a *messenger* to *prepare the way of the Messiah*;
2. Demonstration: John the Baptist comes as a *messenger* who preaches and announces one mightier than he;
3. Conclusion: Therefore, John the Baptist *prepares the way of the Messiah*.

Through the portrayal of John the Baptist as the messenger sent by God, the narrator asks the reader to draw the logical conclusion that John the Baptist prepares the way of the Messiah. Then, the conclusion in the first syllogism is the link in a chain of argumentation as it becomes the assertion at the beginning of a second syllogism. The second syllogism is as follows:

1. Assertion: *John the Baptist* prepares *the way of the Messiah*;
2. Demonstration: *John the Baptist* preaches and is arrested, killed, and buried;
3. Conclusion: Therefore, *the way of the Messiah* will be to preach and to be arrested, killed, and buried.

Through the portrayal of John the Baptist preaching, being arrested, killed, and buried, the narrator asks the reader to draw the conclusion that these activities represent the way of the Messiah. Then, the conclusion in the second syllogism becomes the assertion at the beginning of a third syllogism. The third syllogism is as follows:

1. Assertion: *The way of the Messiah* will be to *preach and to be arrested, killed, and buried*;
2. Demonstration: Jesus *preached and was arrested, killed, and buried*;
3. Conclusion: Therefore, Jesus fulfilled *the way of the Messiah*.

The logic at work in the three syllogisms is essentially the logic of promise and fulfillment so well known in biblical literature. The narrator asks the reader to accept the conclusion that John the Baptist is the messenger promised by Isaiah and that Jesus is the mightier one promised by the Baptist. The logic is grounded in the action and speech of the people involved. That is to say, the logic proceeds in a chain of argumentation that portrays the action and speech of people as a fulfillment of expectations raised by the action and speech of other people. The portrayal of the action and speech of the people is perceived by the author to demonstrate the assertions. By this means, the action and speech of persons in the narrative acquire logical progressive form that presents a chain of argumentation which calls for the conclusion that Jesus fulfilled the way of the Messiah.

The second type of argumentation arises from qualitative progressive forms in the narrative. In contrast to a logical progression that extends the terms of an original assertion, a qualitative progression unfolds attributes of action and speech that appear to be appropriate to the initial assertions of quality. In Mark, qualitative progressive form emerges through the assertion by the Baptist that he who comes after him is mightier than he

(1:7) and the assertion by God that Jesus is his beloved Son in whom he is pleased (1:11). As the attributes of Jesus' action and speech unfold in the narrative, the reader sees a demonstration of the mightier qualities of Jesus (e.g., his miracles, his teaching, and his resurrection). The reader also observes demons, God, Jesus himself, and a centurion assert that Jesus is the Son of God (3:11; 5:7; 9:7; 14:61–62; 15:39). This qualitative progression leads to an extended portrayal of the attributes of Jesus that demonstrates his qualities as mightier than the messenger and worthy of God's beloved Son. This produces a rhetorical progression in which the action and speech of Jesus unfold attributes and qualities appropriate to the initial assertions. The progression proceeds as follows:

1. Assertion: The Messiah is mightier than John the Baptist (1:7) and has the attributes of God's beloved Son (1:11);

2. Demonstration: While John the Baptist preached a baptism of repentance and was arrested, killed, and buried; Jesus preached the Gospel of God (1:14–15); taught with authority [and not as the scribes] (1:22; 11:27–33); forgave sins and enacted lordship over the Sabbath as Son of man (2:1–12, 23–28); performed exorcisms and healings as the Holy One and Son of God (1:24; 3:11; 5:7); acted and taught authoritatively in Jerusalem as Lord and Son of David (10:46—12:44); was rejected, arrested, tried, abused, and killed as Son of man, King of the Jews, and Son of God (8:31; 9:31; 10:32–34; 14:1—15:41); was buried (15:42–47); and arose from death (16:1–8);

3. Conclusion: Therefore, Jesus is the Messiah, Son of God (1:1), who will return as the Son of man in the glory of the Father with the holy angels (8:38; 13:26–27; 14:62).

Logical and qualitative progressive forms in the portrayal of Jesus are closely interrelated in Mark. They dovetail and overlap in such a manner that they produce an integrated rhetorical progression which introduces a complex thesis, demonstrates the thesis, and calls for a conclusion. The integrated progression that merges the chain of argumentation in the logical progression with the unfolding attributes in the qualitative progression is as follows:

1. Assertion: A messenger will prepare the way for the Messiah who is mightier than the messenger and who has the attributes of God's beloved Son;

2. Demonstration: While John the Baptist prepared the way for Jesus by preaching and being arrested, killed, and buried; Jesus was mightier than the Baptist through his preaching of the gospel of God; his teaching with authority (and not as the scribes); his forgiveness of sins and lordship over the Sabbath as Son of man; his

performance of exorcisms and healings as the Holy One of God and
Son of God; his authoritative action and teaching as Son of man,
King of the Jews, and Son of God; his burial; and his resurrection;
3. Conclusion: Therefore, Jesus fulfilled the way of the Messiah, Son of
   God, who will return as the Son of man in the glory of the Father
   with the holy angels.

Logical and qualitative progressive forms merge to present an extended
rhetorical argument that Jesus is the Messiah, Son of God, who will
return as Son of man.

In the midst of the demonstration of the thesis that Jesus is the
Messiah, the Gospel of Mark introduces a second thesis concerning
discipleship. This thesis is demonstrated through a teacher/disciple cycle
that occurs as a result of a sequence of relationships between Jesus and a
group of companions whom he gathers around him. The cycle produces
qualitative progressive form throughout the narrative, but, unlike the
portrayal of Jesus, the portrayal of the disciples does not acquire logical
progressive form that extends through the entire narrative. A number of
minor logical progressions occur. For example, Jesus' assertion, on the
basis of Scripture, that the shepherd will be smitten and the sheep will be
scattered (14:27) has its logical fulfillment in the flight of the disciples
(14:50). Likewise, Jesus' assertion that Peter will deny him three times
(14:30) has its logical fulfillment in Peter's denials in the courtyard outside
the trial before the Sanhedrin (14:66–72). These, however, are not extended logical progressions that unify the entire narrative like the logical
progressions concerning John the Baptist and Jesus. As minor logical
progressions, they raise and fulfill expectations in a limited span of the
text.

The lack of an extended logical progression in the portrayal of the
disciples results in a lack of fulfilled expectation in the qualitative progression concerning discipleship. Qualitative progression unfolds the requirements of discipleship as Jesus instructs the disciples and they respond to
the instruction after Jesus has called them. Since the logic of progressive
form has been established by the portrayal of Jesus, the reader expects a
qualitative progression in which the disciples fulfill the requirements of
discipleship. Such a progression would unfold as follows:
1. Assertion: Jesus makes those who follow him into fishers of men
   (1:17) who deny themselves, take up their crosses, and save their
   lives by losing them for the sake of Jesus and the gospel (8:34–35);
2. Demonstration: The disciples, except Judas who handed Jesus over,
   left their vocations and kinfolk; followed Jesus by preaching repentance, casting out demons, and healing; watched as Jesus was taken

to the cross, killed, and buried; and preached the gospel, after the resurrection, with sufferings and tribulations;
3. Conclusion: Therefore, the disciples, except Judas, fulfilled the expectations of discipleship, denying themselves, taking up their crosses, and saving their lives by losing them for the sake of Jesus and the gospel.

This progression, however, is not what the reader encounters. At first, expectations of fulfillment are raised as the initial promise that the disciples will be made fishers of men appears to be fulfilled. The progression emerges as follows:
1. Assertion: Jesus makes those who follow him into fishers of men (1:17);
2. Demonstration: Twelve disciples follow Jesus throughout Galilee and are sent out to preach. They are given authority to cast out demons and acquire the ability to heal (6:7–13);
3. Conclusion: Therefore, twelve disciples become fishers of men in Galilee.

As the narrative progresses, however, additional stipulations are introduced for following Jesus, and these stipulations are unfulfilled as the narrative ends. The unfulfilled part of discipleship emerges as follows:
1. Assertion: Followers of Jesus deny themselves, take up their crosses, and save their lives by losing them for the sake of Jesus and the gospel (8:34–35);
2. Unfulfilled Demonstration: Judas handed Jesus over, Peter denied Jesus, and the rest of the disciples fled;
3. Conclusion: *If* the disciples, except Judas, deny themselves, take up their crosses, and save their lives by losing them for the sake of Jesus and the gospel, they will be true followers of Jesus.

As a result of the unfulfilled expectations in the qualitative progression in the narrative, the disciples have not completely manifested the attributes of true followers of Jesus. As a result, the activity of the disciples in the future has a rhetorical implication that differs significantly from the activity of Jesus as Son of man in the future. By his action and speech in the narrative, Jesus has already manifested the attributes of the Messiah. Therefore, there is a basis for certainty about Jesus' action in the future. This certainty produces a rhetorical assertion in which the protasis is a direct rationale for the apodosis: *Since* Jesus fulfilled the way of the Messiah while on earth, he will come in the future as the Son of man to gather his elect. In contrast, the disciples have not yet manifested the attributes of true discipleship. In fact, they have shown enough lack of perception to create significant uncertainty concerning their ability to respond satisfactorily. This uncertainty requires that any statement of hope concerning the disciples be constituted in an apodosis qualified by a conditional statement in the protasis: *If* the disciples deny themselves and save their lives by losing them for the sake of Jesus and the gospel, they will fulfill the requirements of following Jesus.

Since an initial promise that the disciples will become fishers of men (1:17) appears to be fulfilled by their mission during the ministry of Jesus (6:12–13, 30), the lack of fulfillment of the requirement to deny oneself, take up one's cross, and save one's life by losing it (8:34–35) creates a conflict between rhetorical forms in the narrative. In other words, the progressive forms in the portrayal of discipleship do not contain the coherence of the interrelated rhetorical forms in the portrayal of Jesus. We recall that all the progressive forms concerning the portrayal of Jesus can be merged into a rhetorical progression that contains no statements of qualification concerning Jesus' fulfillment of the expectations concerning the Messiah. In contrast, the conflict of rhetorical forms in the portrayal of the disciples produces a statement of qualification, introduced by the adversative conjunction "but" in both the demonstration and the conclusion of the rhetorical progression:

1. Assertion: Jesus makes those who follow him into fishers of men (1:17) who deny themselves, take up their crosses, and save their lives by losing them for the sake of Jesus and the gospel (8:34–35);
2. Partially Fulfilled Demonstration: Twelve disciples followed Jesus throughout Galilee and were sent out to preach. They were given authority to cast out demons, and acquired the ability to heal (6:7–13); *but* Judas handed Jesus over, Peter denied Jesus, and the rest of the disciples fled;
3. Conclusion: Twelve disciples became fishers of men in Galilee; *but* only if the eleven disciples save their lives by losing them for the sake of Jesus and the gospel will they be true followers of Jesus.

The conflict of rhetorical forms in the portrayal of the disciples produces a distinctive rhetorical quality for Mark's gospel among literature featuring disciple-gathering teachers. For example, a comparison of the conclusion of Xenophon's *Memorabilia* with the conclusion of Mark reveals differences in the midst of similarities in rhetorical form concerning the portrayal of discipleship. The author, who portrays himself in conversation with Socrates (*Memorabilia* 1.3.8–13), presents his own personal conclusions about Socrates to the reader. In his words:

All who knew what manner of man Socrates was and who seek after virtue continue to this day to miss him beyond all others, as the chief of helpers in the quest of virtue. For myself, I have described him as he was: so religious that he did nothing without counsel from the gods; so just that he did no injury, however small, to any man, but conferred the greatest benefits on all who dealt with him; so self-controlled that he never chose the pleasanter rather than the better course; so wise that he was unerring in his judgment of the better and the worse, and needed no counsellor, but relied on himself for his knowledge of them; masterly in expounding and defining such things; no less masterly in putting others to the test, and convincing them of error and exhorting them to follow virtue and gentleness. To me then he seemed to be all that a truly good and happy man must be. But if there is any doubter, let him set the character of other men beside these things; then let him judge (*Memorabilia* 4.8.11).

In this conclusion, the author presents himself as a true disciple of Socrates. He is thoroughly committed to the system of thought and action manifested by Socrates during his life, and he challenges the opinion of anyone who doubts the wisdom and truth of what he says. In this setting, the conditional rhetorical onus lies on the person who does not believe the thesis demonstrated by the document: "*If* there is any doubter, let him set the character of other men beside these things; then let him judge" (*Memorabilia* 4.8.11).

In contrast, the Gospel of Mark ends with the assertion by a young man at the empty tomb that Jesus has risen and that the women should go and tell his disciples and Peter that he is going before them to Galilee (16:7). When the women flee from the tomb and tell nothing to anyone because they are afraid, none of the followers of Jesus shows the reader that he or she is fully committed to the system of thought and action manifested by Jesus. The young man is a symbol of a person who could accept the charge to preach the gospel to all nations.[3] Yet he only announces the resurrection, and, if he is the same young man who followed for a short time after Jesus' arrest (Mark 14:51–52), he too is one who flees when abuse and potential death confront him.

The differences in the portrayal of discipleship in Xenophon's *Memorabilia* and Mark's gospel do not annul basic similarities in rhetorical form between the two documents. First of all, the action and speech of the disciple-gathering teacher in both documents fulfill the expectations raised by the narrator. Second, the requirements of true discipleship are displayed to the reader by means of progressive forms in the narrative. Third, both documents distinguish between disciples who break the teacher/disciple relationship during the lifetime of the teacher and disciples who attempt to be faithful to the relationship and to fulfill the responsibilities of the system of thought and action transmitted to them.[4]

The existence of similarities in progressive form between Xenophon's *Memorabilia* and Philostratus's *Life of Apollonius of Tyana* creates an almost parallel set of similarities and differences between Philostratus's *Apollonius* and the Gospel of Mark. Philostratus's *Apollonius* unfolds attributes within Apollonius that admirably fulfill the expectations of the reader. The requirements of true discipleship are well displayed and the narrator distinguishes between disciples who break the teacher/disciple relationship during the lifetime of the teacher and those who attempt to be faithful to the relationship and to the system of thought and action.[5] In these ways, all three documents are similar to one another. Then, in similarity with the *Memorabilia*, Philostratus's *Apollonius* exhibits Damis as a true disciple of Apollonius and credits Damis with much of the author's knowledge about Apollonius (1.3, 19; 8.29). In other words, Mark's gospel differs from both Xenophon's *Memorabilia* and Philostratus's *Apollonius* in the portrayal of a lack of fulfillment of true discipleship by anyone in the narrative. In rhetorical terms, the portrayal of discipleship is presented with a concessive qualification that introduces the conjunction "although" rather than a conditional qualification:

> *Although* Critias and Alcibiades were unfaithful disciples of Socrates (*Memorabilia* 1.2.12–28), Criton, Chaerophon, Chaerecrates, Hermogenes, Simmias, Cebes, Phaedondas, and others committed themselves wholeheartedly to discipleship (*Memorabilia* 1.2.48).

> *Although* the number of Apollonius's disciple-companions was reduced from thirty-four to eight when he visited Rome (*Apollonius* 4.37), a number of people including Damis committed themselves wholeheartedly to discipleship.

The lack of fulfillment of true discipleship in these documents pertains only to a certain group of people. Others manifested the attributes of true discipleship to the teacher both during and after his life.

The lack of fulfillment of true discipleship in Mark may contribute to the reasons why the narrative has been called a gospel rather than a life or a memorabilia, and why its form has been considered unique among Mediterranean literature. Certainly the major reason for calling the Gospel of Mark a gospel is the occurrence of the term in the first verse of the document. Moreover, the assertion by the narrator that Jesus preached the gospel of God (Mark 1:14) and the occurrences of the term "gospel" throughout the narrative (1:15; 8:35; 10:29; 13:10; 14:9) made this designation secure. The particular rhetorical form of the portrayal of discipleship, however, may have contributed to the conclusion that Mark was an altogether different type of literature from Xenophon's *Memorabilia* or Philostratus's *Apollonius*. Since no one in Mark's gospel fully adopts the system of thought and action taught and enacted by Jesus, the reader is the object of a special summons to perpetuate the system of thought and action "to all nations for the sake of Jesus and the gospel." No one in the document fully responds to the persuasive manifestation of the system enacted by Jesus. Even though the reader has considerable anxiety about attempting to fulfill the requirements of the system, Jesus, who was sanctioned by God himself, issues a summons again and again throughout the narrative. Since the reader has not vicariously experienced a full response to this summons in the narrative, he or she feels a special necessity to respond. The reader of Xenophon's *Memorabilia* or Philostratus's *Apollonius* has experienced a successful transition from the teacher to the disciple in the narrative and can respond with a calm resolution to remember the teacher and to follow aspects of the system of thought and action that appear to be beneficial. In contrast, the reader of Mark is left with the fear and flight of the women in addition to the fear and flight of the disciples. Possessed by noticeable uncertainty, the reader is asked to respond with greater resolution and sustained commitment than anyone featured in the narrative actually did. Such a rhetorical summons by the narrative itself is likely to have contributed to a conclusion that this document is unique among the literature of its time.

THE PRESERVATION OF THE GOSPEL OF MARK

An understanding of Mark based on the interrelation and conflict of rhetorical forms provides an explanation for the preservation of Mark's gospel within early Christianity. Since 99 percent of the content of Mark is present in either Matthew or Luke, the Gospel of Mark was not preserved because it was a resource for sayings and stories that were unique to it. It is easy to see why the Gospel of Matthew was preserved, since it contains so many quotations from the Old Testament, traditions about the heritage and birth of Jesus, and the Sermon on the Mount containing the Beatitudes and the Lord's Prayer. It is also easy to see why the Gospel of Luke was preserved with its beautiful hymns to Mary and Zechariah, its parables of the good Samaritan and prodigal son, and its dramatic stories about the resurrected Jesus. Why, however, was Mark preserved?

The Gospel of Mark was preserved because it perpetuated an image of Jesus, an understanding of discipleship, and a teaching/learning cycle compatible with ideology in Mediterranean society. Within Mark a system of thought and action that attacked established religious and political leadership was enacted by a suffering teacher-king who refused to play the role of a tyrant. Even when he returns with all authority, his major interest will be to gather together the elect (Mark 13:27), rather than to assure the destruction of people who have transgressed the stipulations of a covenant system (cf. Matthew 25). The preservation of Mark's gospel reveals the significant inroads that itinerant Christians made into the village-town culture of the Mediterranean world. Moreover, it reveals how sociocultural structures, patterns, conventions, and traditions were incorporated into Jewish prophetic-apocalyptic ideology within early Christianity. With Mark, early Christianity possessed a document in which a teacher-king enacted a role that was honored in Greco-Roman society. Jesus' programmatic introduction of an alternative system of thought and action in a cultural setting where the established leaders demanded his execution presented a structure of understanding that had pervaded virtually every sector of Greco-Roman society since the time of Socrates. Within this structure of understanding, Mark presented the gospel of the death, resurrection, and return of its hero in the setting of proverbial wisdom that perpetuated an identity system based on a critique of people who wielded social, religious, and political power.

The ordinary people who are influenced by Jesus' life must not be ignored in Mark. The five disciples whom Jesus calls were all engaged in a job requiring daily toil—four in fishing and one in collecting taxes. Also a blind man who had been forced to live by begging responded (10:45–52). Only the rich man who is called by Jesus refuses to respond (10:17–22). The social implication of this action is the formation of a subcultural elitism by means of an itinerant group that does not have the sanction, or support, of the established sociopolitical leaders. Without the prestige of proper tutelage, or appointment to public office, a band of disciple-companions perform an elite type of service in village-towns throughout the Mediterranean world. The itinerant task of mission includes the skills of preaching, casting out unclean spirits, healing, and serving the needs of people. But this is not simply a trade. The role is perceived as an elite, or "elect," role into which a person can be initiated only through a lengthy association with a teacher.

The proposal that Greco-Roman traditions played a role in the formulation of the Gospel of Mark is based both on literary and on social premises. It is customary for specific social movements to arise in the setting of a general social movement or cultural drift.[6] The specific movements share common ideology and patterns of behavior even when direct influence is not demonstrable.[7] The preservation of the Gospel of Mark was evidently linked with the sympathies of a significant sector of early Christianity toward a general social movement in eastern Mediterranean society that gave special importance to a wandering mode of life, to a poignant wisdom that left opponents speechless, and to a critique of established social and political leadership.[8] In the process of enacting an alternative to the Zealot movement, followers of Jesus related to people in popular society with role enactment which people understood, with forms to which they responded, and with an overall merger of teacher with king that people in Mediterranean society earnestly desired to see.[9]

The acceptance of rejection, suffering, and death as the way to salvation in Mark appears to have been an achievement that sustained the importance of this document for many members of early Christianity. In contrast to the gospels of Matthew and Luke, the Gospel of Mark accepts rejection, suffering, and death from the inside. The members of early Christianity do not presuppose that they will be able to overcome this experience while on earth, nor do they presuppose that those who reject them will be destroyed in an eternal punishment. Rejection, suffering, and death are accepted without the pronouncement of curses upon those who cause the rejection, suffering, and death. The emphasis has shifted to rejection, suffering, and death as necessary experiences through which salvation is achieved. Therefore, Mark does not share the sayings in Matthew and Luke, commonly attributed to the Q-material, that present the rejection of Jesus and the disciples in the prophetic-apocalyptic mode. In this mode the prophet pronounces a curse upon those who reject him and envisions a time when he will sit on a throne as a judge over those who have rejected him.[10] In Mark the disciple-companions will not ever be allowed to rule over others as judges (10:35–45). The suffering teacher-king is truly king over men, but his rule emphasizes service to all people and salvation of the elect (10:45; 13:26–27), rather than judgment of the wicked. The language of blessings and curses has been replaced with language about giving one's life as a means of salvation.

While the Gospel of Mark does not emphasize the prophetic-apocalyptic tradition of the punishment of the wicked, neither does it emphasize the power of God to give life in the manner of the Gospel of John (cf. 20:31). John presents the other side of Jewish ideology in a new form. Instead of emphasizing the rejection of the prophet that brings a curse upcn those who reject him, it emphasizes the mighty acts that demonstrate the triumphant power of God over darkness and death. In Mark, God's power to give life is asserted in a much more subtle manner, a manner that would be more compatible with the ideology concerning life and death that had been nurtured by Socratic tradition.

One of the major reasons interpreters have missed the analogy with democratized Socratic tradition in the Gospel of Mark is the emphasis on Plato's dialogues rather than Xenophon's *Memorabilia* within scholarship.[11] Much as Xenophon's *Memorabilia* has taken second place to Plato's dialogues because it lacked sophistication, coherence, and integration, so the Gospel of Mark has taken second place to Matthew and Luke. Nevertheless, both Xenophon's *Memorabilia* and Mark were preserved. Why? Our thesis is that these documents presented their protagonists in a more folkloric fashion that communicated with less elite circles in the culture. The nature of the documents as more loosely connected traditions about their hero provided greater freedom and ability to perpetuate the stories and discussions in circles of society that did not have the social advantage of formal education. In a similar manner to the way in which Xenophon's *Memorabilia* appealed to people during the first and second centuries who perpetuated the ideals of wandering Cynic-Stoics,[12] so the Gospel of Mark appealed to Christians who perpetuated the ideals of itinerant disciples of the suffering, teacher-Messiah Jesus.

The structuring of experience and validation of the system of thought and action in both Xenophon's *Memorabilia* and Mark attacks the "sophisticated" reasoning of the official perpetrators of wisdom in society. In Mark the desire for integrity has led to the internalization of rejection, suffering, and death. Jesus' authoritative acceptance of rejection, suffering, and death stands as a model for this system of thought and action. This mode of understanding goes beyond the prophetic-apocalyptic tradition by portraying Jesus' acceptance of rejection, suffering, and death on the basis of internalized authority interacting with the external authority of God (14:36). His death is not simply imposed upon him by God. It is internally accepted as a benefit to others through insight into the will of God. Jesus' acceptance of rejection, suffering, and death in the setting of his own authority breaks out of the sphere of Jewish ideology into the sphere of the internal decision to accept death as a benefit to others, as it had thus emerged within nonelitist groups in Greco-Roman society.

The rhetorical form of Mark's gospel reflects a time when both Judaism and Christianity were adapting to a new cultural milieu that was emerging in the Mediterranean world. The Gospel of Mark represents a group of early Christians who were taking Jewish ideals away from established Jewish tradition and participating in the well-established cultural streams of tradition in eastern Mediterranean culture. This move was heightened by the Jewish-Roman wars that led to the destruction of Jerusalem and its Temple. As this group of Christians took Jewish tradition into the new social and cultural sphere, it faced a crisis of identity. The members of this group did not have prestigious social status in major urban centers. Rather, they performed a respected role among people throughout towns and villages in eastern Asia Minor, Syria, and Palestine. In the role of the itinerant teacher-healer, they had a ready-made avenue into the village-town culture. In order to perform this role, however, they had to be able to accept the suffering, persecution, and hatred from established leaders who felt that their positions were threatened. In the midst of their suffering, they perpetuated positive dimensions from both Jewish and Greco-Roman traditions, since they did not consider the regular members of society to be responsible for the suffering (cf. Mark 9:40). To counter the rejection, they understood themselves to be followers of an itinerant teacher who gathered disciple-companions and refused to violate the system of thought and action when he was rejected and killed. Also, they considered themselves to be followers of the Jewish Messiah who would affirm their thought and action in the final days of the age. They found an integrated life as they focused their identity and energy in mission by means of a particular selection of values and patterns of action from both Greco-Roman and Jewish society and culture. For them the promises of God reached their fulfillment in a social and cultural framework of understanding that required suffering and rejection as a way of identity and integrity until the Son of man would come in the glory of the Father with the holy angels (8:34—9:1; 13:9–13, 26).

NOTES

1. Cf. F. J. Matera, *The Kingship of Jesus*, 111–13.
2. E.g., Matt. 7:19; 8:12; 13:42, 50; 22:13; 24:51; 25:30, 41, 46.
3. See R. Scroggs and K. I. Groff, "Baptism in Mark."
4. Cf. Mark 3:16–19; Xenophon, *Memorabilia* 1.2.12–28, 48.
5. Cf. Philostratus, *Life of Apollonius of Tyana* 1.3; 4.12, 25, 37–38, 42; 5.43; 6.3, 12–16, 28, 31; 8.31.
6. See J. Wilson, *Introduction to Social Movements*, 11–13.
7. See, e.g., the interrelation of ideology and behavior patterns presented by J. Freeman in *Politics of Women's Liberation*, 1–70.
8. See. G. Theissen, "Itinerant Radicalism"; idem, *Sociology of Early Palestinian Christianity.*
9. It is especially the popularity of Alexander's discussion with Diogenes within Greek literature that suggests this conclusion. See R. Höistad, *Cynic Hero and Cynic King*, 150–222.
10. See R. A. Edwards, *A Theology of Q*, concerning the prophetic-apocalyptic ideology in that material. Cf. Matt. 11:21–24//Luke 10:13–15; Matt. 19:28//Luke 22:28–30 with Mark 10:42–45.
11. See, e.g., H. D. Betz, *Der Apostel Paulus und die sokratische Tradition.*
12. See A. J. Malherbe, *The Cynic Epistles*, 27, 226–27, 230–31, 252–53, 258–61, 266–69.

Bibliography

I. TEXTS, TRANSLATIONS, AND EDITIONS OF ANCIENT TEXTS

Aristophanes. *The Clouds*. Translated by B. B. Rogers. Vol. 1 of LCL. Cambridge: Harvard University Press; London: William Heinemann, 1924. See also the commentary of Kenneth J. Dover, ed. *Aristophanes: Clouds*. Oxford: Clarendon Press, 1968.

Athenaeus. *The Deipnosophists*. Translated by C. B. Bulick. LCL, 7 vols. Cambridge: Harvard University Press; London: William Heinemann, 1927–51.

The Babylonian Talmud. Edited by I. Epstein. 35 vols. London: Soncino Press, 1935–52 (reprinted in 18 volumes, 1961).

Cicero. *[Cicero] Rhetorica ad Herennium*. Translated by H. Caplan. Vol. 1 of LCL. Cambridge: Harvard University Press; London: William Heinemann, 1954.

Cynics. *The Cynic Epistles: A Study Edition*. Edited by Abraham J. Malherbe. SBLSBS 12. Missoula, Mont.: Scholars Press, 1977.

Dio Chrysostom. Translated by J. W. Cohoon and H. L. Crosby. LCL, 5 vols. Cambridge: Harvard University Press; London: William Heinemann, 1932–51.

Diogenes Laertius. *Lives of Eminent Philosophers*. Translated by R. D. Hicks. LCL, 2 vols. Cambridge: Harvard University Press; London: William Heinemann, 1970.

Eusebius. *Die Demonstratio Evangelica*. Edited by I. A. Heikel. Die griechischen christlichen Schriftsteller 23. Leipzig: J. C. Hinrichs, 1913.

Horace. *Odes*. Translated by C. E. Bennett. LCL. Cambridge: Harvard University Press; London: William Heinemann, 1968.

Isocrates. Translated by LaRue Van Hook. Vol. 3 of LCL. Cambridge: Harvard University Press; London: William Heinemann, 1945.

Josephus. *Against Apion*. Translated by H. St. J. Thackeray. Vol. 1 of LCL. Cambridge: Harvard University Press; London: William Heinemann, 1966.

Josephus. *Jewish Antiquities*. Translated by H. St. J. Thackeray. Vols. 4–10 of LCL. Cambridge: Harvard University Press; London: William Heinemann, 1961.

Justin Martyr. *Iustini philosophi et Martyris Opera*. Edited by Ioann. Theod. Otto. 2d ed. Corpus Apologetarum Christianorum Saeculi Secundi, vols. 1–5. Jena: F. Mauke, 1876–81.

Midrash Tanhuma. Translated by Shlomo Buber. Jerusalem: Orteseo, 1964.

Pausanias. *Descriptions of Greece*. Translated by W. H. S. Jones and H. A. Ormerod. Vol. 3 of LCL. Cambridge: Harvard University Press; London: William Heinemann, 1933.

Philo. Vols. 2 and 3 translated by F. H. Colson and G. H. Whitaker. Vols. 6 and 9 translated by F. H. Colson. LCL. Cambridge: Harvard University Press; London: William Heinemann, 1953, 1959, and 1968.

Philostratus. *The Life of Apollonius of Tyana.* Translated by F. C. Conybeare. LCL, 2 vols. Cambridge: Harvard University Press; London: William Heinemann, 1969.

Plato. Vols. 1 and 7 translated by H. N. Fowler. Vols. 3 and 12 translated by W. R. M. Lamb. LCL. Cambridge: Harvard University Press; London: William Heinemann, 1914, 1921, 1925, and 1927. In addition to LCL, see also Francis Cornford. *Plato's Theaetetus.* New York: Liberal Arts Press, 1959; Paul Friedlander. *Plato.* Bollingen Series 59, 3 vols. New York: Pantheon, 1964.

Plutarch. *Parallel Lives.* Vols. 1 and 6 translated by B. Perrin. LCL. Cambridge: Harvard University Press; London: William Heinemann, 1914, 1919.

Septuagint (LXX). Hanhard, Robert, ed. *Esther.* Septuaginta: Vetus Testamentum Graecum VIII.3. Göttingen: Vandenhoeck & Ruprecht, 1966; Ziegler, Joseph, ed. *Susanna-Daniel-Bel et Draco.* Septuaginta: Vetus Testamentum Graecum XVI.2. Göttingen: Vandenhoeck & Ruprecht, 1954.

Tacitus. *Histories.* Translated by C. H. Moore. Vol. 3 of LCL. Cambridge: Harvard University Press; London: William Heinemann, 1931.

Tatianus. *Oratio ad Graecos.* Edited by Ioann, Theod. Otto. Corpus Christianorum saeculi secundi 6. Wiesbaden: M. Sändig, 1851 (reprint, 1969).

Xenophon. *Memorabilia.* Translated by E. C. Marchant. Vol. 4 of LCL. Cambridge: Harvard University Press; London: William Heinemann, 1968.

II. GENERAL

Abrahams, Roger D. "Introductory Remarks to a Rhetorical Theory of Folklore." *JAF* 81 (1968): 143–58.

Achtemeier, Paul J. " 'And He Followed Him': Miracles and Discipleship in Mark 10:46–52." *Semeia* 11 (1978): 115–45.

———. "Gospel Miracle Tradition and the Divine Man." *Int* 26 (1972): 174–97.

———. "The Origin and Function of the Pre-Marcan Miracle Catenae." *JBL* 91 (1972): 198–221.

———. "Toward the Isolation of Pre-Markan Miracle Catenae." *JBL* 89 (1970): 265–91.

Albertz, Martin. *Die synoptischen Streitgespräche.* Berlin: Trowitzsch, 1921.

Alsup, John E. *The Post-Resurrection Appearance Stories of the Gospel Tradition: A History-of-Tradition Analysis with Text-Synopsis.* Calwer Theologische Monographien 5. Stuttgart: Calwer Verlag, 1975.

Alter, Robert. *The Art of Biblical Narrative.* New York: Basic Books, 1981.

Aune, David E. s.v. "Magic in Early Christianity." *ANRW* 11.23.2 (1981): 1531–35.

———. *Prophecy in Early Christianity and the Ancient Mediterranean World.* Grand Rapids: Wm. B. Eerdmans, 1983.

———. "Septem Sapientium Convivium (*Moralia* 146B–164D)." In *Plutarch's*

Ethical Writings and Early Christian Literature, edited by Hans Dieter Betz, 51–105. SCHNT 4. Leiden: E. J. Brill, 1978.

Bacon, Benjamin W. *The Gospel of Mark: Its Composition and Date.* New Haven, Conn.: Yale University Press, 1925.

Baeck, Leo. *The Pharisees and Other Essays.* New York: Schocken Books, 1947.

Baker, Dom Aelred. "Form and the Gospels." *Downside Review* 88 (1970): 14–26.

Barr, David L. "Toward a Definition of the Gospel Genre: A Generic Analysis and Comparison of the Synoptic Gospels and the Socratic Dialogues by Means of Aristotle's Theory of Tragedy." Ph.D. diss., Florida State University, 1974.

Bascom, William. "Four Functions of Folklore." *JAF* 67 (1954): 333–49.

Beach, Curtis. *The Gospel of Mark: Its Meaning and Making.* New York: Harper & Brothers, 1959.

Beckman, James. *The Religious Dimension of Socrates' Thought.* SRSup 7. Waterloo, Canada: Wilfred Laurier University Press, 1979.

Best, Ernest. *Following Jesus: Discipleship in Mark.* JSNTSup 4. Sheffield: JSOT Press, 1981.

———. "The Role of the Disciples in Mark." *NTS* 23 (1976–77): 11–35.

Betz, Hans Dieter. *Der Apostel Paulus und die sokratische Tradition: eine exegetische Untersuchung zu seiner Apologie 2 Korinther 10–13.* BHT 45. Tübingen: J. C. B. Mohr (Paul Siebeck), 1972.

———. "In Defense of the Spirit: Paul's Letter to the Galatians as a Document of Early Christian Apologetics." In *Aspects of Religious Propaganda in Judaism and Early Christianity,* edited by Elisabeth Schüssler Fiorenza, 99–114. Notre Dame, Ind.: University of Notre Dame Press, 1976.

———. "Jesus as Divine Man." In *Jesus and the Historian: Written in Honor of Ernest Cadman Colwell,* edited by F. Thomas Trotter, 114–33. Philadelphia: Westminster Press, 1968.

———. "The Literary Composition and Function of Paul's Letter to the Galatians." *NTS* 21 (1975): 353–79.

———. "The Sermon on the Mount: Its Literary Genre and Function." *JR* 59 (1979): 285–97.

Betz, Hans Dieter, ed. *Plutarch's Ethical Writings and Early Christian Literature.* SCHNT 4. Leiden: E. J. Brill, 1978.

———. *Plutarch's Theological Writings and Early Christian Literature.* SCHNT 3. Leiden: E. J. Brill, 1975.

Bickerman, Elias J. "The Civil Prayer for Jerusalem." *HTR* 55 (1962): 163–85.

———. "The Maxim of Antigonus of Socho." *HTR* 44 (1951): 153–65.

Bickerman, Elie. "La chaine de la tradition pharisienne." *RevB* 59 (1952): 44–54.

Bilezikian, Gilbert G. *The Liberated Gospel: A Comparison of the Gospel of Mark and Greek Tragedy.* Grand Rapids: Baker Book House, 1977.

Blatherwick, David. "The Markan Silhouette?" *NTS* 17 (1970–71): 184–92.

Bonner, Stanley F. *Education in Ancient Rome: From the elder Cato to the younger Pliny.* Berkeley and Los Angeles: University of California Press, 1977.

Boomershine, Thomas E. "Mark 16:8 and the Apostolic Commission." *JBL* 100 (1981): 225–39.

Boomershine, Thomas E., and G. L. Bartholomew. "The Narrative Technique of Mark 16:8." *JBL* 100 (1981): 213–23.

Bowersock, Glen W. *Greek Sophists in the Roman Empire.* Oxford: Clarendon Press, 1969.

Braulik, G. *Die Mittel deuteronomischer Rhetorik.* AnBib 68. Rome: Biblical Institute, 1978.

Broide, I. "The Speeches in Deuteronomy, Their Style and Rhetoric Devices." In Hebrew. Dissertation, Tel Aviv University, 1970.

Brown, Raymond E. "Jesus and Elisha." *Perspective* 12 (1971): 85–104.

Bultmann, Rudolf. *History of the Synoptic Tradition.* New York: Harper & Row, 1963.

Burch, Ernest W. "Tragic Action in the Second Gospel: A Study in the Narrative of Mark." *JR* 11 (1931): 346–58.

Burke, Kenneth. *Counter-Statement.* Berkeley, Los Angeles, and London: University of California Press, 1931.

———. *Language as Symbolic Action: Essays on Life, Literature, and Method.* Berkeley and Los Angeles: University of California Press; London: Cambridge University Press, 1968.

———. *A Rhetoric of Motives.* Berkeley, Los Angeles, and London: University of California Press, 1950.

Cadbury, Henry J. *The Book of Acts in History.* New York: Harper & Brothers; London: A. & C. Black, 1955.

———. *The Making of Luke-Acts.* New York: Macmillan Co., 1927.

———. *The Style and Literary Method of Luke.* HTS 6. Cambridge: Harvard University Press, 1920.

Carre, Henry B. "The Literary Structure of the Gospel of Mark." In *Studies in Early Christianity,* edited by Shirley Jackson Case, 105–26. New York: Century, 1928.

Carrington, Philip. *The Primitive Christian Calendar: A Study in the Making of the Marcan Gospel.* Cambridge: Cambridge University Press, 1952.

Church, F. Forrester. "Rhetorical Structure and Design in Paul's Letter to Philemon." *HTR* 71 (1978): 17–33.

Clark, Donald L. *Rhetoric in Greco-Roman Education.* New York: Columbia University Press, 1957.

Cohn, Robert L. "The Literary Logic of 1 Kings 17—19." *JBL* 101 (1982): 333–50.

Collins, Adela Y. "The Early Christian Apocalypses." *Semeia* 14 (1979): 61–121.

Collins, John J. "Introduction: Towards the Morphology of a Genre." *Semeia* 14 (1979): 1–19.

Dahl, Nils A. *The Crucified Messiah and Other Essays.* Minneapolis: Augsburg Publishing House, 1974.

Danker, Frederick W. *Luke.* Philadelphia: Fortress Press, 1976.

Daube, David. "Alexandrian Methods of Interpretation and the Rabbis." In *Festschrift Hans Lewald,* 21–44. Basel: Helbing & Lichtenhahn, 1953.

———. *The New Testament and Rabbinic Judaism.* London: University of London, Athlone Press, 1956.

Davies, W. D. *The Setting of the Sermon on the Mount.* New York and Cambridge: Cambridge University Press, 1966.

Dewey, Kim E. "Peter's Curse and Cursed Peter." In *The Passion in Mark: Studies in Mark 14—16,* edited by Werner H. Kelber, 96–114. Philadelphia: Fortress Press, 1976.

————. "Peter's Denial Reexamined: John's Knowledge of Mark's Gospel." *SBL Seminar Papers* 16, edited by Paul J. Achtemeier, I:109–12. Missoula, Mont.: Scholars Press, 1979.

Dibelius, Martin. *From Tradition to Gospel.* Translated by Bertram Lee Woolf. New York: Charles Scribner's Sons, 1935.

Donahue, John R. *Are You the Christ? The Trial Narrative in the Gospel of Mark.* SBLDS 10. Missoula, Mont.: Scholars Press, 1973.

Dormeyer, Detlev. *Die Passion Jesu als Verhaltensmodell.* NTAbh 11. Münster: Aschendorff, 1974.

Dudley, Donald R. *A History of Cynicism.* London: Methuen & Co., 1937.

Eckstein, Jerome. *The Platonic Method: An Interpretation of the Dramatic-Philosophic Aspects of the Meno.* New York: Greenwood, 1968.

Edwards, Richard A. *A Theology of Q: Eschatology, Prophecy, and Wisdom.* Philadelphia: Fortress Press, 1976.

Eissfeldt, Otto. *The Old Testament: An Introduction Including the Apocrypha and Pseudepigrapha, and Also the Works of Similar Type from Qumran; The History of the Formation of the Old Testament.* Translated by P. R. Ackroyd. New York: Harper & Row, 1965.

Elliott, John H. *A Home for the Homeless: A Sociological Exegesis of 1 Peter, Its Situation and Strategy.* Philadelphia: Fortress Press, 1981.

Esser, D. "Formgeschichtliche Studien zur hellenistischen und zur früh christlichen Literatur unter besonderer Berucksichtigung der Vita Apollonii des Philostrat und der Evangelien." Diss., Bonn, 1969.

Field, G. C. s.v. "Sophists." *OCD,* 2d ed. (1970), 1000.

Fischel, Henry A. *Essays in Greco-Roman and Related Talmudic-Midrashic Literature.* New York: KTAV Publishing House, 1974.

————. *Rabbinic Literature and Greco-Roman Philosophy: A Study of Epicurea and Rhetoric in Early Midrashic Writings.* SPB 21. Leiden: E. J. Brill, 1973.

————. "Story and History: Observations on Greco-Roman Rhetoric and Pharisaism." In *American Oriental Society, Middle West Branch, Semi-Centennial Volume,* edited by Dennis Sinor, 59–88. Oriental Series 3. Bloomington, Ind.: Indiana University Press, 1969.

————. "Studies in Cynicism and the Ancient Near East: The Transformation of a Chria." In *Religions in Antiquity,* edited by Jacob Neusner, 372–411. SHR-Numen Supp. 14. Leiden: E. J. Brill, 1970.

Fowler, Alastair. "The Life and Death of Literary Forms." In *New Directions in Literary History,* edited by Ralph Cohen, 77–94. Baltimore: Johns Hopkins University Press, 1974.

Freeman, Jo. *The Politics of Women's Liberation: A Case Study of an Emerging Social Movement and Its Relation to the Policy Process.* London: Longman, 1975.

Fuller, Reginald H. *The Foundations of New Testament Christology*. New York: Charles Scribner's Sons, 1965.

Gager, John. *Kingdom and Community: The Social World of Early Christianity*. Englewood Cliffs, N.J.: Prentice-Hall, 1975.

Gaiser, Konrad. *Proptreptick und Paränese bei Platon*. TBAW 40. Stuttgart: Kohlhammer, 1959.

Geertz, Clifford. *The Interpretation of Cultures: Selected Essays*. New York: Basic Books, 1973.

Georgi, Dieter. "The Records of Jesus in the Light of Ancient Accounts of Revered Men." *SBL Seminar Papers*, edited by Lane C. McGaughy, II: 527–42. Missoula, Mont.: Scholars Press, 1972.

Gerhardsson, Birger. *Memory and Manuscript: Oral Tradition and Written Transmission in Rabbinic Judaism and Early Christianity*. Translated by E. J. Sharpe. ASNU 22. Uppsala: C. W. K. Gleerup, 1961.

Gitay, Yehoshua. *Prophecy and Persuasion: A Study of Isaiah 40—48*. FThL 14. Bonn: Linguistica Biblica, 1981.

Gnilka, Joachim. *Das Evangelium nach Markus (Mk 8, 27—16, 20)*. EKKNT II.1–2. Zürich, Einsiedeln, Köln: Benziger; Neukirchen-Vluyn: Neukirchener, 1979.

Goldin, Judah. *The Fathers According to Rabbi Nathan*. New Haven, Conn.: Yale University Press, 1955.

Goulder, Michael D. *The Evangelist's Calendar: A Lectionary Explanation of the Development of Scripture*. London: SPCK, 1978.

———. *Midrash and Lection in Matthew*. London: SPCK, 1974.

Grant, Robert M. *The Earliest Lives of Jesus*. New York: Harper & Row, 1961.

Grässer, Erich. "Jesus in Nazareth (Mark VI.1–6a)." *NTS* (1969): 1–23.

Guelich, Robert A. " 'The Beginning of the Gospel': Mark 1:1–15." *BR* 27 (1982): 5–15.

Gunn, Giles. "The Semiotics of Culture and the Interpretation of Literature: Clifford Geertz and the Moral Imagination." *Studies in the Literary Imagination* 12 (1979): 109–28.

Habel, Norman. "The Form and Significance of the Call Narrative." *ZAW* 77 (1965): 297–323.

Hadas, Moses. *Hellenistic Culture: Fusion and Diffusion*. New York: Columbia University Press, 1959.

Hadas, Moses, and Morton Smith. *Heroes and Gods: Spiritual Biographies in Antiquity*. RP 13. New York: Harper & Row, 1965.

Hahn, Ferdinand. *The Titles of Jesus in Christology*. London: Lutterworth Press, 1969.

Harnack, Adolf von. *Marcion*. TU 45. Berlin: Akadamie Verlag, 1921.

Hartmann, Gerhard. *Der Aufbau des Markusevangeliums mit einem Anhang: Untersuchungen zur Echtheit des Markusschlusses*. NTAbh XVIII.2–3. Münster: Aschendorff, 1936.

Hatch, Edwin, and Henry A. Redpath. *A Concordance to the Septuagint*. Oxford: Clarendon Press, 1897.

Hengel, Martin. *Acts and the History of Earliest Christianity.* Translated by John Bowden. Philadelphia: Fortress Press, 1980.

——. *The Atonement: The Origins of the Doctrine in the New Testament.* Translated by J. Bowden. Philadelphia: Fortress Press, 1981.

——. *The Charismatic Leader and His Followers.* Translated by J. Greig. New York: Crossroad, 1981.

——. *Crucifixion in the Ancient World and the Folly of the Message of the Cross.* Translated by John Bowden. Philadelphia: Fortress Press, 1977.

——. *Jews, Greeks, and Barbarians: Aspects of the Hellenization of Judaism in the Pre-Christian Period.* Translated by John Bowden. Philadelphia: Fortress Press, 1980.

——. *Judaism and Hellenism: Studies in Their Encounter in Palestine during the Early Hellenistic Period.* Vols. 1–2. Translated by John Bowden. Philadelphia: Fortress Press, 1974.

——. *The Son of God: The Origin of Christology and the History of Jewish-Hellenistic Religion.* Translated by John Bowden. Philadelphia: Fortress Press, 1976.

Hirzel, Rudolf. *Der Dialog: Ein literarhistorischer Versuch.* Vols. 1–2. Leipzig: S. Hirzel, 1895.

Hobbs, Edward C. "Norman Perrin on Methodology in the Interpretation of Mark: A Critique of 'The Christology of Mark' and 'Toward an Interpretation of the Gospel of Mark.'" In *Christology and a Modern Pilgrimage: A Discussion with Norman Perrin,* edited by Hans Dieter Betz, 79–91. Claremont, Calif.: New Testament Colloquium, 1971.

Hock, Ronald F. "Paul's Tentmaking and the Problem of His Social Class." *JBL* 97 (1978): 555–64.

——. "Simon the Shoemaker as an Ideal Cynic." *GRBS* 17 (1976): 41–53.

——. *The Social Context of Paul's Ministry: Tentmaking and Apostleship.* Philadelphia: Fortress Press, 1980.

Höistad, Ragnar. *Cynic Hero and Cynic King.* Lund: Bloms, 1948.

Holladay, William L. *The Architecture of Jeremiah 1—20.* Lewisburg, Pa.: Bucknell University Press, 1976.

Holman, C. Hugh, William F. Thrall, and Addison Hibbard. "Structure." In *A Handbook to Literature,* 3d ed., 513–14. New York: Bobbs-Merrill, 1972.

Howe, Allen H. *The Teaching Jesus Figure in the Gospel of Mark: A Redaction-Critical Study in Markan Christology.* Diss., Northwestern University, 1978.

Johnson, Earl S., Jr. "Mark 10:46–52: Blind Bartimaeus." *CBQ* 40 (1978): 191–204.

Johnson, Sherman. "Greek and Jewish Heroes: Fourth Maccabees and the Gospel of Mark." In *Early Christian Literature and the Classical Intellectual Tradition: In Honorem Robert M. Grant,* edited by William R. Schoedel and Robert L. Wilken. TH 53. Paris: Gabriel Beauchesne, 1979.

Jonge, M. de. "The Use of the Word 'Anointed' in the Time of Jesus." *NovT* 8 (1966): 132–48.

Judge, Edwin A. "Contemporary Political Models for the Inter-Relations of the New Testament Churches." *RTR* 22 (1963): 65–76.

————. "The Early Christians as a Scholastic Community." *JRH* 1 (1960–61): 5–15, 125–37.

————. "Paul's Boasting in Relation to Contemporary Professional Practice." *ABR* 16 (1968): 37–50.

————. "St. Paul and Classical Society." *JAC* 15 (1972): 19–36.

————. "St. Paul and Socrates." *Interchange* 14 (1973): 106–16.

————. "St. Paul as a Radical Critic of Society." *Interchange* 16 (1974): 191–203.

————. *The Social Pattern of the Christian Groups in the First Century: Some Prolegomena to the Study of New Testament Ideas of Social Obligation.* London: Tyndale Press, 1960.

Juel, Donald. *Messiah and Temple: The Trial of Jesus in the Gospel of Mark.* SBLDS 31. Missoula, Mont.: Scholars Press, 1977.

Kähler, Martin. *The So-Called Historical Jesus and the Historic Biblical Christ.* Translated by C. E. Braaten. Philadelphia: Fortress Press, 1964.

Keck, Leander E. "The Introduction to Mark's Gospel." *NTS* 12 (1966): 352–70.

————. "Mark 3:7–12 and Mark's Christology." *JBL* 84 (1965): 341–58.

————. *The New Testament Experience of Faith.* St. Louis: Bethany Press, 1976.

————. "On the Ethos of Early Christians." *JAAR* 42 (1974): 435–52.

Kee, Howard C. "Aretalogy and Gospel." *JBL* (1973): 402–22.

————. *Community of the New Age: Studies in Mark's Gospel.* Philadelphia: Westminster Press, 1977.

Keesing, Roger M. "Toward a Model of Role Analysis." In *A Handbook of Method in Cultural Anthropology,* edited by Raoul Naroll and Ronald Cohen, 423–53. Garden City, N.Y.: Natural History Press, 1970.

Kelber, Werner H. "The Hour of the Son of Man and the Temptation of the Disciples (Mk 14:32–42)." In *The Passion in Mark: Studies on Mark 14—16,* edited by Werner H. Kelber, 41–60. Philadelphia: Fortress Press, 1976.

————. *The Kingdom in Mark: A New Place and a New Time.* Philadelphia: Fortress Press, 1974.

————. "Mark 14:32–42: Gethsemane. Passion Christology and Discipleship Failure." *ZNW* 63 (1972): 166–87.

————. *Mark's Story of Jesus.* Philadelphia: Fortress Press, 1979.

Kelber, Werner H., ed. *The Passion in Mark: Studies on Mark 14—16.* Philadelphia: Fortress Press, 1976.

Kennedy, George. "Classical and Christian Source Criticism." In *The Relationships Among the Gospels,* edited by William O. Walker, Jr., 125–55. TUMSR 5. San Antonio: Trinity University Press, 1978.

Kim, Chan-Hie. *Form and Structure of the Familiar Greek Letter of Recommendation.* SBLDS 4. Missoula, Mont.: Scholars Press, 1972.

Kingsbury, Jack Dean. "The Gospel of Mark in Current Research." *RSR* 5 (1979): 101–7.

Kittel, G. s.v. "akolouthein." *TDNT* 1 (1964): 210.

Knigge, Hans-Dieter. "The Meaning of Mark." *Int* 22 (1958): 53–70.

Koester, Helmut. "One Jesus and Four Primitive Gospels." In *Trajectories Through Early Christianity,* edited by James M. Robinson and Helmut Koester, 158–204. Philadelphia: Fortress Press, 1971.

————. *Synoptische Überlieferung bei den Apostolischen Vätern.* TU 65. Berlin: Akademie Verlag, 1957.

Köpke, Ernst. *Über die Gattung der Apomnēmoneumata in der griechischen Literatur.* Brandenburg: Adolph Müller, 1857.

Kübler-Ross, Elisabeth. *On Death and Dying.* New York: Macmillan Co., 1969.

Kuhn, Heinz-Wolfgang. *Ältere Sammlungen in Markusevangelium.* SUNT 8. Göttingen: Vandenhoeck & Ruprecht, 1971.

Kurz, William S. "Hellenistic Rhetoric in the Christological Proof of Luke-Acts." *CBQ* 42 (1980): 171–95.

Kürzinger, Josef. "Die Aussage des Papias von Hierapolis zur literarischen Form des Markusevangeliums." *BZ* 21 (1977): 245–64.

Ladoucleer, David. "Hellenistic Preconceptions of Shipwreck and Pollution as a Context for Acts 27—28." *HTR* 73 (1980): 435–59.

Lane, William L. *Commentary on the Gospel According to Mark: The English Text with Introduction, Exposition and Notes.* NICNT. Grand Rapids: Wm. B. Eerdmans, 1974.

Lang, Friedrich G. "Kompositionsanalyse des Markusevangeliums." *ZThK* 74 (1977): 1–24.

Lease, Emory B. "The Number Three, Mysterious, Mystic, Magic." *CP* 14 (1919): 56–73.

Liddell, Henry G., Robert Scott, and Henry S. Jones. *A Greek-English Lexicon.* 9th ed. Oxford: Clarendon Press, 1968.

Lieberman, Saul. *Greek in Jewish Palestine: Studies in the Life and Manners of Jewish Palestine in the II–IV Centuries C.E.* New York: Jewish Theological Seminary of America, 1942.

————. *Hellenism in Jewish Palestine: Studies in the Literary Transmission, Beliefs and Manners of Palestine in the I Century B.C.E.–IV Century C.E.* New York: Jewish Theological Seminary of America, 1950.

Liefeld, Walter L. *The Wandering Preacher as a Social Figure in the Roman Empire.* Diss., Columbia University, 1967.

Lindars, Barnabas. "Elijah, Elisha, and the Gospel Miracles." In *Miracles,* edited by C. F. D. Moule, 61–80. London: A. R. Mowbray, 1965.

Lundbom, Jack R. *Jeremiah: A Study in Ancient Hebrew Rhetoric.* SBLDS 18. Missoula, Mont.: Scholars Press, 1975.

————. "Poetic Structure and Prophetic Rhetoric in Hosea." *VT* 29 (1979): 300–308.

Mack, Burton L. "The Elaboration of the Chreia in the Classroom." Paper presented at the annual meeting of the Society of Biblical Literature, San Francisco, 1981, and circulated privately.

————. "IMITATIO MOSIS: Patterns of Cosmology and Soteriology in the Hellenistic Synagogue." *Studia Philonica* 1 (1972): 27–55.

Malherbe, Abraham J. s.v. "Cynics." *IDBSup* (1976): 201–3.

————. *Social Aspects of Early Christianity.* 2d ed., enlarged. Philadelphia: Fortress Press, 1983.

Marrou, H. I. *A History of Education in Antiquity.* New York and London: Sheed & Ward, 1956.

Marxsen, Willi. *Mark the Evangelist: Studies on the Redaction History of the Gospel.* Translated by J. Boyce, D. Juel, W. Poehlmann, and R. A. Harrisville. Nashville: Abingdon Press, 1969.

Matera, Frank J. *The Kingship of Jesus: Composition and Theology in Mark 15.* SBLDS 66. Chico, Calif.: Scholars Press, 1982.

Meeks, Wayne A. "*Hypomnēmata* from an Untamed Sceptic: A Response to George Kennedy." In *The Relationships Among the Gospels,* edited by William O. Walker, Jr., 157–72. TUMSR 5. San Antonio: Trinity University Press, 1978.

——. *The Prophet-King: Moses Traditions and the Johannine Christology.* NovTSup 14. Leiden: E. J. Brill, 1967.

——. "The Man from Heaven in Johannine Sectarianism." *JBL* 91 (1972): 44–72.

Meeks, Wayne A., and Robert L. Wilken. *Jews and Christians in Antioch in the First Four Centuries of the Common Era.* SBLSBS 13. Missoula, Mont.: Scholars Press, 1978.

Merton, R. K. *Social Theory and Social Structure.* Glencoe, Ill.: Free Press, 1957.

Metzger, Bruce M. *The Text of the New Testament: Its Transmission, Corruption, and Restoration.* New York and London: Oxford University Press, 1964.

——. *A Textual Commentary on the Greek New Testament.* New York: United Bible Societies, 1971.

Michel, Hans-Joachim. *Die Abschiedsrede des Paulus an die Kirche Apg 20, 17–38.* SANT 35. Munich: Kösel, 1973.

Miles, Gary B., and Garry Trompf. "Luke and Antiphon: The Theology of Acts 27—28 in the Light of Pagan Beliefs about Divine Retribution, Pollution, and Shipwreck." *HTR* 69 (1976): 259–67.

Momigliano, Arnaldo. *The Development of Greek Biography.* Cambridge: Harvard University Press, 1971.

Mundle, Wilhelm von. "Die Geschichtlichkeit des messianischen Bewusstseins Jesu." *ZNW* 21 (1922): 299–311.

Neirynck, Frans. *Duality in Mark: Contributions to the Study of Markan Redaction.* BETL 31. Leuven: Leuven University Press, 1972.

——. "L'Evangile de Marc (II): A propos de R. Pesch, *Das Markusevangelium,* 2 Teil." *ETL* 55 (1979): 27–42 [= AnLBO Ser. 5, Fasc. 42 (1979): 52–72].

Neusner, Jacob. *Development of a Legend: Studies on the Traditions of Yohanan ben Zakkai.* SPB 16. Leiden: E. J. Brill, 1970.

——. *The Rabbinic Traditions about the Pharisees Before 70. Part 1: The Masters.* Leiden: E. J. Brill, 1971.

Nickelsburg, George W. E. "The Genre and Function of the Markan Passion Narrative." *HTR* 73 (1980): 153–84.

Nock, Arthur D. *Conversion.* New York and London: Oxford University Press, 1961.

Normann, Friedrich. *Christus Didaskalos.* MBT 32. Münster: Aschendorff, 1967.

Olrik, Axel. "Epische Gesetze der Volksdichtung." *Zeitschrift für Deutsches Altertum* 51 (1909): 1–12.

O'Neill, Edward N. "The Chreia in Greco-Roman Literature and Education." In *The Institute for Antiquity and Christianity Report,* edited by Marvin W. Meyer, 19–22. Claremont, Calif.: Institute for Antiquity and Christianity, 1981.

Perelman, C., and L. Olbrechts-Tyteca. *The New Rhetoric: A Treatise on Argumentation.* Translated by J. Wilkinson and P. Weaver. Notre Dame, Ind.: University of Notre Dame Press, 1969.

Perrin, Norman. "The Literary *Gattung* 'Gospel'—Some Observations." *ExpTim* 82 (1970): 4–7.

———. "Towards an Interpretation of the Gospel of Mark." In *Christology and a Modern Pilgrimage: A Discussion with Norman Perrin,* edited by Hans Dieter Betz, 1–78. Claremont, Calif.: Society of Biblical Literature, 1971.

———. *What Is Redaction Criticism?* GBS. Philadelphia: Fortress Press, 1969.

Pesch, Rudolf. *Naherwartungen: Tradition und Redaktion in Mk 13.* KBANT. Düsseldorf: Patmos-Verlag, 1968.

Petersen, David L. *The Roles of Israel's Prophets.* JSOTSup 17. Sheffield: JSOT Press, 1981.

Petersen, Norman R., Jr. "The Composition of Mark 4:1—8:26." *HTR* 73 (1980): 185–217.

———. *Literary Criticism for New Testament Critics.* Philadelphia: Fortress Press, 1978.

———. "So-called Gnostic Type Gospels and the Question of the Genre." Paper presented and circulated at the annual meeting of the Society of Biblical Literature, New York, 1970.

Petzke, G. *Die Traditionen über Apollonius von Tyana und das Neue Testament.* SCHNT 1. Leiden: E. J. Brill, 1970.

Plümacher, Eckhard. *Lukas als hellenistischer Schriftsteller.* SUNT 9. Göttingen: Vandenhoeck & Ruprecht, 1971.

Rad, Gerhard von. *The Problem of the Hexateuch and Other Essays.* New York: McGraw-Hill, 1966. Pp. 1–78.

Renaud, B. "Jér 1: Structure et théologie de la rédaction." In *Le Livre de Jérémie: Le Prophète et son Milieu avec les Oracles et leur Transmission,* edited by P.-M. Bogaert, 177–96. BETL 54. Leuven: Leuven University Press, 1981.

Rengstorf, Karl H. s.v. "mathētēs." *TDNT* 4 (1967): 426–31.

Reploh, Karl-Georg. *Markus—Lehrer der Gemeinde.* SBM 9. Stuttgart: Katholisches Bibelwerk, 1969.

Rhoads, David, and Donald Michie. *Mark as Story: An Introduction to the Narrative of a Gospel.* Philadelphia: Fortress Press, 1982.

Riddle, Donald W. *The Gospels: Their Origin and Growth.* Chicago: University of Chicago Press, 1939.

Robbins, Vernon K. "By Land and By Sea: The We-Passages and Ancient Sea Voyages." In *Perspectives on Luke-Acts,* PRS-SSS 5, edited by C. H. Talbert, 243–56. Macon, Ga.: Mercer University Press; Edinburgh: T. & T. Clark, 1978.

———. "The Healing of Blind Bartimaeus (Mark 10:46–52) in the Marcan Theology." *JBL* 92 (1973): 224–43.

———. "Last Meal: Preparation, Betrayal, and Absence (Mark 14:12–25)." In *The*

Passion in Mark, edited by Werner H. Kelber, 21–40. Philadelphia: Fortress Press, 1976.

———. "Laudation Stories in the Gospel of Luke and Plutarch's *Alexander.*" In *SBL Seminar Papers* 20, edited by Kent Harold Richards, 293–308. Chico, Calif.: Scholars Press, 1981.

———. "Mark as Genre." In *SBL Seminar Papers* 19, edited by Paul J. Achtemeier, 371–85. Chico, Calif.: Scholars Press, 1980.

———. "Mark I.14–20: An Interpretation at the Intersection of Jewish and Graeco-Roman Traditions." *NTS* 28 (1982): 220–36.

———. "Prefaces in Greco-Roman Biography and Luke-Acts." *PRS* 6 (1979): 94–108.

———. "Summons and Outline in Mark: The Three-Step Progression." *NovT* 23 (1981): 97–114.

Robinson, James M. *The Problem of History in Mark: And Other Marcan Studies.* Philadelphia: Fortress Press, 1982.

Roth, Wolfgang. "The Biblical Matrix of Literary Structure and Narrative Execution of the Synoptic Gospel." Paper presented at the Chicago Society for Biblical Research, Evanston, Ill., April 1980, and circulated privately.

Ryle, Gilbert. *The Concept of Mind.* New York: Barnes & Noble, 1949.

Sarbin, Theodore R., and Vernon L. Allen. "Role Theory." In *The Handbook of Social Psychology,* vol. 1, edited by Gardner Lindzey and Elliott Aronson, 488–567. 2d ed. Reading, Mass.: Addison-Wesley, 1968.

Schenk, Wolfgang. *Der Passionsbericht nach Markus.* Gütersloh: Gerd Mohn, 1974.

Schmidt, Karl Ludwig. *Der Rahmen der Geschichte Jesu.* Berlin: Trowitzsch, 1919.

———. "Die Stellung der Evangelien in der allgemeinen Literaturgeschichte." In *Eucharisterion: Studien zur Religion und Literatur des Alten und Neuen Testaments Hermann Gunkel zum 60. Geburtstag,* edited by Hans Schmidt, 50–134. FRLANT, N.F. 19.2. Göttingen: Vandenhoeck & Ruprecht, 1923.

Schoedel, William R. *Polycarp, Martyrdom of Polycarp, Fragments of Papias.* The Apostolic Fathers 5. Nashville: Thomas Nelson & Sons, 1967.

Schulz, Siegfried. "Die Bedeutung des Markus für die Theologiegeschichte des Urchristentums." In *Studia Evangelica II,* edited by F. L. Cross, 135–45. TU 87. Berlin: Akademie Verlag, 1961.

Schweizer, Eduard. "Anmerkungen zur Theologie des Markus." In *Neotestamentica et Patristica,* edited by W. C. van Unnik, 35–46. Leiden: E. J. Brill, 1962.

———. *The Good News According to Mark.* Translated by Donald H. Madvig. Richmond: John Knox Press, 1970.

Scroggs, Robin. "The Earliest Christian Communities as Sectarian Movement." In *Christianity, Judaism and Other Greco-Roman Cults: Studies for Morton Smith at Sixty, Part Two: Early Christianity,* edited by Jacob Neusner, 1–23. SJLA 12. Leiden: E. J. Brill, 1975.

Scroggs, Robin, and Kent I. Groff. "Baptism in Mark: Dying and Rising with Christ." *JBL* 92 (1973): 531–48.

Smith, Jonathan Z. "Good News is No News! Aretalogy and Gospel." In *Christianity, Judaism and Other Greco-Roman Cults: Studies for Morton Smith at Sixty, Part One: New Testament,* edited by Jacob Neusner, 21–38. SJLA 12. Leiden: E. J. Brill, 1975.

──────. *Map Is Not Territory.* SJLA 23. Leiden: E. J. Brill, 1978.

Smith, Morton. "The Image of God." *BJRL* 50 (1958): 473–512.

──────. "Palestinian Judaism in the First Century." In *Israel: Its Role in Civilization,* edited by Moshe Davis, 67–81. New York: Jewish Theological Seminary of America, 1956.

──────. "Prolegomena to a Discussion of Aretalogies, Divine Men, the Gospels and Jesus." *JBL* 90 (1971): 174–99.

Soden, Hermann F. von. *Die Schriften des Neuen Testaments I.1.* Göttingen: Vandenhoeck & Ruprecht, 1911.

Steck, Odil H. *Israel und das Gewaltsame Geschick der Propheten.* WMANT 23. Neukirchen-Vluyn: Neukirchen, 1967.

Stein, Robert H. "A Short Note on Mark xiv.28 and xvi.7." *NTS* 20 (1974): 445–52.

Stein, Siegfried. "The Influence of Symposia Literature and the Literary Form of the Pesach Haggadah." *JJS* 8 (1957): 13–44.

Stendahl, Krister. *The School of St. Matthew.* Philadelphia: Fortress Press, 1968.

Szarek, Gene. "A Critique of Kelber's 'The Hour of the Son of Man and the Temptation of the Disciples: Mark 14:32–42.'" In *SBL Seminar Papers* 10, edited by George MacRae, 111–18. Missoula, Mont.: Scholars Press, 1976.

Talbert, Charles H. "Biographies of Philosophers and Rulers as Instruments of Religious Propaganda in Mediterranean Antiquity." In *ANRW* II.2, 1619–51. Berlin and New York: Walter de Gruyter, 1978.

──────. "The Concept of Immortals in Mediterranean Antiquity." *JBL* 94 (1975): 19–36.

──────. *Literary Patterns, Theological Themes and the Genre of Luke-Acts.* SBLMS 20. Missoula, Mont.: Scholars Press, 1974.

──────. "Prophecies of Future Greatness: The Contribution of Greco-Roman Biographies to an Understanding of Luke 1:5—4:14." In *The Divine Helmsman: Studies on God's Control of Human Events, Presented to Lou H. Silberman,* edited by James L. Crenshaw and Samuel Sandmel, 129–41. New York: KTAV, 1980.

──────. *What Is a Gospel? The Genre of the Canonical Gospels.* Philadelphia: Fortress Press, 1977.

Tannehill, Robert C. "The Disciples in Mark: The Function of a Narrative Role." *JR* 57 (1977): 386–405.

──────. "The Gospel of Mark as Narrative Christology." *Semeia* 16 (1980): 57–95.

──────. *The Sword of His Mouth.* SS 1. Philadelphia: Fortress Press; Missoula, Mont.: Scholars Press, 1975.

Tavenner, Eugene. "Three as a Magic Number in Latin Literature." *TAPA* 47 (1916): 117–43.

Taylor, R. O. P. *The Groundwork of the Gospels.* Oxford: Basil Blackwell, 1946.

Taylor, Vincent. *The Gospel According to Mark.* London: Macmillan & Co., 1963.

Theissen, Gerd. "Itinerant Radicalism: The Tradition of Jesus Sayings from the Perspective of the Sociology of Literature." *Radical Religion* 2 (1975): 84–93.

———. *The Social Setting of Pauline Christianity: Essays on Corinth.* Edited and translated by John H. Schütz. Philadelphia: Fortress Press, 1982.

———. *Sociology of Early Palestinian Christianity.* Translated by John Bowden. Philadelphia: Fortress Press, 1978.

Thompson, J. A. "The Use of Repetition in the Prophecy of Joel." In *On Language, Culture and Religion in Honor of E. A. Nida,* edited by M. Black and W. A. Smalley, 101–10. The Hague and Paris: Mouton, 1974.

Tiede, David L. *The Charismatic Figure as Miracle Worker.* SBLDS 1. Missoula, Mont.: Scholars Press, 1972.

Trocmé, Etienne. *The Formation of the Gospel According to Mark.* Philadelphia: Westminster Press, 1975.

Veltman, Fred. "The Defense Speeches of Paul in Acts." In *Perspectives on Luke-Acts,* PRS-SSS 5, edited by C. H. Talbert, 243–56. Macon, Ga.: Mercer University Press; Edinburgh: T. & T. Clark, 1978.

Vivas, Eliseo. "Literary Classes: Some Problems." *Genre* 1 (1968): 97–105.

Votaw, Clyde W. *The Gospels and Contemporary Biographies in the Greco-Roman World.* FB. Philadelphia: Fortress Press, 1970 [= *AJT* 19 (1915): 45–73, 217–49].

Wagner, Walter H. "Philo and Paideia." *Cithara* 10 (1971): 53–64.

Weeden, Theodore J. *Mark—Traditions in Conflict.* Philadelphia: Fortress Press, 1971.

Weinfeld, M. *Deuteronomy and the Deuteronomic School.* New York and London: Oxford University Press, 1972.

Weiss, Christian H. *Die Evangelische Geschichte kritisch und philosophisch bearbeitet.* Leipzig: Breitkopf, 1838.

Weiss, Johannes. *Das älteste Evangelium.* Göttingen: Vandenhoeck & Ruprecht, 1903.

Wendling, Emil. *Die Enstehung des Marcus-Evangeliums.* Tübingen: J. C. B. Mohr (Paul Siebeck), 1908.

Westerholm, Stephen. *Jesus and Scribal Authority.* ConBNT 10. Lund: C. W. K. Gleerup, 1978.

White, John L. *The Form and Function of the Body of the Greek Letter: A Study of the Letter-Body in the Non-Literary Papyri and in Paul the Apostle.* SBLDS 2. Missoula, Mont.: Scholars Press, 1972.

———. *The Form and Structure of the Official Petition: A Study in Greek Epistolography.* SBLDS 5. Missoula, Mont.: Scholars Press, 1972.

White, John L., and Keith A. Kensinger. "Categories of Greek Papyrus Letters." In *SBL Seminar Papers* 10, edited by George MacRae, 79–91. Missoula, Mont.: Scholars Press, 1976.

Wilcoxen, Jay A. "The Making of Israel." Unpublished paper.

———. "Narrative." In *Old Testament Form Criticism,* edited by John M. Hayes, 57–98. TUMSR 2. San Antonio: Trinity University Press, 1974.

Wilde, James A. "The Social World of Mark's Gospel: A Word About Method." In

SBL Seminar Papers 14, edited by Paul J. Achtemeier, II:47–70. Missoula, Mont.: Scholars Press, 1978.

Williams, Sam K. *Jesus' Death as Saving Event: The Background and Origin of a Concept.* HDR 2. Missoula, Mont.: Scholars Press, 1975.

Wilson, John. *Introduction to Social Movements.* New York: Basic Books, 1973.

Wohlenberg, Gustav. *Das Evangelium des Markus.* KNT 2. Leipzig: Diechert, 1910.

Wrede, William. *The Messianic Secret.* Translated by J. C. G. Greig. Cambridge: James Clarke & Co., 1971.

Wuellner, Wilhelm H. "Der Jakobusbrief in Licht der Rhetorik und Textpragmatik." *LingBib* 43 (1978): 5–66.

———. *The Meaning of "Fishers of Men."* NTL. Philadelphia: Westminster Press, 1967.

———. "Paul's Rhetoric of Argumentation in Romans: An Alternative to the Donfried-Karris Debate over Romans." *CBQ* 38 (1976): 330–51.

Index of Passages

*Indicates numerous references to this book or chapter in the citation(s).

OLD TESTAMENT AND APOCRYPHA

Genesis
12—50—132
12:1—115
12:1–3—115,
  120n.20
12:1–9—120n.17,
  129
12:2—115
12:2–3—131
12:13—129
12:14–18—129
15:1–17:14—129
15:2—129
17—129
17:10–14—129
17:12—129
17:15–18:15—130
17:17—130
18:12—130
18:16–19:29—130
18:17–21—130
18:22–27—130
18:22–33—130
19:20–22:24—131
19:27–28—133
22:1–14—131
22:2—80
22:17–18—131
24:16–20—96
37—50—185
47:29–49:33—174

Exodus
1—13:16—132
3:1–4:17—120n.17,
  133
3:7–10—120n.20
3:10—115
4:18–18:27—133
12:21–15:27—132
13:17–18:27—132
16—34:28—133
16:2—133
17:3—133
17:9–10—97
19—Num. 15:41—
  133

19:1—Num. 10:36—
  132
19:23–24—134
23:20—80, 120n.16
32:11–13—134
32:31–34—134
33:12–23—134
34:29—Num.
  10:36—133

Numbers
11:1–15:41—133
11:1—Deut. 34—132
11:11–23—134
14:2—133
14:11–35—134
16—25:18—133
16—Deut. 4:49—133
16:15—133
26—133
26—Deut. 30:20—
  133
27:18–23—98

Deuteronomy
  —70n.14
31:1–34:38—174
31:14–15—98
32:51—134

Joshua
1—24—132
23:1–24:30—174

1 Samuel
3:1–14—120n.17
3:11–14—120n.20
12:1–25—174

*1 Kings**
  —70nn.15–22
2:1–9—174
17—19—120n.24
17:1—56, 84
17:1–24—84
17:2–7—84
17:8–24—84

17:17–24—123n.86
17:18—85
17:24—85
18:15—56
19:16—85, 99
19:19–21—85, 99,
  136
19:20—100
22:19—56

*2 Kings**
  —70nn.15–22
2—136
3:14—56
4:18–37—123n.86
5:14—56
5:16—56
7:1—56
7:16—56
10:10—55
10:17—56

1 Chronicles
25:8—87, 121n.30
28—29—174

2 Chronicles
15:3—121n.30

Esther
  —121nn.31–32,
  185
6:1—87

Psalms
2:7—80
118—187
119:99—121n.30

Proverbs
5:13—121n.30

*Isaiah**
  —70nn.34–35,
  71nn.36–38
6—120n.18
6:7–13—120n.20

30:20—121n.30
40:3—80, 120n.16
42:11—80
52:7—79
52:13—53:12—185

*Jeremiah**
  —69n.9,
  70nn.14, 23–
  31
1—20—70n.14
1:1–2—57
1:4–19—120n.18
1:5–10—120n.20
13:21—94
20:11—94
26:9—94, 121n.51

*Ezekiel**
  —70nn.32–35,
  71nn.35–36,
  39
1—2—120n.18
2:3–7—120n.20

Daniel
  —151n.51
1:3—94
2:14—94
3—185
6—185

Hosea
  —70n.14
1:1—70n.32
1:2—79
1:2–11—120n.17
1:5—71n.37
3:1—70n.34
4:1—71n.36
5:1—71n.36

Joel
  —70n.14
1:1—70n.32

OLD TESTAMENT PSEUDEPIGRAPHA AND OTHER JEWISH LITERATURE

NEW TESTAMENT

EARLY CHRISTIAN LITERATURE AND
THE ANCIENT CHURCH

GREEK AND LATIN AUTHORS

Ion
—121n.45

Lysis
207D—92
207E—10D—92

Menexenus
—121n.45

Meno
—121n.45, 136,
144, 147,
169n.18
70A—142
70A—79E—142
70B—D—142
71E—72A—142
72A—D—143
72D—143
73C—D—143
75C—143
75C—76A—143
76A—143
76C—143
79A—143
79B—C—143
79C—143
79E—143
79E—89C—142,
144, 145, 153
80A—B—144
80A—82A—145
80B—D—144
80D—144
81A—144
81E—82A—144
82C—85B—144
86C—D—144
89D—144
89D—100C—142,
145
90A—95A—145, 155
91A—95A—146
92A—145
92D—146
92D—E—146

94E—145
95A—145, 146
100C—145

Minos
—121n.45

Phaedo
—17n.52

Phaedrus
—121n.45

Protag.
—120n.26,
121n.46

Theaet.
—71n.58, 136—
42, 144, 146,
147, 169n.17
143D—51D—136
144D—89
148C—D—89
151B—C—89
151D—89
151E—60E—137,
138, 139
152C—138
152E—139
160E—139
160E—69D—139,
143
160E—86E—137
162C—D—139
168C—84B—139
169A—139
187A—210D—137,
140, 144, 153
187C—D—141
189C—141
192D—141
204B—141
210B—C—141

Plutarch
Alex.
—15n.6

1.1—72n.60

Amator.
771D—50n.33,
194n.11
De def. orac.
—194nn.11, 14
De E apud Delph.
—194nn.11, 14
De facie
937C—50n.33,
194n.11
De Pythia orac.
—194n.11
De sera num.
—194n.11
Non posse suav.
1086D—50n.33,
194n.11
Romulus
28.4—195n.48
28.5—195n.48
28.6—196n.48
Sept. sap. conv.
—23n.87,
194n.11

Rhet. ad Her.
4.42.54—29, 64

Stilpo
—61

Tacitus
Histories
4.81—123n.86

Varro
De re rustica
1.1.2—178
1.2.1—178
1.3.1—178

Xenophon
Mem. (Apomn.)
—54, 60–61,
63–68,
72*nn.63–71,
75, 93, 167,
200, 209, 211,
212
1—3—120n.27
1.2.12–28—208,
213n.4
1.2.17—64
1.2.48—208, 213n.4
1.3.8–13—206
4—120n.27, 129,
172, 173
4.1.1–5—126
4.1.5—86
4.1.5–4.2.40—86
4.2.1—86
4.2.1–40—126
4.2.40—86
4.3.1–2—126
4.3.1–18—126
4.3.18—126
4.4.1–25—127
4.4.4—127
4.4.5–25—127
4.4.25—127
4.5.1–12—127
4.5.9—127
4.6.1–15—128
4.6.2–14—128
4.7.1–10—172
4.7.9—172
4.8.1–11—173
4.8.9–10—173
4.8.11—207

Zeno
Apomn. Krat.
—61